The Social Benefits of Education

The Social Benefits
of Education

JERE R. BEHRMAN AND NEVZER STACEY,
EDITORS

Ann Arbor
THE UNIVERSITY OF MICHIGAN PRESS

2000   1999   1998   1997   4   3   2   1

A CIP catalog record for this book is available from the British Library.

Library of Congress Cataloging-in-Publication Data

The social benefits of education / Jere R. Behrman and Nevzer Stacey,
    editors.
        p.   cm. — (The economics of education)
    Revisions of papers originally commissioned by the Office of
Research of the U.S. Dept. of Education and then presented at a
conference in Washington, D.C., in January 1995.
    Includes bibliographical references and index.
    ISBN 0-472-10769-0 (alk. paper)
    1. Education—Social aspects—United States—Congresses.
2. Education and state—United States—Congresses.   3. Education—
United States—Evaluation—Congresses.   I. Behrman, Jere R.
II. Stacey, Nevzer.   III. Series.
LC191.4.S63   1996
370.19'0973—dc20   96-43405
                                                                        CIP

The views expressed in this book are part of ongoing research and analysis at the Office of Educational Research and Improvement and do not necessarily reflect the position of the U.S. Department of Education.

Contents

Contributors

Kenneth J. Arrow, Joan Kennedy Professor of Economics, Emeritus, and Professor of Operations Research, Emeritus, Stanford University

Jere R. Behrman, W. R. Kenan, Jr., Professor of Economics, University of Pennsylvania

David L. Crawford, President, Econsult Corporation, Philadelphia

Michael Grossman, Professor of Economics, City University of New York Graduate School; Faculty Research Fellow, National Bureau of Economic Research, New York

Robert Kaestner, Assistant Professor of Economics, Baruch College, Rider College; Faculty Research Fellow, National Bureau of Economic Research, New York

Rebecca A. Maynard, Trustee Professor, Graduate School of Education, University of Pennsylvania

Daniel J. McGrath, Ph.D. candidate, Graduate School of Education, University of Pennsylvania

V. Kerry Smith, Arts and Sciences Professor of Economics and University Fellow, Resources for the Future, Economics, Duke University

Nevzer Stacey, National School to Work Office, Washington, D.C. (Formerly U.S. Dept. of Education, Office of the Assistant Secretary for Educational Research and Improvement, Washington, D.C.)

Ann Dryden Witte, Professor of Public Administration, Florida International University; Professor of Economics, Wellesley College; Faculty Research Fellow, National Bureau of Economic Research

CHAPTER 1

Introduction

Jere R. Behrman, David L. Crawford, and Nevzer Stacey

The "social benefits of education" may have different meanings to different people. In this book we use this phrase to refer to the benefits of education other than the enhancement of labor market productivity and earnings. For decades, the primary argument in justifying education has been based on its direct economic effects. Yet it is widely perceived that the effects of education spread beyond direct economic effects to include "social benefits" for individuals and society at large. Such benefits include a better way of taking care of ourselves and consequently creating a better society in which to live. The quantification of these social benefits is difficult, but more systematically analyzing these benefits not only would improve our understanding of the full effects of education but also would improve the informational basis for considering policies related to education.

To promote better understanding of the social benefits of education, the Office of Research of the U.S. Department of Education recently commissioned a series of papers on measuring these effects of education. These papers were presented at a conference in Washington, D.C., in January 1995, then revised in light of comments and critiques and assembled in this volume. The first of these chapters, by Kenneth J. Arrow, provides perspective with its consideration of education and preference formation. The next, by Jere R. Behrman, considers general conceptual and measurement issues in assessing the social benefits of education and policies related to education. The next four chapters consider conceptual and measurement issues related to the effects of education on particular social benefits. All are written by experts in the substantive fields— Michael Grossman and Robert Kaestner on health; Rebecca A. Maynard and Daniel J. McGrath on family structure, fertility, and child welfare; V. Kerry Smith on the environment; and Ann Dryden Witte on crime. Chapter 8 provides concluding thoughts.

Three common themes regarding the analysis of the social benefits of education emerge in the chapters in this volume. First, there are measurement issues with regard to what we mean by education and its benefits. Second, there are basic analytical issues regarding how to assess the causal impact of education on these social benefits using behavioral data. Third, there is the question of whether the social benefits of education provide rationales for public policy interventions. The reviews of studies on particular social benefits of education in chapters 4 through 7 indicate that these issues have been explored much more for some topics—particularly health—than for others. As discussed in chapter 8, however, there are substantial possibilities of future contributions to our understanding of all the social benefits of education through improvements in dealing with three analytical issues: measurement of education and its effects, assessment of the impact of education, and the basis for policy interventions.

Measurement of Education and Its Effects

One common theme in these chapters concerns how "education" and "benefits" are best measured for empirical efforts to assess the "effects" or "benefits" of education. Historically, education most generally has been represented in empirical studies by the number of years or grades an individual has completed in formal instruction. The term most often used is "educational attainment" or what some have called "the extensive margin of education."

Another way of measuring education is by the significant characteristics of an individual's schooling experience such as type of school, curriculum, public or private provision, class size, expenditures per student, and teacher qualifications. This is called the "intensive margin" or "quality" of education.

Yet another way of measuring education is to use test scores or course grades as indicators of what an individual knows. As often has been formalized with regard to at least formal schooling, education can be considered a process that produces such outcomes as cognitive achievement or specific knowledge using a series of inputs including time in formal schooling and other experiences, school quality and similar indicators of the quality of other educational experiences, and individual and family background characteristics. Such a conceptualization points to the importance of using output measures for education. Particular inputs, such as time in formal schooling, may be very poor indicators of education, particularly if there is considerable variation in the other inputs and substitution in the production process.

The choice among these three types of measures definitions should be guided by two considerations. The first of these is data availability. In most cases we do not have the luxury of designing data sets for our own purposes. Rather we are often forced to use data sets designed by others for other purposes. In such cases we are stuck with whatever educational measurements were chosen for those data sets. To the extent that we have the luxury of designing new data sets, we would want to think carefully about the choice of education measures.

The other consideration is the nature of the question that we aspire to answer. There are different important questions that would lead us to each of the three types of measures. If we are concerned about high school dropouts or if we wish to examine the payoffs to one or two years of postsecondary education, then our focus would be on the extensive margin, and we would want a measure of years in school or the highest level completed. If we are asking about most school reform issues, then our inquiry would be on the intensive margin, and we would want data on the characteristics of schools, teachers, and students. We can manipulate the extensive and intensive margins through public policy, but we cannot manipulate learning directly. Nevertheless, data on learning would be useful if we wanted to understand the linkages through which changes on the extensive or intensive margins affect various outcomes.

The measurement issues also are pervasive regarding the outcomes on which education may have important "effects" or "benefits." These apply to all the areas considered in this volume. For example, indicators of health are more available for physical than for psychological conditions, those for the environment are relatively sparse for many forms of household and workplace pollution, and those for crime are more available for "blue collar" than for "white collar" crime and are fairly fragmented for "domestic" crime within families and households. As a result, certain aspects of the social benefits of education may receive disproportionate emphasis (relative to their importance for efficiency or distributional reasons) in the literature. Further, the outcome indicators that are available in many cases may be contaminated by systematic errors. To illustrate, reports of some health, parenting, environmental, and crime problems may be systematically related to education or income for the same objective, actual experiences. Such biases may result in underestimates of the true effects of education on these outcomes.

Assessment of the Impact of Education

A second common theme of the papers in this volume concerns the difficulties of ascertaining the causal effects of education from behavioral data in the presence of unobserved factors such as abilities and preferences. Education might generate benefits in three ways: by changing individuals' preferences, by changing the constraints individuals face, or by augmenting the knowledge or information on which individuals base their behavior. Ascertaining the causal impact of education, as opposed to associations of education with various outcomes, is extremely difficult because education is a process in which there are many inputs, some of which reflect choices of individuals, families, and communities. These choices are made in the presence of important factors that are not observed by analysts in most data sets used to analyze the effects of education.

For example, a recurring theme of the conference and of the chapters in this volume is the enormous importance of family background as a determinant of children's eventual earnings, health, treatment of their own children, dealings

with the environment, and illegal activity. Systematic empirical analysis, anecdotes, personal experience, and common sense about the importance of family
background are so compelling as to be undeniable. Because education is also
correlated with family background, it is difficult to measure the independent
effects of education. There are two ways to sort things out. One approach is
to use data based on random, or nearly random, assignment of individuals to
different educational treatments. This approach eliminates the correlation between education and family background and thereby simplifies the measurement
problems enormously.

Unfortunately we seldom have the opportunity to design such experimental
data, so we have to rely on behavioral data that have been generated by a
number of choices in the presence of factors that are imperfectly observed
or unobserved by analysts. In order to use such data to assess the social
benefits of education, it is essential to control for behavioral choices and
measurement problems related to various inputs. Otherwise the impact of
education may be grossly overestimated or underestimated because of the
attribution to education of effects of other factors. If, for example, children from
better family backgrounds tend to attend school longer and there is no control for
family backgrounds, analysts may overstate the effect of school attainment by
attributing to such attainment the correlated impact of unobserved components
of family background. If, on the other hand, resources are directed particularly
toward improving the education of individuals with poor family background
but important aspects of family background are not controlled in the analysis,
the impact of those resources is likely to be underestimated. To obtain good
estimates of the social effects of education, it is essential that the analyst be
mindful of the data generation process.

Basis for Policy Interventions

A third common theme in the chapters in this volume is that, for policy purposes,
it is critical to distinguish between private benefits of education and benefits
that are external to the individual being educated. Economists usually focus
on the costs and benefits of any activity they want to understand whether
it be a firm's production, a consumer's purchases, or a student's education.
Traditionally these costs and benefits are decomposed into private and external
components. The social benefits of education that are addressed in this volume
fall into both categories. If people's college degrees cause them to earn more
money, live longer and/or healthier lives, avoid environmental hazards, and
derive more joy from the arts, these are private benefits. If the same college
degrees cause people to avoid spreading diseases, recycle bottles and cans, and
not kill anybody, these are all external benefits because they accrue to someone
other than the college graduates themselves.

Those who remind us of the importance of family in education often suggest that this importance should somehow deter us from pursuing other avenues to achieve the social benefits of education and other outcomes we all seek. Some observers have been making this same mistake since the Coleman Report (Coleman et al. 1966) was first misinterpreted. We should not give up on education just because educational policy variables explain a relatively small amount of variance in adult outcomes. Education still may be the most effective channel for inducing change. The unfortunate fact is that opportunities to influence family environments are extremely limited. Resources can be pumped in, but we cannot be sure that those resources will get to the children. Family support services can be offered, but we cannot be sure parents will use them. And it is virtually impossible to use public policy to induce parents to love and protect their children. Public policy does have direct access to children for significant periods of time when those children are in school and in some forms of subsequent informal education. The basic policy question is whether we can use that time to enhance the future of our children in ways that improve the social and economic benefits they receive. That is, are there market failures or distributional reasons to advocate educational interventions?

Until very recently virtually no one but economists would question the propriety of government involvement in education. Economists always struggle with the rationale for any type of government intervention in society. The standard economics argument is that government should only get involved when it is clear that the market system is going to fail to reach the appropriate balance of costs and benefits or for distributional reasons. In such cases of so-called market failure, there is at least the potential that government intervention can improve the situation. There is, of course, no guarantee that government action produces a preferred outcome. Government interventions have distortion and other resource costs as well as potential benefits.

Economists differ on the assignment of the burden of proof regarding the promise of government intervention. Some would require proof that a government solution will be no worse than the market solution before advocating intervention. Others might look to government as soon as the market failure is identified. Still others, perhaps most, would have views between these two extremes.

Several conference participants called for a focus on the external benefits of education, some suggesting that private benefits were not of policy interest. This suggestion appears to be based on the notion that external benefits are the only basis for government intervention in education. External benefits, however, are only one of several categories of market failures that might justify such intervention.

Economists have long discussed other types of market failures that are clearly relevant to the case of education. It is widely agreed that imperfect capital markets limit the ability of students and their parents to borrow against future earnings to finance educational investments. Without public subsidies, lower income families may have to forego some educational investments with attractive rates of return from a social point of view. A private market approach to education in such a case would lead to inefficient outcomes. Before we can try to correct the problem, we need to know all of the private as well as the external benefits of education.

Economists also understand that the efficiency of market solutions often depends crucially on decision makers, in this case parents and students, having access to good information. In the case of education it seems clear that students and their parents could easily fail to understand the promise of investments in education. After all, the social scientists assembled at the conference expressed considerable uncertainty regarding the existence and magnitude of payoffs to education. Again, if we are going to try to adjust the market outcome, we would want an assessment of all the private benefits.

Another efficiency problem can arise because parents make many educational decisions on behalf of their children. Some would suggest that parents internalize the benefits that accrue to their children so that there is no loss of efficiency. When we see substance abuse by pregnant mothers and a variety of postnatal child abuse, however, it is hard to see how anyone could assume that all parents will internalize the private educational gains that will accrue to their children.

Beyond these efficiency arguments there are equity arguments for public intervention in education. It provides a vehicle for investment in the future of disadvantaged children, an investment that does not depend on the intermediation of benevolent parents. Once we admit a redistribution rationale, we become interested in all of the private benefits of education so that we can measure the amount of redistribution accomplished.

Our general concern for human welfare and distributional goals, moreover, has led us to set up safety nets that have the effect of externalizing certain private benefits. If a person fails to invest in education and consequently has low income and major health problems, taxpayers will assume the cost of health care that might never have been required if the person had made more sensible decisions. Given our humanitarian concerns, there may be a public policy interest in substituting an ounce of early educational intervention for a pound of later health care if the health benefits are large enough.

Policymakers must decide how much evidence they need before moving forward. The statistical methods commonly used by economists and other social scientists may stack the deck against conclusions of policy efficacy. When we insist that the impact of education on health be statistically significant, we are saying that we are going to assume that there is no effect until we can prove it's there. This approach is analogous to placing the burden of proof on the prosecution of criminal offenses. In that situation we strongly prefer to let the guilty go free rather than punish the innocent. It seems unlikely that more education, however defined, is going to hurt anyone, so perhaps we should not overemphasize the presence of statistically significant outcomes. On the other hand, education has costs as well as benefits. So it probably is neither socially optimal nor politically effective to assume unquestionably that education has substantial benefits that warrant large public support. While questions about policy support for education have to be made on the basis of imperfect knowledge, it is important to attempt to improve that knowledge so that future policies will be based on better understanding.

Summary of Subsequent Chapters

As we ponder greater investment in our children, at an early age through the school system and in subsequent informal education, we need to understand the social as well as the economic benefits throughout the lifetimes of individuals. It is more important now than ever to see the extent to which education can affect outcomes such as health, parenting and child welfare, the environment, and crime. This volume includes two chapters that provide perspective and a conceptual framework for considering these issues and four chapters by leading experts on the effects of education in each of four substantive areas.

Chapter 2, by Kenneth J. Arrow, is on "The Benefits of Education and the Formation of Preferences." This chapter places the benefits of education into a historical perspective. Then it discusses how education may facilitate understanding the nature of benefits and how it may affect preferences and thereby the evaluation of benefits. The latter possibly raises some difficult questions regarding what values are to be reinforced and how policy evaluations can be made if preferences are endogenous.

Chapter 3, by Jere R. Behrman, is on "Conceptual and Measurement Issues." This chapter discusses in considerably greater detail the three themes summarized previously: (1) measurement of education and of outcomes, (2) identifying causality rather than association given observations on behavioral data in the presence of important unobserved factors, and (3) the problem of understanding and identifying the reasons why we need to intervene and what policy interventions are likely to be effective.

Chapter 4 is by Michael Grossman and Robert Kaestner, who report on the "Effects of Education on Health." This chapter summarizes trends in the educational attainment and health of the U.S. population since 1960, placed in the context of some international experience. It focuses on empirical research using U.S. data as they attempt to establish a causal relationship between more schooling and better health. It considers externalities and possible rationales for governmental intervention in the health care of its citizens, including better education.

Rebecca A. Maynard and Daniel J. McGrath, in chapter 5, discuss on "Family Structure, Fertility, and Child Welfare." This chapter outlines a behavioral model that highlights the role that education plays in various aspects of social welfare and vice versa. Then it discusses trends in education and key social outcomes in the context of this model. It reviews research literature on the effectiveness of various social policy interventions and concludes that government intervention to improve outcomes for youths has been discouraging. But it concludes that as long as families with low levels of education experience high levels of economic difficulty we should persist in our efforts to improve the educational outcomes of young people. Finally, it reflects on what may be promising future demonstration projects and policy initiatives.

In chapter 6, V. Kerry Smith discusses "Feedback Effects and Environmental Resources." This chapter reinforces what many have suspected: systematic evidence on education's effects outside markets is very limited. However, the analysis of how education promotes private behavior and enables individuals to protect themselves from negative environmental effects introduces a new perspective on the possible social benefits of education. Given that there is very little research on education's role in improving environmental quality, this chapter reviews studies of peoples' behavior in avoiding environmental hazards, looking for indirect evidence of a causal link between education and increased activities meant to improve the environment. It then raises a question: if we indeed find a causal relationship, how can we infuse that information into environmental policy making?

Chapter 7, by Ann Dryden Witte, is on "Crime." It reviews the literature and discusses models that suggest possible crime-reducing effects of education. It presents a thorough review of all the theoretical research available on the topic but finds that empirical evidence regarding the effects of education on crime is limited. The chapter concludes with a convincing discussion on the potential economic justification for education programs to combat crime and on directions for future research.

Chapter 8 concludes. First the importance of considering the social benefits of education is re-emphasized. Then three common themes, mentioned previously, are revisited: (1) measurement issues with regard to what is meant by education and the outcomes affected by education; (2) basic analytical issues regarding how to use behavioral data to assess the causal impact of education on these social outcomes; and (3) the question of whether the social benefits of education provide rationales for public policy interventions. The literatures on different types of social benefits vary considerably in how well they deal with these themes. This final chapter summarizes how these different literatures have done so, and points thereby to research issues for which the potential payoffs might be considerable.

The authors provide insightful discussions about measuring the contribution of education to specific social domains with a basic assumption that an attempt to measure outcomes would indeed lead to better understanding and more informed policy making. While these discussions focus on a subset, albeit an important one, of the overall social benefits of education, the measurement and conceptual issues that they raise have important implications for analyzing other benefits of education. Hopefully they will inform debates on analyzing those benefits as well as on the substantive areas covered in this book.

REFERENCES

Coleman, J.S., et al. 1966. *Equality of Education Opportunity*. Washington, DC: U.S. Government Printing Office.

CHAPTER 2

The Benefits of Education
and the Formation of Preferences

Kenneth J. Arrow

Education has occupied a central position in the formation of modern adulthood. From the Age of Enlightenment on, universal education has been seen as a major, perhaps the major, step in the creation of a world in which all have a chance and in which otherwise undetected talent may flourish and benefit the entire society. The eighteenth-century poet Thomas Gray brooded over gravestones beneath which were buried "some mute inglorious Milton" and "some village Hampden that with dauntless breast / The little tyrant of his fields withstood." "But Knowledge to their eyes her ample page, / Rich with the spoils of time did ne'er unroll." In short, the dead might have created social benefits had they had the opportunity to be educated.

The advanced thought of the late eighteenth and entire nineteenth centuries was increasingly determined that "a gem of purest ray serene" should no longer be confined to "the dark unfathomed caves of ocean." Even before the adoption of the Constitution, the U. S. government decided that as Western land was sold to settlers the proceeds of a fixed proportion were to be devoted to education. The Duke of Brunswick was persuaded by Enlightenment ideas to adopt universal education at about this time; among the peasants' sons so educated, the talent of one of the world's greatest mathematicians, Carl Friederich Gauss, was discovered.

Why all this generosity? Why, indeed, do we find that the upper classes gave away their monopoly on education? I am not a historian of education and cannot give a social-historical answer. The idea that society benefits from the wider net for talent was certainly one motivation; egalitarian ideas were another. A powerful force, at least at some point, was the perceived need for an educated electorate; when the British extended their franchise to virtually

---

This chapter is a revised version of the keynote address delivered at the conference "Social Benefits of Education: Can They Be Measured?" sponsored by the Office of Educational Research and Improvement, U.S. Department of Education, 4–5 January 1995, Washington, D.C.

all adults in 1867, a leading statesman said: "We must educate our masters."
The belated commitment of the British to universal education dates from
this time.

I don't know whether education was thought of as taming the unruly and
weaning them from a life of crime. There was a widely quoted proverb, "The
devil finds work for idle hands." But I suppose that employment might have
been just as good as schooling.

On this occasion, I want to bring to your consideration two aspects of
the measurement of social benefits for education. The first aspect relates to the
term *benefits* and the second especially to the term *education*. But both have to
do with the way positive analyses of the relation between education and other
social consequences are to be used for normative purposes, particularly in the
formation of policy in a democratic polity.

The first aspect I want to discuss is the representation of benefits. The
second is the meaning of preferences and in particular the role of education in
forming them. Both of these were suggested to me when I served on a committee
formed to evaluate the use of contingent valuation methods for environmental
damage.

With regard to the first, economists have developed a tradition of expressing benefits in terms of monetary equivalents. It is natural to our preferred areas
of analysis, the commercial and industrial sectors dominated by the market. The
use of monetary equivalents for public goods policy analysis goes back to Jules
Dupuit's classic paper of 1844, in which he sought the criteria for justifying
expenditures on a bridge or a highway (his job, after all, was inspector of
bridges and highways). Dupuit could have used time saved in transportation
as a representation of benefits. A more modern analyst of highways might add
lives saved, reduction of nonfatal accidents, and respect for the natural contours
of the land. But he used, not time saved, but its monetary equivalent.

There is, of course, one obvious explanation. Highways and bridges use
resources, and the ones that come to mind most naturally are marketed goods,
construction labor, cement, steel, and so forth. The measuring rod of money
works well for them. To compare benefits and costs, then, it is convenient
indeed to express the benefits also in money terms.

The world, however, is frequently not convenient. How do we compare
benefits with money? Indeed, the individual consumer in the economist's
standard story does not make any such comparison. The ends for which we
consume are compared with each other but not with money as such. Public
goods are no different in principle, and money measurement is more difficult
in practice because of the absence of markets. I can know that the marginal
strawberry is worth $1.89 a pound to me because I find myself paying that
amount. But I cannot appeal to my own or anyone else's market transactions
for the money value of a reduction in crime.

The analogous questions have arisen in the evaluation of environmental costs or benefits. Contingent valuation has been one response: ask respondents to make the comparison. The results have been controversial. Some responses, at least, are paradoxical. Some comparisons with market behavior suggest a tendency to overestimate. I personally think the method gives useful and interesting but certainly not conclusive results. Certainly the results are not so clearly reliable that other approaches should not be considered.

The political process of decision making in fact is only mildly influenced by quantitative benefit-cost analysis. The field where benefit-cost analysis was first employed in the United States is that of water resources; yet even there the outcomes are determined by many factors, of which the analysis is only one. I think it is true that *extremely* low benefit-cost ratios are a serious bar to acceptance of a project; but beyond that there can be considerable debate. In any case, the methodology is not used even in cases much more favorable to its use than, say, analysis of environmental effects or the social benefits of education.

A critical point about the political process is that it is a *process*. It takes place over a period of time in which there is a dialogue. I do not want to suggest that this leads to better decisions; in many cases, it clearly does not. But there is one point at which a process approach does better; it at least admits the possibility of achieving a *clarification of values*.

Suppose it were established that increased expenditures on education reduce crime. A benefit-cost approach would be to try to put a money value on the crime reduction to be compared with the increased educational expenditures. Compare this with simply presenting the relation. Then citizens and politicians can argue over different levels of expenditure using the crime reduction as an example. Concrete proposals are made, defended, and attacked. It is probably a mistake to assume that each individual carries around an indifference map between crime and expenditures on private goods, at least not an indifference map that is readily available for introspection. Instead, each individual concerned with the decision-making process can be thought of as engaged in research on his or her own values. These values are influenced by others' and are clarified and discovered in the dialogue.

This is, of course, an ideal picture, and much thought has to be given to the institutional framework in which the debate takes place. There is hardly time for an extended discussion here, and in any case there is much that is unknown about the optimal conditions for value clarification in the political process.

In a context like this, it seems clear to me that the role of the social scientist is first and foremost the development of the empirical and structural relations, linking education, say, to crime, health, and other similar values. It is the political decision-making arena in which, in a democratic society, the tradeoffs are determined.

There is one important qualification to what I have just said. If we assume that values are rational in the technical sense of the word, the social scientist can point out inconsistencies in the tradeoff patterns. There are allegedly many ways to reduce crime; education may be one, and longer sentences or more police expenditures may be others. We can argue and have argued that the implicit prices in different policies may differ. This certainly is true about safety measures in different fields, where benefits are reported in units of probability of death. But, although this comparative cost analysis has been made repeatedly, it has not had much effect, I regret to say. The political system appears to agree rather with Walt Whitman: "Do I contradict myself? Very well, I contradict myself."

I have been emphasizing that values should frequently not be regarded as given but may only be revealed in the course of dialogue. This leads to the second aspect of evaluation of the social benefits of education: the role of education as a source of values or preferences.

Economists have built a structure of welfare evaluation based on given individual values. Not only do the standard arguments for the usefulness of the market and for benefit-cost analysis take the values of individuals as given, but so do the theories of social choice and of political choice, theories that have had influence on political science and sociology.

I have already argued that values are likely to be formed or at least clarified in the course of public debate. But an even sharper problem of preference formation accompanies the development of the child. We clearly cannot take preferences as given; they develop over the period of maturation. It is a commonplace that learning from others by precept and example is a powerful source of values.

Parenthetically, I have become aware that the welfare analysis of children is a totally neglected topic. In positive theory, children appear as part of household utility functions; the research agenda includes such topics as family equivalence scales and the demand for children. Welfare economics, theoretical or applied, has implicitly adopted the same stance. This leads to a number of blind spots. We can say nothing in this language about the transition from childhood, unrepresented in the social welfare functions, to adulthood, where there is full representation. There are all sorts of very practical issues connected with the transition. At what age should people be allowed to vote, drive, or enter into contracts? What are the parents' varying responsibilities for the costs of a child's education at different ages?

At an earlier age, there is a similar problem. How do we justify compulsory education? It is true that there are externalities, but in fact the private benefits of primary and secondary education are sufficiently high that the fairly drastic step of compulsion should be unnecessary. The only discussion I have seen refers to conflict of interest between child and parent, a reasonable argument but one that implies that children count separately from parents in welfare analysis.

Let me return from this digression on the need for a welfare economics of childhood. One reason for this lack is precisely the ill-formed nature of a child's preferences. Like everything else interesting about human beings, preferences are a mixture of heredity and environment. Schools must surely have a major part, if only because they occupy a large part of a child's day.

It is a traditional view that not only does education influence values but it ought to do so. It is only to the last few generations that *indoctrination* has become pejorative. The social benefits with which this conference is concerned derive in good measure from putative changes in values, as can easily be demonstrated from the papers presented here. Admittedly, there is a fine line between providing information and changing values, but typically there is little to be gained by pursuing this distinction.

There are two problems created by recognition that education creates and changes values, one normative and one descriptive or positive. The positive question is: how do schools change values and how controllable is the process? Let me illustrate with a related issue. There seems to be consistent evidence that additional schooling adds to income in later life, even though it may contribute little to directly measured cognition as measured by standard achievement tests. It is, I believe, an old view of educators that the mode of operation of the school system as such imparts values by rewarding diligence, performance, conformity, cooperation, and competition. We may approve or disapprove of some of these values, but they are the ones that are reinforced and, for the most part, improve subsequent achievement in our economic system. The progressive education movement of the 1920s and 1930s sought to create a more democratic and interactive classroom environment with the avowed aim of fostering creativity and laying the basis for future participation in democratic government.

I use these illustrations to exemplify that the ways in which schools change values and thereby create social benefits are fairly complicated. Both the manifest content of the curriculum and the latent content of the school organization are involved.

Finally, there is the normative problem: how do we choose the values to be imparted? Usually, we argue from given individual preferences or values to actions. But we are now choosing values themselves. Not very long ago, it was held by some that crime was a justifiable rebellion of the oppressed. The inculcation of anticriminal values might have been thought of as an infringement of freedom. Similarly, teaching what have traditionally been thought of as the classics in literature or music is today regarded in many educational circles as oppressive, as imposing the culture of DWEM's—"dead white European males."

The social benefits discussed at this conference seem safe, that is, they correspond to the values most universally held, at least by the classes and social groups represented here. Family structure, with its sexual implications, may be the most dubious; the recent resignation of the surgeon general shows the fine lines to be observed. But none of the topics is actually without value controversy, certainly at the level of specifics.

It is clear that we cannot avoid making some definite choices as to the values to be inculcated. I can only suggest that there has to be a respect for minority views such as those on abortion. If values are widely accepted, they can reasonably be diffused through the educational system, if we can, in fact, do so. If there is real clash, the educational system cannot be in the position of imposing a limited view.

CHAPTER 3

Conceptual and Measurement Issues

Jere R. Behrman

Education is the process of learning—acquiring knowledge, cognitive skills, problem-solving skills—through formal schooling or through many other experiences. Education, or indicators of education, is correlated with many outcomes that most members of most societies generally consider good.[1] There are vast literatures that document these correlations for the United States and for many other countries. But correlation does not necessarily imply causality. Correlation may be due in part to causal effects of education, but it also may reflect reverse causality or the fact that both education and other outcomes of interest respond to other determinants such as innate ability, motivation, and family connections. The purpose of this volume is to consider some major effects of education "beyond those on income and economic productivity" and assess what we currently know and how we might learn more about these "nonincome" or "social" benefits of education. These effects may be private in the sense that they

This paper was written while Behrman served as a consultant for Pelavin Associates on behalf of the Office of Research of the U.S. Department of Education for the conference on "Social Benefits of Education: Can They Be Measured?" sponsored by the Office of Research of the U.S. Department of Education and held at the Meridian International Center in Washington, D.C., on 4–5 January 1995. Behrman acknowledges the help of and thanks various coauthors of papers related to the topics discussed in this chapter, including Harold Alderman, Nancy Birdsall, Anil Deolalikar, Victor Lavy, David Ross, Richard Sabot, Barbara Wolfe, and particularly Andrew Foster, Robert A. Pollak, Mark Rosenzweig, and Paul Taubman. He also thanks participants at the conference for helpful comments, particularly Hope Corman, David Crawford, Erik Hanushek, Charles Manski, Rebecca Maynard, Llad Phillips, and Anita Summers. Behrman alone is responsible for all material in this chapter.

1. Most of these correlations use formal schooling—particularly schooling attainment—to represent education, in part because formal schooling is a major form of education in most societies and in part because more information is available on formal schooling than on most other forms of education. Some forms of education, broadly defined, such as training, moreover, are directly focused on the productive effects of education rather than the non-labor market benefits (though they may have some effect on these benefits). The applied studies that we review in this volume focus on formal schooling, though they also consider some other forms of education. This chapter, as well as some of the others in this volume, discusses some of the limitations in the representations of education that have been used in empirical analysis.

affect the individual educated and/or they may affect others through markets and through mechanisms external to markets with whom educated individuals come into contact in their families or their daily activities. We are interested in both the private effects and the total effects in order to understand better the causal impact of education. From a policy perspective, of course, an important issue is to what extent the total effects of education include effects beyond the private ones because the existence of such effects might call for policy interventions.

The income effects of education are immensely important. These effects also have been the subject of a vast literature, particularly in economics but also in other social sciences and policy analysis. But to keep the topic manageable and to focus on newer material, we consider in this volume only nonincome benefits of education, on which there has been a somewhat smaller, albeit rapidly growing, literature. Such an emphasis is timely because of increasing concern about the extent to which education can have benefits in a wide range of areas such as improving health and health-related behaviors, reducing crime, improving parenting and child welfare and reducing fertility, and improving the environment. This volume includes contributions by leading experts on the effects of education in each of these substantive areas—Michael Grossman and Robert Kaestner, Anne Dryden Witte, Rebecca A. Maynard and Daniel J. McGrath, and V. Kerry Smith. These contributions assess what we know and what we do not know regarding the nonincome benefits of education in these selected and yet fairly broad areas. They focus on taking stock regarding what we know and what we might learn about such benefits of education in the United States, but they also offer some insights gained from studies or experience in other countries.

But it is important to note that the conceptual and measurement issues that make evaluation of these benefits of education difficult also plague not only efforts to assess the income and economic productivity effects of education but also most other topics in the social sciences and policy evaluation. The basic problem is that usually it is not feasible to conduct carefully controlled double-blind experiments because of a combination of cost and ethical concerns. Therefore, most inferences must be drawn from observations of imperfect indicators of both education and the outcomes affected by education from nonexperimental behaviors that respond not only to observed characteristics but also to unobserved prices, tastes, innate abilities, motivations, and other endowments. Thus, the conceptual, measurement, and estimation issues that are considered in this volume with reference to important substantive topics regarding the nonincome benefits of education also are of central importance more broadly in the analysis of human behavior.

This chapter helps to set the stage for the more focused analysis on selected topics related to particular nonincome effects of education in the subsequent chapters by considering three major, general problems in going from the associations of education with good outcomes that dominates much of the social science literature to having a confident social science basis for understanding the impact of education on both private outcomes and broader social outcomes and for advocating policy support of education.

1. As noted previously, there is the problem of identifying *causality* rather than just *association*, given the behavioral data with which most assessments of the impact of education are made. This is a problem not only with regard to the proximate determinants of the outcomes of interest, such as health or child quality, by households and individuals but also with regard to the determination of the location and quality of schools by educational systems and legislative bodies.

2. There are numerous other data inadequacies—beyond those associated with unobserved heterogeneities across individuals and families that may affect observed behavior—that may affect the analysis of the social benefits of education. Both the outcomes affected by education and education itself are measured imperfectly in ways that may limit our capacity for measuring the effects of education. Most of the literature, as noted previously, uses fairly limited indicators of education—such as schooling attainment—rather than measures of knowledge, cognitive achievement and problem-solving capacities that constitute education.

3. There is the problem of understanding and identifying reasons for policy interventions and, if policy interventions are warranted, what are likely to be more effective policy interventions.

The remainder of this chapter has a section devoted to each of these three problems.

3.1. Modeling Behavior Underlying Associations between Education and Social Outcomes

Most analyses of the effects of education must use data (usually cross-sectional data) that were collected from real world situations so that the observed outcomes reflect the behavior of individuals being educated and individuals educating others.[2] Casual observations and systematic analysis by social scientists and educators all indicate, for example, that the amount of education that individuals receive is not random but is related to factors such as ability, motivation, habits, and family and community background. If those factors

---

2. In some cases, however, experimental data are available for investigating these issues (e.g., see chapters 5–7).

are not controlled in the assessment of the impact of education and if they affect the outcomes of interest, simple associations between education and outcomes of interest reflect not only the impact of education per se but also the correlated impact of these factors. Likewise, there is growing recognition of the implications for systematic analysis of the fact that educational (and other) program placement and the quality of those programs are not distributed randomly but purposively given the objectives of legislative and operational bodies. If there is not control for the possibility that educational programs are distributed in part in response to characteristics that are not observed in the data (that may be related, for example, to the political power of those better off or to society's desire for lessening poverty), the impact of such programs may be misunderstood. Therefore, in assessing the causal impact of education on social benefits, it is essential to control for underlying behaviors that may be responsive to heterogeneities in unobserved characteristics.

How can one control for such behaviors when attempting to analyze the social effects of education with nonexperimental data? The answer to this question is that, whether implicit or explicit, guidance is provided for controlling for such behavior by simple socioeconomic models of behavior. This section considers such models, first for the proximate determinants of individual or household behavior that directly determine education and the social outcomes of interest and then for governmental behavior related to educational programs. While the presentations here are kept relatively simple, they illustrate some of the critical problems that arise in assessing the social effects of education.

3.1.1. Household Models and Own Impact of Education

There are many estimates of the impact of education, or usually proxies for education, on own outcomes such as own health, consumption patterns (with implications for pollution and other environmental concerns), time use (including criminal activities), and fertility. Few of these studies, however, recognize that education is a choice variable that is related to unmeasured factors, inclusive of endowments, that may directly affect the outcomes that are hypothesized to be influenced by education, a phenomenon emphasized in the household models in Becker (1965, 1991), Becker and Tomes (1976), Behrman, Pollak, and Taubman (1982), and Griliches (1979) and the household demand relations for human resources derived from those models emphasized in Grossman (1972a, 1972b) and many other studies. For own health, for example, innate robustness or genetic predispositions toward illness may be important directly in addition to any effects through education and may reflect in part endowments. Fertility may be affected by such endowments through biological channels but also by affecting the opportunity cost of time for childbearing and rearing, the knowledge of and the efficacy of use of contraception, and the tradeoffs between parental consumption of child services and own consumption.

In the marriage market considered in section 3.1.2, appearance, intelligence, and personality may be relevant in addition to education and again may reflect in part endowments. Such possibilities have been recognized in some of the empirical literature, and efforts have been made to eliminate the covariance between measured education and the disturbance term in a relatively small, though increasing, proportion of econometric studies.

A simple one-period household model illustrates such phenomena and the related difficulties of obtaining good estimates of the impact of education even if there are no measurement problems for education and for the outcomes of interest. Consider the ith individual in the hth household in the cth community. Assume that the household objective function includes directly or indirectly among its arguments education E for the ith individual and some outcome H for the ith individual,[3] and that there is heterogeneity across households in preferences as indicated by δ:[4]

$$U = U(E_{ihc}, H_{ihc}, \ldots \mid \delta). \tag{1}$$

All of the factors that enter into this objective function could be vectors. While only outcomes for the ith individual are indicated explicitly, outcomes for other individual—for example, the ith child's sister—also in general are included in the objective function. Preference heterogeneity may have many components, including difference across households in preference tradeoffs between parental and child consumption, differences across households in preferences for healthy versus educated children, and differences across households in time preferences, which affect the willingness to wait for longer-run investment returns such as those from formal schooling.[5] For concreteness I refer to H as health, but it could as well refer to any other outcomes of interest affected by education.

---

3. These may be of interest in themselves or because they affect future productivity and earnings capacities.

4. This objective function is written to be consistent with there being a unified household preference function that is maximized by the household. If there is household bargaining and bargainers differ in their preferences, then such preference differences need to be indicated in the objective function. But such complications would not add to the basic points being made here, so for simplicity I abstract from them. However, if the bargaining power of individuals in the household matters and that bargaining power depends on the education of individuals, then it may be important for applied analysis to specify how education affects such bargaining. Some recent studies suggest that which household members control resources may matter in household decision making (see e.g., Schultz 1990; and Thomas 1990). But it is not clear that the empirical representations used identify whether who has command over resources matters or unobserved differences in productivity and preferences (see Behrman 1994, 1996).

5. In an influential paper Fuchs (1982) argues that differences in predetermined time preference are important in explaining differences in health, but the point applies more generally to human resource investments, including those in education. That is, individuals who have low discount rates for future events are more likely to make longer-run investments than are individuals who have high discount rates for future events (and thus are very oriented toward current

This objective function is maximized subject to production function constraints and a full-income constraint, given household assets (broadly defined to include endowments), preferences, market prices, and community characteristics. By endowments are meant attributes such as innate ability and healthiness that are given independent of household resource allocation decisions and have affects, directly or indirectly, on outcomes of interest.[6] Two critical production functions for the present interest are those for education E and for health H:

$$E_{ihc} = E(H_{ihc}, S_{ihc}, I_{ihc}, F_{hc}, C_c, I_{ihc}^u, F_{hc}^u, C_c^u, X_{ihc}^u, e_{ihc}). \tag{2}$$

$$H_{ihc} = H(E_{ihc}, I_{ihc}^h, F_{hc}^h, C_c^h, I_{ihc}^{hu}, F_{hc}^{hu}, C_c^{hu}, X_{ihc}^{hu}, e_{ihc}^h). \tag{3}$$

where

E_{ihc} is education;

H_{ihc} is outcome of interest on which education has an impact (in this illustration health);

S_{ihc} is schooling attainment;

I_{ihc} is a vector of observed predetermined individual characteristics (e.g., gender);

F_{hc} is a vector of observed predetermined family (household) characteristics that contribute to the learning environment that the individual i experiences;[7]

C_c is a vector of observed predetermined community characteristics that affect child education;

I_{ihc}^u is a vector of unobserved predetermined individual characteristics that affect education (e.g., innate ability);

F_{hc}^u is a vector of unobserved predetermined family (household) characteristics that affect education (e.g., intellectual atmosphere);

C_c^u is a vector of unobserved predetermined community characteristics that affect education (e.g., general intellectual atmosphere, expected

---

consumption). There have been a number of efforts to test this possibility as well as some recent efforts by Becker and Mulligan (1993) to model the possibility that time preferences, rather than explaining differences in human resource investments, are affected by investments in education. This literature is discussed more extensively in succeeding chapters, particularly in chapter 4.

6. Therefore, the value of biological endowments varies depending on the markets (or nonmarket activities) in which one obtains returns from those endowments. In poor agricultural societies, for example, there may be much more value to endowments associated with physical robustness and strength relative to intelligence in comparison with the relative values in high-tech economies.

7. Parental education often is considered such a characteristic and can be thought of as an example for this section. But, as is discussed in section 3.1.3, if there are intergenerational correlations in unobserved endowments due to genetic linkages, parental education is not likely to be predetermined in the critical sense of being orthogonal to the disturbance term, so ordinary least squares (OLS) estimates of coefficients of parental schooling also are likely to be biased.

returns on investing in education given technology and structure of local community);

X_{ihc}^u is a vector of unobserved resources allocated by the household that affect individual i's education (e.g., parental time and reading material);

e_{ihc} is a stochastic disturbance term;

subscript i refers to the ith individual;

subscript h refers to the household (family) of the ith individual;

subscript c refers to the community of the ith individual;

superscript o means observed in the data;

superscript u means unobserved in the data (though observed by decision makers in the processes being investigated); and

superscript h means that the variables are defined for health in relation 3 parallel to those in relation 2 for education.

Note, first, that education in relation (2) is not the same as formal schooling attainment. Formal schooling attainment is but one of a number of inputs into the production of education, and, because of variations in these other inputs across people, individuals with the same level of formal schooling attainment may have very different levels of education. Moreover, education, as previously noted, may have multiple dimensions, the correct specification of which is important for empirical analysis and policy evaluation. Second, note that education is posited to affect health, but it also may be the case that health affects education, so there may be a basic problem of determining the direction of causality, for which reason, in estimating relation 3, the analysis must take into account the possibility of this reverse causality.

The full-income constraint states that full income is equal to time and other resource expenditures on the items that enter into the relevant production relations and the objective function:

$$Y = P_S S + P_C C_c + P_{Co} C_c^u + P_X X_c + P_{Ch} C_c^h + P_{Chu} C_c^{hu} + \ldots \tag{4}$$

The constrained maximization of the objective function leads to reduced-form demand relations for all outcomes determined by the household (the vector W)—including education for individual i, health for individual i, schooling attainment and other education-related choice inputs for individual i (whether observed or not), health-related choice inputs for individual i (whether observed or not)—as dependent on household taste parameters, all predetermined assets broadly defined to include endowments and prices (including their monetary and their time components):

$$W = W(I_{ihc}, F_{hc}, C_c, I_{ihc}^u, F_{hc}^u, C_c^u, I_{ihc}^h, F_{hc}^h, C_c^h, I_{ihc}^{hu}, F_{hc}^{hu}, C_c^{hu}, \tag{5}$$
$$\delta, P_S, P_C, P_{Co}, P_X, P_{Ch}, P_{Cho}, \ldots).$$

It is important to note that the left-side vector W in relation 5 includes outcomes for all other members of the household and that on the right side of relation 5 are the observed and unobserved predetermined characteristics of all individuals in the household. That means that a decision or intervention that improves the health or education of individual i may have ramifications, positive or negative, on the health and education (and other outcomes) of other household members. Such interconnectedness of household members, for example, may be important in understanding the effects of policy interventions. A subsidized preschool program that provides food to poor children, for example, may have "leakages" that benefit other household members through feeding the children less at home (and thereby less benefits to the targeted children than might have been expected if such leakages were not anticipated). It is also important to note that some behaviors may affect whether or not we observe certain variables in the data. For example, only individuals (or their parents or other respondents) who perceive themselves to be sick (or to have been sick within some reference period) can report what curative medical services they used when sick. But this means that analysis of curative medical care choices based on only those who reported that they were sick is based on a selected sample and the estimates cannot be generalized to the populations unless there is control for who selected to perceive themselves as sick.

Within this simple model, education for individual i has an impact on the health of individual i only within the health production function in relation 3. Those who are more educated, for example, may produce better health from a given level of other choice or given inputs, which often is referred to as "productive efficiency" following Grossman (1972a, 1972b).[8] That is, education may be included in interaction with other observed variables, such as public health services or behavioral choices, as is found in estimates for other societies (Rosenzweig and Schultz 1982; Barrera 1990a, 1990b; Strauss 1990). If education of individual i were predetermined (as it might be in a multiperiod framework) so that it is included among the right-side variables in the reduced-form demand relation 5, education of individual i also would reflect the choice of inputs used in the production of health for individual i (e.g., through improving information about the health impact of consumption of various goods and services), which is referred to in the literature as better allocative efficiency (e.g., Rosenzweig and Schultz 1981, 1982).[9] In such a case good estimates of the health production function in relation 3 would give the

---

8. Here *efficiency* means more productive but not more efficient in the sense that the term is used in welfare economics to refer to equating social marginal with private marginal costs (i.e., Pareto optimality) as in section 3.3.

9. This identification of education with allocative efficiency assumes that education does not affect preferences that also are in the reduced-form demand relations.

direct productive effect (or "productive efficiency" effect) of own education on own health and good estimates of the reduced-form demand relation for health would give the total (i.e., "productive efficiency" plus "allocative efficiency") effect of own education on own health. Chapter 4 explores at some length the evidence for possible "productive efficiency" versus "allocative efficiency" effects of education on health.

What is required to obtain good estimates of the direct impact of the education of individual i on health of individual i in relation 3? Ignoring measurement problems for education and health, what is required is that the representation of education used in the estimation be independent of the disturbance term in this relation, which is the critical aspect of being "predetermined" in the way in which that term is used in this chapter. The estimation problem is that in ordinary least squares (OLS) estimates of the linear approximation of relation 3, the disturbance term is $v_{ihc}^h = I_{ihc}^{hu} + F_{hc}^{hu} + C_c^{hu} + X_{ifc}^{hu} + e_{ifc}^h$. If education depends on any of the components of v_{ihc}^h—the unobserved individual, family, or community characteristics and pure stochastic terms that affect health or on the determinants of unobserved resources allocated by the household that affect health—the OLS coefficient estimate of the impact of education on health is biased because education represents in part these unobserved factors in the estimates. But an implication of the reduced-form demand relation 5 for education is precisely the one that in general education depends on $I_{ihc}^{hu} + F_{hc}^{hu} + C_c^{hu}$, the unobserved individual, family, and community characteristics that affect health (and are among the determinants of unobserved resources allocated by the household that affect health). Therefore, the OLS coefficient estimate of education in the health production function is inconsistent unless there is a good reason to assume that education is independent of $I_{ihc}^{hu} + F_{hc}^{hu} + C_c^{hu}$—such as that education is distributed randomly as in a controlled experiment. Likewise, casual observations about the impact of education on health are biased unless they control (implicitly, perhaps) for such unobserved factors—which is very difficult for most people to do.

It still might be very useful to know the OLS estimates of the impact of education on health if they were a bound (either upper or lower) on the true effect of education on health. But without more information on the health production function and how the determinants of its inputs fit into the household decision-making process, unfortunately, it is not possible to know even the direction of the bias since it is easy to think of possibilities that would lead to either an upward or a downward bias.

The following factors, for example, in isolation would lead to an *upward bias*:

1. *Unobserved predetermined individual characteristics affect in the same direction the production of both health and education.* An individual

who is more robust has better health and, through greater energy, learns better, so that I_{ihc}^{u} and I_{ihc}^{hu} are positively correlated.

2. *Heterogeneity in unobserved predetermined family endowments that affect the production of child quality.* Some parents are more productive than others in producing all forms of child quality in ways that are not captured in observed representations of parents' characteristics, such as their schooling, so such parents have more F_{fc}^{u} and F_{fc}^{hu}, and the ith individual has better health and education.

3. *Heterogeneity in tastes regarding child quality versus parental consumption.* Some parents care more about child quality relative to their own consumption than do others, which is reflected in a different value of δ and leads to both better health and better education for individual i.

4. *Unobserved heterogeneity across households in access to capital markets.* Poorer households may have less capital market access, or access on less favorable terms, than do better-off households, and capital markets may limit investment in E_{ihc} and in X_{ifc}^{hu} with the result that the OLS coefficient estimate for education is biased upward since it proxies for other unobserved investment inputs that affect health.

5. *Heterogeneity in unobserved predetermined community endowments that affect the production of child quality.* Some communities have characteristics that are more conducive than others in producing all forms of child quality in ways that are not captured in observed representations of communities' characteristics, so such communities have more C_{c}^{u} and C_{c}^{hu}.

In all of these cases the disturbance term in the health production function represents factors such as those just discussed that have effects in the same direction on health and education, so the OLS estimated effect of education on health is upwardly biased because observed education is in part representing these factors.[10]

There also are factors that, considered one at a time, may lead to a *downward bias* in the OLS estimated coefficient of the impact of education on health in relation 3:

1. *Heterogeneity in unobserved individual characteristics that affect the production of education versus health.* Some individuals have more inherent intellectual curiosity, which increases their education (beyond any observed control for ability), and others have greater physical exuberance, which improves their physical health (through their relatively active physical life), so that I_{ihc}^{u} and I_{ihc}^{hu} are negatively correlated.

---

10. It also is the case that introducing this residual into the reduced-form estimates in relation 5 should result in positive coefficient estimates for this residual for both health and education.

2. *Unobserved heterogeneity in parental tastes regarding the education versus health composition of individual quality.* Suppose that because of inherent preferences some parents value highly a child (individual i) who succeeds intellectually, while others value highly a child who is physically robust, as is reflected in δ. If education is valued relatively highly due to pure taste considerations, more unobserved resources are likely to be allocated to individual i's education and less to that individual's health than in an otherwise identical household with preferences that favor health.[11]

3. *Unobserved heterogeneity across households in the expected returns to education versus health.* Suppose that some parents want an individual who succeeds intellectually, while others want an individual who is physically robust because of different expected returns to such characteristics in different labor markets. If education is valued relatively highly due to higher expected returns considerations, more unobserved resources are likely to be allocated to individual i's education and less to i's health than in an otherwise identical household with higher expectations for the relative returns of health versus education.

4. *Heterogeneity in parental unobserved endowments regarding their relative efficiency in producing individual education and individual health.* Suppose that some parents are relatively better at creating a home environment that is conducive to education (e.g., through articulating their curiosity about how things work) and others are relatively better at creating a home environment that is conducive to physical health (e.g., through being role models with good health and nutrition habits) so that F_{hc}^{u} and F_{hc}^{hu} are negatively correlated.

5. *Heterogeneity in unobserved prices for unobserved inputs used to produce individual cognitive achievement versus individual health/nutrition.* Suppose that P_X/P_{Xh} varies across households. Then otherwise identical households facing relatively low prices for unobserved inputs used for education relative to those used for health tend to purchase more X_{ihc} relative to X_{ihc}^{h} so that X_{ihc} and X_{ihc}^{h} are negatively correlated and E_{ihc} and X_{ihc}^{h} are negatively correlated.

6. *Heterogeneity in community unobserved endowments regarding their relative conduciveness in producing education and health.* Suppose that some communities are more conducive to improving education (e.g., through the greater emphasis on intellectual activities and greater links with the rest of the world) and others are more conducive to better

---

11. Under the plausible assumption that for affecting health alone the most effective use of resources at the margin is not likely to be through improving education but through more direct health-related investments.

physical health (e.g., through less congestion and pollution and more scope for more physical activity for individuals) so that C_c^u and C_c^{hu} are negatively correlated.

In all of these cases the disturbance term in the health production function represents factors such as those just discussed, which may have effects in the opposite direction on health and education, so the OLS estimated effect of education on health is downwardly biased because observed education is in part representing these factors.[12]

As I have argued, within this model the natural relation for investigating the effect of education on health is relation 3. However, often in the literature, instead, people estimate what they interpret to be a conditional demand function similar to relation 5 but conditional on education. What might underlie such a function? It is useful to consider simplified linear versions of relation 5 for education and health with right-side variables being the prices (P) for education and health that the household faces, the predetermined observed assets (A) that it has, the unobserved individual endowments (I) that it has, and a stochastic disturbance term (e):

$$H = a_{11}P_H + a_{12}P_E + a_{13}A + a_{14}I + e_1 \qquad \text{and} \qquad (5A)$$

$$E = a_{21}P_H + a_{22}P_E + a_{23}A + a_{24}I + e_2. \qquad (5B)$$

If these two relations are estimated, it is possible to indicate the effect of any of the observed right-side variables on both H and E, which would seem of interest. But they do not reveal anything about the direct effect of E on H. Of course, these two relations can be manipulated to obtain an expression for H in terms of E by eliminating one variable, such as:

$$H = a_{35}E + a_{31}P_H + a_{33}A + a_{34}I + e_3, \qquad (5C)$$

in which P_E has been eliminated. It might seem that one could investigate the impact of E on H by estimating this relation, and that conveniently P_E is available as an identifying instrument that breaks the correlation between E and the disturbance term $a_{34}I + e_3$, which exists because the disturbance term includes both I and e_1 (though I have not made the latter explicit, it is part of e_3). While it is true that one can obtain a consistent estimate of a_{35} through such a process, the question remains, as to how should it be interpreted. The manipulation to obtain relation 5C from 5A and 5B means that a_{35} is just the

---

12. It also is the case that introducing this residual into the reduced-form estimates in relation 5 should result in coefficient estimates for this residual that are opposite in sign for both health and education.

ratio of the coefficients of the excluded variable P_E (i.e., $a_{35} = a_{12}/a_{22}$), which would not seem to be what people mean when they talk of the impact of E on H. To reinforce this point, note that one alternatively could eliminate P_H or A to obtain two other relations with H as the dependent variable and E on the right side as in relation 5C, but the coefficients of E would differ because they would refer to ratios of different excluded variables.

If one moves to a two-period model in which E is determined in the first period (e.g., "childhood") and considers the dynamic decision rule for determining the health stock in the second period (e.g., "adulthood") conditional on all assets (including E) at the end of the first period, then a relation with H dependent on E results. But there remains the question of the endogeneity of E since E is not independent of the endowments in the disturbance term for H (I in the preceding example). First-period market shocks or other shocks that affect second-period health only through changing E and A at the end of the first period could provide identification and permit estimation of such a relation. This may be the rationale underlying the many estimates of demand functions conditional on education. But it is generally not made clear, nor are the implications generally followed regarding what is needed to obtain consistent estimates of the impact of E.

Moreover, it should be noted that within a multiperiod framework the education level determined prior to the current period may have important effects on noneconomic outcomes not only directly through either the production function in relation 3 or the reduced-form demand relation 5 but also indirectly through other right-side variables in these relations. If income or assets are affected in part by education, for example, education may work indirectly through a number of channels via the command over resources. The total effect of education on an outcome within a multiperiod framework, thus, consists not only of the direct effect through the production function plus any additional explicit effects through the reduced-form demand relation but also the indirect effects through any other variables such as assets that may be predetermined in part by past education and that enter into the reduced-form demand relations and perhaps the production relations explicitly. To obtain the total effect of education all of these channels must be considered by recognizing the possible effect of past levels of education on variables that are predetermined from the point of view of the current period decision rule.

Finally, within such a multiperiod model there may be uncertainty about future periods that may affect educational investments and returns to those investments in at least two ways. *First,* potential investors in education who are basing such investments in part on expected longer-run returns may be risk averse and thus lessen their investments if there is considerable dispersion in the possible returns. Some claim, moreover, that poorer members of society have greater risk aversion than those better off, so that they make lesser longer-run investments than do those who are better off, controlling for all other determinants of investments.[13] *Second,* one's current stock of education is often claimed to facilitate one's capacity to cope with uncertainty, adjust to changes, and exploit well new opportunities when they become available (Welch 1970; T. W. Schultz 1975; Rosenzweig 1995). Education may enable one to deal better with uncertainty by improving one's ability to learn, which is likely to be particularly important in dynamic environments in which there are relatively complex technological innovations and new market opportunities.[14] Education can affect the production cum learning process through two mechanisms. First, education may increase the precision of the information that an individual has initially because of access to more information sources.[15] In this case experience and education clearly are substitutes—alternative ways of increasing the precision of one's priors. Therefore, the returns to education are high only

---

13. I am unaware of systematic empirical evidence on the relation of risk aversion to wealth for educational investments in the United States, but some studies suggest increased risk aversion among poorer members of other societies (e.g., Binswanger 1980).

14. These notions have been formalized recently in a target-input model in which individuals choose an allocation of resources or inputs knowing the technology of production only up to a stochastic "target" for the level of input use. With repeated production periods, in each period the priors regarding the optimal input use are updated based on past experience. An important implication of a model in which education augments information or learning capacity is that returns to education should be greater if tasks or new technologies are more complex. Several studies, mostly based on other societies, seem consistent with this implication: (1) For relatively simple tasks in traditional agriculture, such as weeding and harvesting, several studies for different Asian contexts (in some cases with control for unobserved characteristics of individuals) find low or insignificant returns to schooling. (2) Variation in schooling in a relatively highly schooled population does not affect efficacy of use of relatively simple new technologies, but it does affect efficacy of use of more complex technologies in the same population. Rosenzweig and Schultz (1989) provide an example for contraceptive use in the United States in 1973. Whether women had a maximum of high school or college education did not affect the efficacy of use of relatively simple though relatively new contraceptives (e.g., the IUD or the pill) but had a substantial effect on the efficacy of the more complex rhythm method. (3) The availability of complex new technologies increases the returns to schooling. The new Green Revolution technologies in India, which could be used only where soil and water were appropriate and the profitability of which is sensitive to the nature of the use of other inputs such as fertilizer and water, provides an example. Estimates indicate that (with control for other choices and for unobserved characteristics) net agricultural profits increased significantly if household heads had primary schooling in areas for which the new technologies were appropriate, though not in areas in which schooling was high but the soil and water conditions were not appropriate such as Kerala (Foster and Rosenzweig 1994; Behrman, Rosenzweig, and Vashishtha 1995). Further exploration of the initial stages of the Indian Green Revolution adoption experience indicates that schooling conferred upon farmers in appropriate environments the capacity for learning more from their own experience or that of others rather than having an initial information advantage (Foster and Rosenzweig 1995).

15. For example, Thomas, Strauss, and Henriques (1991) give such an interpretation based on how the coefficient estimates of mother's schooling declines as they include use of information sources in their conditional demand relations.

with new technological and market options and decline with more experience with any given technology. Second, education may enable individuals to gain more information from each use of a technology or exploration of a market than they would otherwise be able to gain—the more educated may learn faster and be able to decode information acquired through experience more effectively. If this is the only effect, at low levels of experience, education and experience are complements rather than substitutes so that the returns to education at least initially increase with experience with a given new technology or new market. Thus, whether incorporation of uncertainty into the analysis reduces or increases investment in education depends on whether risk aversion or an increased return due to learning has the greater impact.

In summary:

1. If education and health both reflect in part decisions in response to unobserved (by analysts) characteristics, in general education is correlated with the disturbance term in the health production function so that OLS estimates of the impact of education on health in this production function are biased and do not reveal the true effects; moreover, the direction of this bias cannot be signed without further information on the determinants of the household allocation decisions determining education and health, so it is generally not clear whether the OLS estimates are upper or lower bounds for the true effects.

2. Because education and health in part may reflect decisions and in part may affect one another, to obtain estimates of the impact of education on health it may be necessary to control for what determines education.

3. Demand functions conditional on education that are often estimated do not have an interpretation within an one-period framework.

4. Such conditional demand functions may have a useful interpretation within a multiperiod framework, but the implications of a dynamic decision process in a multiperiod model generally are not spelled out or taken into account in estimation.

5. Also, within such a framework education prior to the current period may have important indirect effects through other channels such as affecting assets in addition to direct effects.

6. Within a multiperiod framework uncertainty may reduce the incentives to invest in education for a given level of expected returns because of risk aversion but may increase the expected returns because of the value of education in processing new information and facilitating adjustment to change.

7. Behavioral decisions may result in critical variables being observed by analysts for part of the sample and thus selectivity bias if this selective behavior is not taken into account in the analysis.

As has been noted, I use health only as an example, but the same considerations hold for assessing the impact of education on behaviors that relate to the other (social and income) effects of education examined in this volume, such as the composition of consumption of goods and services and the related environmental impact, time use in criminal activities, and parenting capacities.

3.1.2. Endowments, Education, Assortative Mating, and Intergenerational Education Effects

How the education of an individual affects whom that individual marries (or shares a household with) has important implications for household decisions relating to health, time use, and consumption choices and for the strength of the relationship between the current and next-generation distributions of human capital, including health and education. Whom people marry may affect their own outcomes, and the education of a spouse may contribute to the healthiness or earnings of her or his mate, as is concluded in many studies that examine correlations between spouses' characteristics. Just as unobservables affect education received by individuals and "own" outcomes such as health in relation 3, unobservables play a role in the marriage market so that regressions of spouse traits inclusive of characteristics and behaviors of in-laws on the education of an individual yield biased and uninterpretable estimates of education effects. In fact, there is a relation parallel to relation 3 in which the outcome is some spouse characteristic such as spouse education or health, where the superscript s refers to spouse (on the left side, a spouse characteristic; on the right side, observed and unobserved characteristics other than education that attract the left-side spouse characteristic in the marriage market):

$$E_{ihc}^{s} = f(E_{ihc}, I_{ihc}^{s}, F_{hc}^{s}, C_{c}^{s}, I_{ihc}^{su}, F_{hc}^{su}, C_{c}^{su}, X_{ihc}^{su}, e_{ihc}^{s}). \tag{6}$$

The coefficient estimate of E_{ihc} is of interest because it indicates whether there is positive or negative assortative mating with respect to education, net of endowments, and other unobservables. The estimate of I_{ihc}^{su} would be of interest because it would indicate the effect of the inherent healthiness of an individual on the education of the person he or she marries via the marriage market, which is important for identifying (obtaining unbiased estimates of) the separate effects of father's and mother's education on the outcomes of their children net of intergenerationally correlated endowment and assortative mating effects (sec. 3.1.2). The estimate of I_{ihc}^{su} in relation 6 with spouse health as the dependent variable would be of interest because it would indicate whether those individuals who are endowed with better health marry spouses who are healthier (which would bias the OLS estimated effect of the education of a spouse on her or his mate's health if not controlled in such estimates). But, of course, estimates of I_{ihc}^{su}, whatever the dependent variable in relation 6, cannot be obtained directly since this endowment variable is not observable (but see sec. 3.1.4). And the problems in estimating the coefficient of own education are exactly parallel to those discussed in section 3.1.1 with regard to estimating the impact of education on own health, once again without even being able to use the OLS estimate to bound the true value without more information.

Much attention in the literature has focused on the impact of parents' education on their children's education and health, time use, and consumption patterns (e.g., Cochrane et al. 1982; Michael 1982; Haveman and Wolfe 1984; King and Hill 1993; and chapters 4, 5, and 7, this volume). It is claimed on the basis of these studies that parental education is an important determinant of these and other outcomes, even though the estimated impact of education ranges considerably, including whether maternal or paternal education is more important. The chapters in this volume that examine health and parenting and child welfare address explicitly the question of the impact of parental education on child health and other indicators of child quality.

The same problems regarding estimates of the own and marriage market impact of education, however, also pertain to these estimates, except that the sources of bias are more complex. This is clear from modifying relation 3 to be explicit about the impact of maternal (subscript m) and paternal (subscript p) education and endowments (but suppressing other observed variables and unobserved allocated variables for greater simplicity):[16]

$$H_{ihc} = H(E_{ihc}, I_{ihc}^{hu}, F_{hc}^{hu}, C_c^{hu}, E_{mhc}, I_{mhc}^{hu}, F_{mhc}^{hu}, C_{mc}^{hu}, E_{phc}, I_{phc}^{hu}, \quad (7)$$
$$F_{phc}^{hu}, C_{pc}^{hu}, e_{ihc}^h).$$

The principal problem is that the disturbance term in these intergenerational relationships presumably includes child endowments ($I_{ihc}^{hu}, F_{hc}^{hu}, C_c^{hu}$) that have direct impact on the child outcomes that are being determined as in relation 3 and correlated parental endowments ($I_{mhc}^{hu}, F_{mhc}^{hu}, C_{mc}^{hu}, E_{phc}, I_{phc}^{hu}, F_{phc}^{hu}, C_{pc}^{hu}$). Therefore, neither own education nor either parent's education is independent of the disturbance term. There has been very limited recognition of this problem in the empirical literature or a clear understanding of its sources or resolution.

3.1.3. Policy Program Placement and Quality

Buchanan, Tollock, and others have stressed that governmental decisions generally are not exogenous but are in response to various incentives. Rosenzweig

---

16. The F and C variables for the mother and father have subscripts m and p, respectively, to refer to the household and community endowments in which the mother and father, respectively, were children.

and Wolpin (1986) and Pitt, Rosenzweig, and Gibbons (1993) have emphasized that local availability of social services provided by higher governmental units may be in response to political pressures, in which case higher-income school districts or those with more political power might be expected to have a higher probability of having higher-quality schools, or they may be in response to equity concerns, in which case lower-income school districts might be expected to have a higher probability of having higher-quality schools. Behrman and Sah (1984), Behrman and Craig (1987), and others have modeled and estimated the allocation of public services among different constituencies as reflecting the implicit constrained maximization of a governmental social welfare function that reflects productivity versus equity tradeoffs. Application of this framework for allocation of school resources across communities in other countries by Behrman and Birdsall (1988) and Gershberg and Schuermann (1994) indicate that governmental allocations of school resources are consistent with governments making some tradeoff between productivity and equity in such allocations but not weighing equity enough to make compensating larger investments in poorer than in richer areas. Schultz (1988) further analyzes national schooling enrollment decisions under the explicit assumption that schooling reflects importantly income and price demand determinants that manifest themselves through the political process to affect school availability and school quality.

Such evidence certainly suggests what again seems consistent with casual observations, that schooling availability and quality and other educational policy programs respond to community characteristics. What implications does this have for estimating the social effects of education through relations such as those indicated previvously? If education is affected by or correlated with community school availability and quality and unobserved community characteristics that affect the nature of the community school system (e.g., the community intellectual atmosphere) also directly affect the outcome of interest, then OLS estimates of the impact of education in relations 3, 6, and 7, as well as relation 5 modified for an appropriate dynamic framework, are biased because of the endogenous policy decision regarding schooling availability and quality. And, once again, the bias for this reason may be in either direction, depending upon exactly what determines the allocation of educational programs, including schooling availability and quality across communities.

3.1.4. Estimation Strategies

Social scientists and policy analysts have become increasing sensitive to the problems outlined previously in assessing the social effects of education from nonexperimental data because of critical unobserved variables, selectivity, and simultaneity.[17] These problems may cause education to be correlated with

---

17. Measurement error in variables is another widespread estimation problem that is discussed in section 3.2.

the disturbance term in the relation being specified to obtain estimates of the impact of education on some outcome of interest so that simple estimators may yield biased and inconsistent estimates of the effects of education. A number of estimation strategies therefore have been proposed and used to attempt to deal with these problems. Under certain assumptions each of these strategies eliminates the estimation problems. But in many cases the required assumptions are very restrictive. And many empirical applications of these methods are (usually implicitly) quite cavalier about what assumptions are required for a particular strategy to yield consistent estimates of the effects of education. It does not help simply to repeat, like a mantra, "instrumental variables," "fixed effects," or "observed indicators of endowment." In fact unthinking "cookbook" applications of some of these methods may result in worse rather than reduced inconsistencies. What are needed, but all too often are wanting, are thoughtful applications of estimation methods that are appropriate given the underlying behavior models, such as those already discussed and/or better data.

For communicating better with most people, estimation methods that are as transparent as possible are desirable. This is the case because greater transparency increases credibility, in part because greater transparency increases the probability that individuals can assess with understanding the analysis for themselves. A basic problem, emphasized previously, is that some critical variables that may affect the behaviors we observe related to educational choices and the effects of those choices generally are not observed by data analysts. As a result, analysis of relations among the observed variables, without control for the unobserved variables, may be very misleading regarding the magnitude and even the sign of the impact of education on various outcomes. If better data change critical, usually unobserved variables into observed variables, the analysis can be undertaken in a much more transparent manner and be more credible to a broader audience, though there still may be other estimation issues such as identifying the direction of causality given that education and the outcomes of interest all may importantly reflect behavioral choices. But data collection is costly, often more so for some of the possibly critical, usually unobserved variables (which may be part of the reason why they usually are unobserved). Therefore, in order to obtain consistent estimates from much of the data that currently are available or will become available fortuitously in the future because of data collection for other purposes, estimation techniques must substitute for data. This well might, as Erik Hanushek suggested in his comments on an earlier draft of this chapter, increase the private and social returns to education of careful analysts with interests in analyzing the effects of education and thereby create employment for econometricians. But, even if clever analysts can deal with the problems created by important unobserved variables in their analysis of the effects of education, they are likely to have limited success in communicating their results to a wider audience because the methods they use are not likely to be sufficiently transparent to give their results much credibility with a broader audience. So there is a basic tradeoff involved between obtaining consistent estimates with such data but having problems in communicating credibly the implications of such estimates and using simpler methods that appear to be transparent by assuming away the missing variable problems so their results are easier to communicate and accepted as more credible, but the results may be biased and inconsistent. In terms of making scientific progress regarding our knowledge of the effects of education, I argue that it is important to obtain the best estimates possible with existing data despite the credibility/communication problem and also to continue to attempt to obtain better data, which will permit more truly transparent analysis leading to consistent estimates (not just analysis that is apparently more transparent because critical real problems are assumed away). Only by adopting such a two-pronged approach are we likely to learn more about the true effects of education on outcomes of interest. This does not mean that descriptive correlations that have not controlled for some of the estimation problems are of no interest. But they should be presented as just that, descriptions of the data, and not interpreted to reflect the casual impact of education.

I now briefly discuss some of the major approaches taken in the literature to dealing with some of the estimation problems, including as illustrations some studies of the effects of education on labor market outcomes in addition to ones that focus on social effects and studies of other countries in addition to ones on the United States.

Instrumental variables. Some studies have instrumented education (schooling) using the individual's family background. For example, Griliches (1977) presents earnings functions estimates with schooling instrumented by mother's schooling, father's occupation, a home culture index, number of siblings, race, and region; he claims that his results imply that "the original simple least squares estimates of the education coefficient may have seriously *under-estimated* rather than over-estimated it" (16). Boulier and Rosenzweig (1984) present the estimated own education effect on the age of women at marriage and their husbands' expected earnings in which the women's education is instrumented by parental background characteristics such as fathers' schooling. However, a good instrument must have two qualities: (1) independence from the disturbance term in the relation being estimated and (2) correlation with the variable being instrumented. If the disturbance term includes endowment components and such components are intergenerationally correlated, parental characteristics such as schooling are not likely to satisfy (1) so the instrumented estimates are not likely to be consistent, as was suggested in section 3.1.2. The data used in these studies do not permit testing of the important identifying assumption that endowments of parents and children are uncorrelated. Alderman, Behrman, Ross, and Sabot (1996) instrument education (measured by cognitive achievement) in earnings functions with the identifying first-stage variables being travel time to local schools of individuals and book prices when they were of school age and find more powerful schooling effects with instrumental variable estimates. These identifying variables would seem more likely to be independent of intergenerational correlations in endowments than are variables such as parental schooling used in other studies, though there still may be some intergenerational correlations in community endowments in the disturbance term. I am not aware, however, of the use of such identifying instruments for investigating the social effects of education.

There also is the question of the quality (2) of the first-stage instruments. Recent contributions to the instrumental variables literature (e.g., Nelson and Startz 1990a, 1990b; Bound, Jaeger, and Baker 1993, 1995; and Deaton 1995) raise a question about the quality of the identifying instruments in the sense of how correlated they are with the variable being instrumented, education in the present case.[18] If the identifying instruments are poor enough in the sense that they explain little of the variation in education, they can lead to large inconsistencies in instrumental variable estimates of the social effects of education even if there is only a weak relation between these instruments and the error terms in the outcome relations of interest. Moreover, in finite samples instrumental variable estimates are biased in the same direction as OLS estimates are, and the magnitude of this bias approaches that of OLS estimates as the R^2 between the instruments and the potentially endogenous explanatory variables approaches zero. Bound, Jaeger, and Baker (1993) present a table with the bias of instrumental variable estimates relative to OLS estimates for values of the F-statistic for the joint statistical significance of the first-stage estimates[19] and for numbers of excluded instruments, and they recommend that the F-statistic and the partial R^2 on the excluded instruments in the first-stage estimates be reported with reference to this table as a rough guide to the quality of the instrumental variables.

Some recent studies for the United States argue forcefully that schooling should be instrumented either because of the behavioral choice that it represents or because of random measurement error. They use as instruments for schooling reports by other individuals, the military service lottery during the Vietnam War, local compulsory schooling laws, the presence of sisters among siblings, and different costs of college due to location (e.g., Angrist and Krueger 1991,

---

18. The relevant set of instruments for the question of how correlated the first-stage estimates are with the variables being instrumented includes only the identifying instruments that do not appear in the post-secondary schooling determination relations because of exclusion restrictions. However, as Cardell and Hopkins (1977) note (also see Blackburn and Neumark 1995), for the second-stage estimates to be consistent the predetermined variables at the second stage should be in the first-stage estimates (or an additional assumption would have to be made about the orthogonality of the first-stage residuals with these variables).

19. Strictly speaking, their test is for the population analogue to this F.

1992a, 1992b; Butcher and Case 1994; and Card 1993). They tend to find higher estimated rates of return than the standard estimates do. But there are still areas of ongoing controversy. The instruments used in some of these studies do not seem to be independent of the disturbance term (e.g., number of sisters if fertility reflects child quality-quantity choices), and in other cases the first-stage relations are so weak that "the cure may be worse than the disease" (e.g., the military service lottery and Bound, Jaeger, and Baker 1993, 1995). Card (1994) argues that the difference between several recent U.S. estimates that attempt to account for the endogeneity of schooling and standard estimates is due primarily to differences in unobserved discount rates with individuals with lower schooling having higher discount rates (and therefore higher marginal returns to schooling) and secondarily to unobserved ability differentials. He also concludes that, rather than further estimates based on standard earnings function specification, "further research on the role of schooling in the labor market could usefully benefit from a more explicit consideration of the issues raised by a well-posed theoretical model" (33). Card further shows that the choice of instruments biases upward the estimated returns to school because they effectively overweight the part of the curve where the response is greatest, a point that is elaborated in a more general framework in Angrist, Graddy, and Imbens (1995). This ferment regarding the recent U.S. estimates, despite the large number of previous studies, points to the difficulties in ascertaining the schooling impact from analysis of behavioral data because of choices made in the presence of unobserved variables and measurement errors.

Measurement of endowments. A few studies have tried to purge the disturbance term of endowments through the inclusion of some indicator of such endowments, most commonly some indicator of IQ in earnings and schooling functions or parental anthropometric measures in relations for child health, sometimes with considerable impact on the estimated effects of education (e.g., Griliches and Mason 1972; Behrman, Hrubec, Taubman, and Wales 1980; Manski and Wise 1983; Boissiere, Knight, and Sabot 1985; Horton 1988; Berger 1988; Barrera 1990a, 1990b; Knight and Sabot 1990; Glewwe and Jacoby 1994; and Thomas, Strauss, and Henriques 1991). These are examples in which data have been obtained to represent what usually have been unobserved variables from the point of view of the analysts. As was previously argued, there is a lot to be said for such an approach in terms of increasing the transparency, and thus probably the credibility to a wider audience, of the estimates. If such an indicator truly reflects only endowments and captures all of the relevant aspects of endowments for the outcome of interest, the covariance between the indicator of education and the disturbance term due to endowments is eliminated. Unfortunately, there are doubts about whether these available indicators (1) measure only underlying endowments and (2) measure all of the characteristics based on endowments other than those that have direct effects on the outcomes of interest and are likely to be correlated with education. Because the first condition is not likely to hold, it is not obvious that such proxies improve the estimates. Indeed, Rosenzweig and Wolpin (1994a) show, using unique data on sibling children, that if a measure of the mother's intelligence is used to "control" for heterogeneity in estimating the effects of maternal education on children's intellectual achievement, the resulting education estimate is more biased than that obtained with no correction at all.

Sibling and cousins estimators. Sibling data have been used to control for common genetic and environmental family background variables through within-sibling fixed effects or variance component (latent variable) models of family effects. Such approaches have been used to estimate the impact of education on wage relations (e.g., Chamberlain and Griliches 1975, 1977; Olneck 1977; and Behrman and Wolfe 1984), own health and fertility (e.g., Behrman and Wolfe 1987, 1989; and Wolfe and Behrman 1986, 1992), and child health and education (Behrman and Wolfe 1984, 1987; Currie and Cole 1993; Geronimus and Korenman 1992; Wolfe and Behrman 1986, 1987)—with the latter studies having as dependent variables within-cousin differences. In some cases the within-sibling estimates differ substantially from individual estimates. Unfortunately, as Griliches (1979) demonstrates, even without measurement error within-sibling estimates generally do not eliminate all of the bias due to endowment components in the disturbance term, nor do they necessarily yield estimates that are less biased than are standard individual estimates. The basic point is that within-sibling estimates, while controlling for unobserved family and community factors, obviously do not control for unobserved individual differences; therefore, biases are likely to persist and may be larger than those without within-sibling control if the biases in the standard OLS individual estimates due to unobserved household and community factors partially offset those due to unobserved individual factors. Rosenzweig and Wolpin (1995) compare cousins and sibling estimators and conclude that instruments are needed in addition to cope with endowment heterogeneity but that the available instruments often do not perform well. Behrman, Rosenzweig, and Taubman (1994, 1996) also present estimates using twins data that suggest that empirically the estimated impact of schooling attainment and school quality indicators in some cases changes substantially if there is control for individual as well as family endowments rather than just the family endowments that alone are controlled with the usual siblings estimates.

Rosenzweig and Wolpin (1994a) use data on sibling children, some of whom were born before their mothers completed schooling, to investigate the impact of mothers' education on child cognitive achievement, and they find a significant positive effect larger than that obtained using least squares. These within-sibling estimates do control for all of the endowments that are common among the children and their parents if all the siblings have the same fathers as well as mothers, but for most populations the proportion of parents who had schooling after childbirth is not large, so this procedure cannot be used. Moreover, biases due to individual-specific differences in endowments among the siblings are not taken into account in this procedure unless the children are identical twins.

Finally, it is important to note that within-siblings (and the special case of within-twins estimators (1) are claimed to be more subject to biases due to measurement errors than individual estimates (see sec. 3.2) and (2) are conditional on the (perhaps transformed) observed outcome of interest being represented as a linear function of the relevant unobserved variables.

Twins estimators. Twins have been used to control for common genetic and environmental family background variables through within-twins fixed effects or variance component (latent variable) models of family effects. Within-identical (monozygotic, or MZ) twins estimates control for all genetic and common environmental variables; differencing relations such as 3, 6, or 7 (or, again, relation 5 from an appropriate dynamic framework) eliminates the common individual endowments for such twins in addition to common unobserved household and community factors. They also control for any selectivity due to families that have twins being different from other families (for similar observations about fixed effects estimates controlling for selectivity in a related context, see Heckman and MaCurdy 1980; and Pitt and Rosenzweig 1990). Behrman, Hrubec, Taubman, and Wales (1980) and Behrman and Taubman (1976), based on a survey of the National Academy of Sciences–National Research Council (NAS-NRC) of white male twins and their offspring, find that control for genetic endowments and common environment makes a substantial difference in the estimated impact of schooling on earnings—reducing the coefficient estimate from 8.0 to 2.6 percent. Behrman, Rosenzweig, and Taubman (1994) also find evidence of significant endowment effects that affect the estimated impact of years of schooling on earnings, anthropometric indicators of health, and marriage market outcomes (in particular, spouse's schooling, as in relation 6) for a sample that combines the NAS-NRC sample and the males in the Minnesota Twin Registry (MTR), which includes all twins born in Minnesota between 1937 and 1955. But Ashenfelter and Krueger (1994) estimate the earnings returns to schooling based on a relatively small sample of male and female twins who attended a twins convention and find little influence of endowments on schooling.[20] Miller, Mulvey, and Martin (1995, 1996), in contrast, find a substantial impact of endowments using a large sample of Australian twins.

---

20. Ashenfelter and Krueger include both men and women; however, the sample is too small (298 male and female MZ twins) to obtain reliable estimates separately for men and women, so the (dubious) assumption that the structure of earnings is the same for each sex could not be tested. The requirement, moreover, that both women in a twin pair be in the labor force in the past year and the lack of information on female work experience may have led to bias in their estimates.

Behrman, Rosenzweig, and Taubman further develop an extended twins model that includes nonidentical (dizygotic, or DZ) twins as well as MZ twins and find that schooling investments respond significantly to reinforce individual endowment differentials, thus indicating that within-sibling estimators do not control for all of the relevant unobserved factors.[21] Behrman, Rosenzweig, and Taubman (1996) further present estimates of the impact of college quality on female earnings, as well as the impact of individual endowments on choices of college quality, and again they find evidence of significant individual endowment effects (again largely reinforcing endowment differences) that would lead to misunderstanding of which dimensions of college quality are important in labor market returns if there is no control for the choice of dimensions of college quality in response to endowments. The reasons for the difference between the Ashenfelter and Krueger results and those from other twins samples are not clear, though the sample design with twins who identified with their twinness sufficiently to attend a twins convention (in contrast to birth-certificate- or military-service-based samples) or the use of females and males together (with the maintained assumption that some aspects of the basic underlying relations are the same instead of possibly differing by gender) may account for these differences.

For intergenerational education relationships such as those in relation 7, within-MZ adult estimates, where the children are cousins, control for all but the random part of the common endowment components from the parents, who are the MZ twins, but they do not control for all of the endowment components from spouses if there is imperfect assortative mating on schooling and endowments. Thus, simple MZ-parent estimates of intergenerational school effects do not eliminate the bias in the estimated impact of parental education

---

21. The standard MZ twins estimators assume a linear form of relation 3 for H (with β being the coefficient of E, and $v = e^h_{ihc}$, and no unobserved allocated resources) and a linear form of relation 5 for E (with u being the disturbance) and calculate the within-family variances and covariances: $\text{Var}(\Delta H^M) = 2\beta^2\sigma_u^2 + 2\sigma_v^2$, $\text{Var}(\Delta E^M) = 2\sigma_u^2$ and $\text{Cov}(\Delta H^M, \Delta E^M) = 2\beta\sigma_u^2$ (where Δ means within differences and the superscript M refers to MZ twins). The left sides of these expressions are observed in the data, so dividing the third of these by the second gives the within-MZ estimator b^w_{MZ}, which yields β without bias (and the two disturbance variances also are identified by these three expressions). Behrman, Rosenzweig, and Taubman (1994) observe that the DZ variances and covariance differ from those for MZ twins only because of terms related to the variance of specific endowments (σ_I^2): $\text{Var}(\Delta H^D) - \text{Var}(\Delta H^M) = 2(1 + \beta I_1 - \beta I_2)^2\sigma_I^2$, $\text{Var}(\Delta E^D) - \text{Var}(\Delta E^M) = 2(I_1 - I_2)^2\sigma_I^2$, and $\text{Cov}(\Delta H^D, \Delta E^D) - \text{Cov}(\Delta H^M, \Delta E^M) = 2(I_1 - I_2)(1 + \beta I_1 - \beta I_2)\sigma_I^2$ (where the subscripts 1 and 2 refer to the two twins). Given the MZ estimate of β, division of the last expression by the penultimate one yields an unbiased estimate of $I_1 - I_2$, the difference between the own and cross effect of child-specific endowment differentials (a positive value of which indicates that the family allocates schooling so as to reinforce endowment differentials), and σ_I^2, the variance in the child-specific component of endowments. Compensatory or reinforcing behavior can thus be identified by combining MZ and DZ twin pairs, which cannot be done using data on siblings, MZ twins alone, or DZ twins alone.

on child human capital. Indeed, no existing study has even recognized the assortative mating problem in estimating parental schooling effects on children. However, in a work in progress, Behrman, Rosenzweig, and Taubman show that, with unbiased estimates of the relationship between parental endowments and own schooling and an individual's endowments on mate's schooling (via the marriage market) obtained for both sexes using MZ and DZ twins data, it is possible to identify (and thus compare) the effects of both maternal and paternal schooling effects on child outcomes net of the influence of their joint correlations with their children's endowments. It is thus necessary to use twins data to estimate jointly intrafamily schooling allocation rules and assortative mating relationships with respect to endowments and schooling to obtain appropriate and interpretable estimates of the impact of parental schooling on child health and schooling. Their estimation of all these relationships jointly will permit the estimation of not only the private returns from increased schooling for men and women, in terms of labor and marriage market outcomes and health, but also the intergenerational effects of these schooling investments on market and nonmarket outcomes and their implications for intergenerational relations. Their comparison of estimates based on the twins experiment with standard estimates will permit assessment of the magnitudes of the biases in the large number of estimates in the literature without such controls and with within-sibling estimates (using the DZ twins) to see whether within-sibling estimates have smaller or larger biases than do standard individual estimates.

Longitudinal data. Longitudinal data can be differenced to eliminate the impact of all unobserved fixed individual, household, and community factors in relations such as 3, 6, and 7. This eliminates the correlation between such factors and differences in time-varying right-side variables. However, such a procedure is rarely of much use in estimating the first-order direct effects of education because the available indicators of education generally are fixed over the time periods of interest (e.g., in postschooling years), so they also are eliminated in such a process and their coefficients cannot be estimated unless they interact with time-varying variables. The Rosenzweig and Wolpin (1994) study is an exception that has data on sibling children, some of whom were born before their mothers completed schooling, and investigates the impact of mothers' education on child cognitive achievement. But such opportunities to exploit longitudinal data in this manner in order to estimate the social effects of education are relatively rare. Nevertheless, the use of longitudinal data to explore the interactive effects of education with time-varying variables in some cases may be of considerable interest.

Longitudinal, or recall, data (still putting aside until sec. 3.2 the question of measurement error) may be useful in identifying educational effects in ways other than those permitting fixed effects estimates. Schooling prices, as noted previously, arguably may be good first-stage variables for instrumenting schooling. Historic information also may help make other distinctions. For example, information on the respondent's and spouse's health characteristics prior to or at marriage may permit the distinction between whether (1) those individuals with higher levels of education are married to spouses with higher levels of endowed health or (2) whether a spouse's education affects her or his spouse's health directly within marriage—a distinction that otherwise could not be made even with twins data.

Putting bounds on estimates. In cases in which observations on critical variables may be missing selectively, it may be possible to put bounds on the estimates without placing as much structure on the analysis as in the other procedures described previously. Consider again the example given after relation 5 of the case in which only individuals who perceive themselves to be sick (or to have been sick within some reference period) report the curative medical services they used when sick. As noted there, this means that analysis of curative medical care choices based on only those who reported that they were sick is based on a selected sample, and the estimates cannot be generalized to the population. One common approach to this problem is to control for those who selected to perceive themselves to be sick, and then estimate, for example, the impact of education on who uses a particular type of curative health care. To follow this approach requires some way of specifying the selection process— in this case, those who perceive themselves to be sick. In many cases there is not a very good theoretical basis for specifying this process. If the interest is in estimating a reduced-form relation for the outcome of interest (i.e., using a particular type of medical care) with control for the selection process, moreover, there may be no way to identify the selection process from the behavior of interest except for arbitrary assumptions about functional form or arbitrary exclusion restrictions because both the selection and the behavior of interest depend on the same set of right-side variables in the reduced form relations in relation 5.

Manski (1989) has proposed the alternative of placing bounds on the estimates. For example, suppose that the question of interest is the probability of obtaining a particular type of medical care for different levels of education, but whether or not people sought this medical care is observed only for those who perceived themselves to be sick. In this case the estimates could be bounded by assuming, first, that all those who did not perceive themselves to be sick would have sought this medical care if they had been sick and then that all those who did not perceive themselves to be sick would not have sought medical care if they had been sick. The range of estimates under these two extreme assumptions then establishes a domain, which may or may not be relatively small, for the relation. If it is relatively small, then it may narrow debates about policy effectiveness considerably. The advantage of this procedure is that in some cases it may yield relatively small ranges of estimated effectiveness of education on some outcome despite selectivity in observations without making strong assumptions on model specification. But it does not always yield useful answers. Moreover, in some contexts it may ignore some possibly important aspects of the problems of analyzing behavior such as the direction of causality between the two variables of interest. Nevertheless, it certainly adds another tool that could be used to analyze the impact of education on various outcomes in the presence of estimation problems, such as selectivity, and might lead to quite informative results in some contexts. However, I am unaware of any use of this procedure for the topics covered in this book, though Manski gives an interesting illustration of calculating bounds on the probability of continued homelessness after six months for a sample on homeless people, as related, alternatively, to their sex and their income, with the selection being sample attrition over the six-month period.

Robustness and repetition. Because of the substantial estimation problems with behavioral data, there is an advantage to making as weak assumptions as possible, to testing how robust results are to alternatives, and to repetition with different data sets in different contexts. There seem to be considerable professional returns to analysts who demonstrate for the first time in a particular context that weakening an assumption changes the estimates considerably. There appear to be considerably smaller private returns to repetition in the social sciences, though the social returns might be considerable. There exist some examples, however, in the literature, such as Rosenzweig and Schultz's (1988) study of birth production functions. There may be considerable social gains from encouraging more such studies. Yet a caveat is in order because it is not clear that continual repetition of studies that make implausible assumptions is of much value. For example, suppose that education is determined in part by family background (i.e., genetics, parental education, parental income, and home environment) and that family background also affects health in many contexts. Then it is not clear that estimating education-health correlations in many contexts with many data sets without controlling for family background helps us to understand the impact of education per se (as opposed to education and correlated dimensions of family background) on health. Yet at times, such as in the schooling-earnings literature, the very repetition of such studies for many data sets in many different contexts is widely interpreted as confirming the robustness of the interpretation that schooling has certain estimated effects.

3.2. Random and Systematic Errors in Indicators of Education and Social Outcomes

There are numerous other data inadequacies that may affect the analysis of the social benefits of education beyond those associated with unobserved hetero-geneities that may affect observed behavior in observing certain variables. The data used to represent education in many studies are crude, with random measurement errors that may bias the estimated effects toward zero and systematic measurement errors (e.g., the use of schooling attainment with no information on school quality, which is positively associated with the indicators of education used such as grades of school) that may bias estimates of educational effects in either direction. The data used to represent outcomes affected by education, particularly for some of the social benefits of particular interest for this volume, also are often very crude and—as noted—may be available only for selected subsamples (e.g., those who elect to go to hospitals or those who choose to have children when they are teenagers). Such data problems can affect what we think we know about the social effects of education and the choice of desirable strategies for attempting to estimate the social effects of education. I here review some of the issues surrounding data problems, first regarding education, and then present some illustrations of outcomes of interest.

Measurement errors in education indicators. If education is measured with error, its effects on social outcomes cannot be identified (estimated without bias) even with information on MZ and DZ twins. There are two sources of error in the empirical representations of education.

The first is that education itself may not be well characterized by a singulate measure such as years of schooling or highest grade completed, even if that measure is itself not error ridden. In the specification of the educational production function in relation 2 schooling attainment is but one of the inputs into the production of education, together with a number of individual, household, and community factors. Among these other inputs, the quality of schooling has been particularly emphasized by Behrman and Birdsall (1983), Behrman, Rosenzweig, and Taubman (1996), Hanushek (1986), Card and Krueger (1992a, 1992b), Harbison and Hanushek (1992), Behrman, Kletzer, McPherson, and Schapiro (1995), Hanushek et al. (1994), Heckman et al. (1994), Betts (1995), and a number of others. Some of these studies report that empirical estimates of the impact of schooling change substantially if school quality is incorporated into the analysis. Behrman and Birdsall, for example, report that the estimated rates of return to years of school are overstated in their Brazilian sample by 80 percent if the true specification includes school quality but quality is excluded from the model and that the social rates of return are at least as high to school quality as to school quantity investments. They provide a simple interpretation of why there is a bias in the estimated returns to years of schooling if school quality is ignored, namely, that more publicly subsidized school quality induces more schooling attainment within a modified version of the Becker (1967) Woytinsky model of human resource investments. Therefore, ignoring school quality is not likely to result in random measurement error but in systematic error that is associated with years of schooling. Hanushek et al. (1994) report benefit-cost estimates for improving the quality of very poor schools in the same society of 10 to 1. Ignoring school quality afflicts most of the estimates in the literature focusing on determining the returns of "education," which generally uses years of schooling. The inclusion of school quality measures (e.g., expenditures per student, library and computer facilities, teachers' education and cognitive achievement, and teachers' salaries) for analysis of the social effects of education would seem essential if education is to be represented by inputs into its production. The consequences of the omission of a quality dimension to schooling is attenuated somewhat using sibling data and somewhat more by using twins data because twins are more likely than "singulate" siblings to attend the same schools (particularly primary and secondary schools) and siblings are much more likely to do so than are randomly chosen individuals. Thus, schooling quality differences are minimized with twins relative to a sample of nontwin siblings and much less for siblings than for unrelated individuals. Studies that use sibling or twin data can estimate how much of the household and community effects are due to observed school quality indicators. Though this discussion, for illustration, has focused on multidimensional aspects of measuring education by means of schooling, once again, even if schooling is perfectly measured there are other factors that affect education—family, individual, and community factors and programs—not just schooling.

Whether a singulate measure of education is satisfactory, however, may depend upon whether the measure is one of educational *inputs,* such as schooling attainment and school quality, or is one of education itself. The leading nominee for the latter may be cognitive achievement as indicated by test scores. Cognitive achievement arguably is produced, as in relation 2, by combining schooling attainment, school quality, individual ability, household and community learning environments, and so on, in the production process. Studies of labor market outcomes in very different societies suggest that cognitive achievement is more consistent with those outcomes than is the years-of-schooling representation of education that dominates the literature (e.g., Alderman, Behrman, Ross, and Sabot 1996; Boissiere, Knight, and Sabot 1985; and Glewwe 1996). However, to my knowledge, such representations of education have not been used much, if at all, to explore social benefits. Of course, while cognitive achievement represents what most consider to be an important product of schooling and an important dimension of education, there may be other dimensions of education—such as self-discipline, problem-solving capabilities, specific skills, general knowledge, and learning how to learn—that also are important in assessing educational effects, but I am unaware of efforts to assess such possibilities systematically for either the economic or the social effects of education.

The second source of error is that indicators of education may not be reported accurately. There has been recent interest, for example, in measurement errors in schooling attainment, the educational indicator that primarily has been used in studies of the impact of education. It is well known that random measurement error in a regressor variable, in this case schooling, biases regression coefficient estimates toward zero. Sibling and twins studies have also been subject to the criticism that measurement error in schooling renders such "within estimates" of schooling effects more biased than individual estimates are (Bishop 1976; Griliches 1979). Griliches claims that a correction for measurement error in estimates for the NAS-NRC twin sample accounts for the difference between the MZ twin and OLS estimates of the impact of schooling obtained in the Behrman-Taubman studies. But his empirical demonstration depends on using a twin's first occupation as an instrument for his schooling, which does *not* seem to satisfy the first condition for a legitimate instrument (section 3.1.4)—independence from the disturbance. It is therefore difficult to know how to interpret this finding, although the theoretical point is important. It is not usually recognized, moreover, that measurement errors include both family and individual components. Grubb (1990), for example, reports that overstatements regarding years of postsecondary education (based on comparison of transcripts with self-reports) in the NLS High School Class of 1972 data are significantly (inversely) related to parents' socioeconomic status. Only that portion of measurement error that is individual-specific, however, afflicts within-family estimators. Therefore, the overall effect of measurement error on within estimates depends on the gain from controlling for common family measurement error versus the loss from exacerbating the effects of the remaining idiosyncratic component of measurement error.

Consider the case in which true schooling S_{ihc} is measured, with random error w containing both family f_{hc} and idiosyncratic e_{ihc} components, such that

$$S'_{ihc} = S_{ihc} + w_{ihc} = S_{ihc} + f_{hc} + e_{ihc}. \tag{8}$$

Bishop and Griliches show that the bias in the estimated β, b^w, from sibling deviation estimators when the measurement error is not correlated across adult siblings,[22] so that $w_{ij} = e_{ij}$ is:

$$\text{plim } b^w = \beta \left\{ 1 - \sigma_w^2 / \left[\sigma_{S'}^2 (1 - \rho_s) \right] \right\}, \tag{9}$$

---

22. These expressions for the biases due to measurement error using within-sibling estimators assume that the correlation across siblings in the measurement error (ρ_w) is zero. If this correlation is not zero because of a family component for the measurement error f_{hc}, for sibling deviation estimates plim $\hat{\beta} = \beta(1 - \phi\sigma_w^2/\sigma_S^2)$, where $\phi = (1 - \rho_w)/(1 - \rho_s)$. Note that the bias due to measurement error in the sibling deviation estimates declines as ρ_w increases and is less than the bias in standard individual estimates if $\rho_w > \rho_s$. I am not aware of direct observations on ϕ or ρ_w. But, if twins tend to attend the same schools and the cross-twin correlation is due to unobserved schooling quality, ρ_w may be fairly large. In any case, this measurement problem has not been dealt with in the literature making use of siblings or twins.

where ρ_s is the correlation across siblings in S.[23] If ρ_s is positive, as is the case for schooling, the measurement error bias toward zero in the sibling deviation estimates is greater than that in the standard individual estimates (for which $\rho_s = 0$) and is even greater for estimates based on twins, for whom correlations in schooling are higher than those for singulate siblings. For example, the cross-sibling correlation in schooling is about 0.55 (as reported for measured schooling in Olneck 1977 and Behrman, Taubman, and Wales 1977), and the cross-twin schooling correlations, based on the MTR sample, are 0.74 for MZ twins and 0.52 for single-sex DZ twins. If idiosyncratic measurement error is about 10 percent of the true variance in schooling for everyone, which is an overestimate given that the best prior estimates of measurement error, by Bielby, Hauser, and Featherman (1977),[24] are of this magnitude for the sum of family and idiosyncratic error components, the bias toward zero in estimates based on individuals would be 9 percent but would be 19 and 35 percent for the DZ and MZ samples, respectively.[25]

Ashenfelter and Krueger (1994) recently identified the schooling impact in earnings relations ß and the measurement error variance in a sample of twins attending a twin convention by utilizing an additional measure of schooling whose idiosyncratic measurement error is not correlated with that in the original measure—one twin's report of the other twin's schooling. With one additional

---

23. In note 21 I give the within-MZ moment expressions based on linear versions of relation 3 for H and relation 5 for E, if there is no measurement error in E, and show that the coefficient on education β in relation 3 is identified. If there is measurement error in E so that $\sigma_w^2 \neq 0$, these moments become: $\mathrm{Var}(\Delta H^M) = 2\beta^2\sigma_u^2 + 2\sigma_v^2$, $\mathrm{Var}(\Delta E^M) = 2\sigma_u^2 + 2\sigma_e^2$, and $\mathrm{Cov}(\Delta H^M, \Delta E^M) = 2\beta\sigma_u^2$, from which it can be seen that β is no longer identified (estimated without bias) from the ratio of the last two of these moments because of the presence of the idiosyncratic error term variance σ_e^2 (though the family component of measurement error causes no problem).

24. Bielby et al. used information on the schooling of a subset of nonblack respondents from the 1973 Consumer Price Survey (CPS) and reports of schooling from the same respondents in a telephone-based follow-up survey to estimate a measurement model. Their estimates indicated that the ratio of total measurement error variance to the true schooling variance was .051 in the 1973 CPS and .13 in the follow-up survey.

25. However, Behrman, Rosenzweig, and Taubman (1994) show that random measurement error in schooling does not affect their conclusions based on their MZ-DZ model regarding (1) whether there is compensation with respect to own schooling for individual-specific endowment differences and (2) whether there is positive assortative mating with respect to spouse's schooling and earnings endowments. They also show that, if the estimates are consistent with reinforcement under the assumption of no measurement error in schooling, it is possible to find the *maximum* proportion of idiosyncratic measurement error in observed schooling that would lead to the rejection of the conclusion that there is compensation, and that for their data this maximum implies that the share of idiosyncratic measurement error variance in the variance of true schooling would have to be 17 percent for this conclusion to be rejected, an extent of idiosyncratic measurement error that is considerably larger than that found in the most error-ridden (in terms of total error) of the two surveys studied by Bielby et al. (1977).

measure of schooling for each sibling (twin) and orthogonality across the idiosyncratic measurement errors of all four schooling indicators (or, rather, $e_{ij} - e_{kj}$ and $e'_{ij} - e'_{kj}$ are orthogonal where the $'$ refers to the additional measure), the true return for schooling ß is identified. Under this latter assumption, these "instrumental" variables add two equations to the model of the form:

$$S'_{ihc} = S_{ihc} + w'_{ihc} = S_{ihc} + f'_{hc} + e'_{ihc}. \tag{10}$$

Ashenfelter and Krueger's (1994) estimates, based on the implementation of this measurement error model applied to sibling schooling reports among MZ twin pairs, imply that the ratio of the variance in the idiosyncratic measurement error to the variance in true schooling is 8 to 12 percent in their sample. Comparisons of self-reported schooling and transcript-recorded schooling in the NLS High School Class of 1972 suggest a similar order of magnitude. In these data, for example, only 6.8 percent of those reporting a B.A. degree as of 1979 did not have one according to the transcript search covering the period 1982–84. The implementation in Behrman, Rosenzweig, and Taubman (1994) of a methodology similar to that of Ashenfelter and Krueger using the reports by the twins' offspring on the twins' schooling applied to the NAS-NRC data indicates that the idiosyncratic error variance in schooling is 8 percent of the true schooling variance. Behrman, Rosenzweig, and Taubman (1996), however, find that with better data on schooling the estimated noise to signal ratio is only 5.9 percent for years of schooling with sibling schooling reports and repeated own reports over time (which have correlated measurement errors over time rather than the independence usually assumed) and specification tests reject the use of measurement error corrections in estimating the impact of schooling on wages.

These explorations of the measurement error in reported schooling attainment have focused on the implications for estimates of labor market outcomes. But they indicate that such measurement errors are large enough to merit serious consideration as well in evaluating the social effects of education, particularly if use is made of various within estimators. I am not aware, however, of similar studies that explore the impact of measurement error in other indicators of education.

Measurement errors in indicators of social benefits of education. Many different indicators of the social benefits of education have been used in different studies. To continue with the health outcome that is used for illustration in section 3.1, for example, such indicators include self-reported health assessments, self-reported morbidity experience, anthropometric measures such as height and the body mass index, clinical measures, and mortality. Further, there are many studies of the impact of education on health-related behaviors such as smoking cigarettes and consuming other addictive substances, dietary patterns, exercise, and using different types of health-related services. Both the health outcomes and the health-related behaviors, moreover, may be for current or past experience, with the latter raising the further question of recall error. In this connection, research on "bounded recall" (Sudman et al. 1984; Loftus and Margurger 1982) suggests that linking retrospective questions to salient life-cycle events, such as weddings, increases significantly recall accuracy. For the other social outcomes of interest in this study there likewise are multiple indicators of outcomes—self-reports and police reports on criminal activities, multiple indicators of child development for evaluation of parenting, multiple reports on chemical composition of air, water, and soil, and of related health problems for environmental concerns.

Since our interest is in these variables as outcomes, as is well known, random errors in them do not cause problems in estimating the impact of education but merely add to the truly stochastic component of the disturbance terms in relations such as 3, 5, 6, and 7. Systematic reporting errors, in particular those related to education, however, cause biases. If, for example, more educated respondents are more likely to report certain illnesses, the true impact of education on preventing such illnesses is likely to be understated. If crime reports relatively understate white-collar crime, the true impact of education on reducing crime is likely to be overstated. Therefore, attention to such systematic reporting errors may be critical for obtaining estimates of the true social benefits of education.

The existence of multiple indicators of outcomes of interest also raises the question of whether some indicators are better representations of the phenomena of ultimate interest than are others. For this reason there have been efforts to assess the validity of alternative indicators. With regard to health indicators, for example, recent surveys by Idler and Kasl (1991, 1995) indicate that self-assessments predict subsequent mortality in existing longitudinal data sets better than "objective" health indicators do. Also, recent surveys of the epidemiological evidence by Ilo and Preston (1992), Fogel (1991a, 1991b), and Cole (1991) indicate that anthropometric indicators such as height and the body mass index (i.e., weight over height squared) are good predictors of the risk of morbidity and mortality. The medical literature further indicates that reports by family members of other family members' health (proxy reporting) are very accurate (Halabi et al. 1992), as are self-reports of weight and height, although there is a small upward bias in reports of height (Stewart 1981; Fortenberry 1992). Only two studies of which I am aware have attempted to assess recall accuracy with regard to anthropometric information on family members (Burns et al. 1987; Seidman and Gale 1988), both of which indicate that mothers reported accurately their children's birth weight up to 23 years after birth. Similar issues exist, of course, with respect to the other social outcomes that may be affected by education. For purposes of the interest in this volume in the social effects of education, the critical point is not whether some indicators have more or less random measurement error than others (which is the focus of much of the data validation literature) since random errors in these indicators do not cause biases in the estimated impact of education. The critical point is whether there are systematic errors, particularly errors related to education.

3.3.   When Are Policy Interventions Warranted?

Within the economics literature the basic reasons for policy interventions usually are summarized as being related to distribution (including poverty) and efficiency. The two are intertwined in that it would seem desirable to achieve distributional aims relatively efficiently since there probably are tradeoffs between the distributional and efficiency goals in most societies' social welfare functions.

From the point of view of efficiency, that education may have some strong positive effects is not in itself a reason for policy intervention and support, though many studies give such an interpretation. In addition, there must be a presumption of "market failures," in the sense that the total effects differ from the private effects, and some presumption that "policy failures" will not be of such magnitude so as to swamp possible gains from policy interventions. In analysis of education, such "market failures" are thought to arise possibly because of imperfect capital and insurance markets (e.g., difficulties in obtaining financing for educational investments and in pooling risks), information problems, and public goods or external aspects of education (e.g., effects on persons other than the individual being educated that are transferred other than through markets). However, much of the applied literature that purports to evaluate the policy implications of the impact of education is not sensitive to the analytical reasons for policy interventions related to education. The papers in this volume attempt to be sensitive to these issues and discuss to what extent the literature being reviewed does evaluate policy options within such an analytic context as well as how further research might be valuable for such reasons.

I now note briefly some simple standard reasons why total returns to education might exceed the private returns.

Technological externalities[26] are often thought to be important in considering policies related to education. Such externalities may be tied to a particular product or to the use of a particular factor, such as educated labor, in the production of a particular product, including outcomes that we are characterizing as "social effects," such as better health, reduced crime, better parenting, and a better environment. If there is a positive externality associated

---

26. The adjective *technological* is used to distinguish externalities that are not transferred through market prices from those that are so transferred, which are called pecuniary externalities.

with the production of a particular product, the social marginal cost curve net of the positive externality can be viewed as being below the private marginal cost curve. Therefore, the private incentive is to produce too small a quantity of the product, so consideration of policy interventions to induce more production is warranted. If there is a positive externality associated with the use of a particular input, such as educated labor in the production of a particular product, there are differences between social and private costs, so again there is a reason for consideration of policy interventions to encourage more use of the input that is generating the externalities.

Such externalities are claimed by some to be substantial for education, particularly with regard to the outcomes that are of interest for this volume. If more-educated individuals act so as to prevent themselves and their families from contracting contagious diseases (private returns) and if that has spillovers in lessening the probabilities of members of other households contracting such diseases, then the total returns to education in terms of preventing diseases exceed the private returns. If more-educated individuals are less likely to engage in nonmarket criminal activities that impose resource costs on other members of society, then the total gains from their education exceed the private gains. If more-educated individuals are likely to choose consumption patterns that are less pollution-intensive ceteris paribus, then the total returns on their education again exceed the private gains. If more-educated individuals are better parents with the result that their children impose less cost on society through delinquency, crime, and welfare transfers, the total returns on their education again exceed the private gains.

Within the framework of section 3.1, such effects can be represented as effects of the education of individual i in household h in community c on outcomes of individual j in household f in community d that are not transferred through markets in a relation such as (where the community subscript d may be the same as c because the two relevant individuals may or may not be in the same community):

$$H_{jfd} = g(E_{ihc}, I_{ihc}, F_{hc}, C_c, I^u_{ihc}, F^u_{hc}, C^u_c, X^u_{ihc}, e^j_{ihc}). \tag{11}$$

The estimation problems are parallel to those that are discussed in section 3.1. To obtain a consistent estimate of the true impact of the education of i on the health (or other outcome) of j, the representation of the education of i must be orthogonal to the disturbance term in relation 11. The problems that arise are akin to the problems in estimating "community effects" discussed by Manski (1993). To evaluate the magnitude of such technological externalities, moreover, it must be ascertained what amount of the effect of the education of i on outcome H for individual j is captured by private prices paid by j to i for goods or services. For example, if i is a better-educated medical doctor, the health of patient j may be improved, but there is no externality if j pays i for medical services the total marginal social value of those services.

A basic issue that must be considered is the entity to which a given effect is external. Often it is claimed, for example, that the impact of parental education on child development, broadly defined, is an external effect, so consideration should be given to public subsidies for education because of this impact. But this would seem to depend on what the relevant entity is. Such an effect is external to the individual (parent) educated. But it is not external to the family. If an individual with greater education increases the productivity of others working in the same firm, that in itself does not create an externality if the individual is paid the value of her or his marginal product to the firm. If a mother having greater education makes other family members more productive, likewise, it may not create an externality from the perspective of the family, though the analogy with the firm may not hold completely because of market imperfections regarding movements of individuals among families and because of possible special considerations concerning the capacities and options of children. Sometimes, for example, it is claimed that society has a greater interest in the future than do individuals, so that the social discount rate is lower than the private discount rate. In this case, society may want to subsidize investments in children, and a means to do so would be to subsidize the education of their parents (or of potential parents). There also seems to be a distributional concern about children because they are seen as more vulnerable and less able to fend for themselves. In a growing economy, of course, there would not seem to be an equity incentive for subsidizing children on the average because on the average children are better off than their parents. But there may be a legitimate social distributional concern about those children who are worse off in various dimensions, enhanced by the perceptions that such children may have limited choices and are more likely to impose external costs on others (e.g., through using public social services or committing crimes). If so, and if parental education lessens the probability of children being in such bad situations, then there may be reason for considering public subsidies again for parental education. But I perceive that often the discussion of the policy reasons for subsidizing education on such parental-child grounds is fairly murky and usefully could be made clearer in order to think better about policy. Even if this short discussion does not clarify completely all these issues, hopefully it will help to provoke needed thought about them.

Uncertainty and related information externalities in a dynamic world are likely to be pervasive. If knowledge about a new market is imperfect and entry into such markets by firms is sequential, for example, Rob (1989) observes that information externalities are created. Effectively, better information about the extent of the market becomes available over time for potential new entrants from the observed experience of previous entrants. But the early entrants do not receive any return from the provision of such information, so they provide it too slowly (by entering the market too slowly) from a social point of view. Rob formally investigates the details and the properties of such a phenomenon. The major results include the findings that: (1) the equilibrium rate of entry is monotonically decreasing over time (since the expanding supply lessens the prospects of further expected profits by further entrants) and (2) at any point in time the private equilibrium entry rate is less than the social one because of the information externalities about the size of the uncertain market. If the capacity to evaluate potential markets depends in part on human resources, a possibly important implication of the second point is that there may be reasons from a social point of view to increase human resources in order to reduce the divergence between the privately optimal and socially optimal rates of entry. Moreover, a similar argument may be made about firms and other entities ranging from police departments concerned with crime, to hospitals concerned with health, to environmental agencies adopting other innovations, such as new sources of inputs or new technology, to the extent that their subsequent behavior lessens information problems for potential following entities.

Finally, I note that technological externalities, in the sense of differences between total and private rates of return, may be negative as well as positive. In a simple pure signaling model in which those with more abilities find schooling less costly and employers cannot directly observe abilities, for instance, the private returns from signaling through schooling of receiving higher earnings exceed the total returns by the cost of schooling since schooling has no effect on productivity. In more complicated cases in which, say, there may be increasing returns to scale from assembling a number of people of similar abilities, there may be social as well as private gains from signaling, so whether the net impact results in positive or negative differences between total and private rates of return is an empirical question.

Increasing returns to scale are a second general reason for market failure and possible governmental policy intervention. If there are sufficient[27] increasing returns to scale in the production of a good or service, the private marginal cost declines with the scale of operation over a range of outputs. Over that output range, with marginal cost pricing a production entity is not able to cover total costs. If the entity has market power in the sense that it can affect the price at which it sells its product by changing the amount that it sells (or, in other words, faces a downward-sloping demand curve), it may be able to cover its costs by restricting its supply sufficiently and charging a price equal or greater than its average cost per unit of output.[28] Such a practice creates a wedge between the marginal unit expenditure (i.e., price) to users of the product and

27. *Sufficient* here means sufficient to offset any diminishing returns to fixed factors over a range of output.

28. If the entity is maximizing its net revenues or profits, then the textbook rule is that it should choose the level of output at which marginal costs equals marginal revenue.

the true marginal social cost of the product, and therefore it is not efficient. Overall welfare could be increased by expanding production and selling at a price equal to the marginal cost. If the marginal cost curve eventually turns up, such a condition can be satisfied by expanding production to the point at which price equals the long-run marginal cost. If the domestic market is not sufficiently large to absorb such a level of output and if the long-run marginal cost curve minimum is below the world price, such a position can be attained by exporting on the world market. If the marginal cost curve does not turn up over the relevant range, however, efficiency with marginal cost pricing can be obtained only with interventions such as subsidization to cover the fixed and part (that part above the marginal cost of the last unit sold) of the variable cost of inframarginal units sold.

How do such considerations relate to human resource investments? First, there may be increasing returns to scale over relevant ranges for some types of specialized education related to the social outcomes of interest (e.g., specialized surgeons). Second, recent growth models in Romer (1986), Lucas (1988), and elsewhere develop formally the implications of increasing returns to scale, together with externalities, in the impact of knowledge on production of goods and services that can include those of interest for the present volume.

Public goods, in a sense, are an extreme form of increasing returns to scale.[29] Public goods are goods for which more use by one individual does not preclude use by others. Therefore, the marginal cost of use by one more entity of such public goods is zero. For such goods my comments on the problems of marginal cost pricing obviously apply. If a private entity is to produce public goods and cover its costs (to say nothing of making a profit), it must price above the zero marginal cost and somehow privatize the public good by restricting access to the product. In doing so, however, inefficiency results because the price that users pay exceeds the true social marginal cost and too little of the good is used. One possibly important manner in which education relates to public goods is that knowledge often is thought to be close to a public good (though perhaps not quite a pure public good if there are relatively small, but still positive, costs of dissemination). And education is thought to be critical in the production and possibly the dissemination of knowledge. Smith, in chapter 6, discusses an interesting possibility in which more education may lead to more effective survey collection of information on which to base environmental policies. If education indeed is critical in the production and the dissemination of knowledge related to social outcomes, policies that increase the availability of knowledge beyond what would occur with private production of knowledge are likely to lead to greater efficiency.

---

29. See chapter 6 for a more extensive discussion of public goods within the particular context of the impact of education on the environment.

Capital and insurance market imperfections also are pervasive in a dynamic world with uncertainty and are thought to affect particularly educational and other human capital investments because of difficulties in establishing collateral in such investments and possibly greater moral hazard and adverse selection problems with human resources than with many other investments. If capital markets allow access to finances for all individuals at the same rate of interest (abstracting from risk differentials and risk aversion), the incentives exist for all individuals, independent of their family background, to invest in education and other human resources until the expected private rate of return on all relevant outcomes equals the interest rates. In the absence of adequate access to capital markets, human resource investments are likely to be less (and probably less than socially optimal), particularly for poorer households that cannot self-finance such investments. The capital market imperfections are likely to be even more constraining for the social effects of education since often these do not result in an increased income stream for the individual in whom the educational investment is made. In the absence of perfect insurance markets, risk-adverse individuals may underinvest in education, though progressive income tax structures and expenditures provide some risk pooling. If, as noted previously, the claim is true that poorer individuals are more risk averse, the lack of insurance is likely to discourage relatively investments in their human capital even if all people face the same risk and have the same means of coping with that risk. But those who are better off may face less risk and be better able to cope with it because, for example, the family background of those who are better off may lessen risk and enable individuals to cope better with bad outcomes (e.g., by working in the family business or for friends). Therefore, mechanisms that improve the possibility of risk pooling in human resource investments from their present level may have both efficiency and equity gains.

There also may be equity gains from minimal levels of educational investments if such investments, by improving the capacity of individuals to cope with unanticipated developments, increase the probability that they do not fall below some poverty, health, or other threshold. For example, it is claimed that more-educated individuals deal better with preventing AIDS, but from the perspective of most investments in education before 1980 this specific return on education was not widely anticipated. Of course, there are private gains to be had from capacities for dealing with unanticipated events and learning, so there are private incentives for investing in education if it improves such capacities. But the point here is that there may be social gains as well if society wishes, through voluntary or governmental processes, to provide support for individuals who are unable to cope with such changes, and those capacities are enhanced by education.

Policy interventions have costs, however, so that just because there is a market failure related to education or a distributional improvement that might be made with interventions related to education does not mean that a policy intervention, or a policy intervention related to education, is warranted. Policy interventions have both direct resource costs and distortion costs through changing incentives for behavior. If health care is subsidized by policies, for example, and education changes the demand for health care, the total marginal resource effects may differ from the private marginal incentives because of such subsidies. Likewise, if schooling is subsidized by policies and more education for women reduces their fertility, the total effects are likely to exceed the private effects because of the schooling subsidies. Therefore policy-induced market distortions may be important and represent a different class of reasons beyond market failures why, within a given policy context, outcomes may not be efficient. In fact, policy failures in many instances may be greater than market failures. That is, though market failures and distributional inadequacies undoubtedly are pervasive for some of the above reasons, there may not be policy interventions that are efficiency enhancing or distribution improving at a cost that society wishes to pay. Even if there are desirable policy interventions, there is the question of which interventions should be selected. Because of distortion costs of policies, unless there is an explicit argument to the contrary because of direct resource costs, distributional considerations, or second-best arguments, the best operating assumption is that interventions focused on the distortion are likely to be preferred both for efficiency reasons and because they are more transparent and thus more subject to monitoring and evaluation. Because more education may help to address some inefficiencies or distributional concerns does not mean that policy support for more education is the best policy. To the contrary, in some cases interventions to make markets work better or reduce policy distortions may be higher in the policy hierarchy. For most of the topics considered in the rest of this book, indeed, public subsidization of general education is not likely to be the best available policy if the only social benefit relates to that particular market failure or distributional problem, though some specific forms of education may be high in policy hierarchies for some problems. However, decisions about public subsidies of general education have to be considered in light of their total, and quite broad, possible effects.

Some forms of policies may work by changing people's preferences, which are assumed to be predetermined in the analysis of section 3.2. Such policies cause a real problem for welfare evaluation. Consider, for example, the case in which a policy is deemed to have good effects by those affected if they judge the policy by their preferences as modified by the policy, but is deemed to have bad effects by those affected if they judge the policy by their prepolicy preferences. How can one come to a judgment as to whether such a policy is good or bad? And, though for emphasis this example is given in which the policy is viewed as bad or good depending on whether the preferences before or after are used, the basic problem exists anytime the effects are viewed differently (including good to different degrees or bad to various degrees) depending on whether pre- or postpolicy preferences are used. For this reason it is not clear what to say about policies that change preferences.

Thus, there often are alleged to be important policy implications because of the social effects of education, and there are a number of a priori reasons why policy interventions to support education on such grounds might be warranted. But empirical assessment of possible efficiency and distributional reasons for such policy interventions and of the relative merits of policy support of education versus other possible interventions is difficult indeed, even if preferences are unaffected (and probably impossible if they are affected). The other chapters presented in this volume devote some of their efforts to assessments of what we know and what we might learn about the policy implications of measured social effects of education in addition to what we know and what we might learn about the effects of education and the distribution of those effects between private and social ones.

REFERENCES

Alderman, H., J. R. Behrman, D. Ross, and R. Sabot. 1996. The Returns to Endogenous Human Capital in Pakistan's Rural Wage Labor Market. *Oxford Bulletin of Economics and Statistics* 58 (February):29–55.

Angrist, J. D., K. Graddy, and G. W. Imbens. 1995. Non-parametric Demand Analysis with an Application to the Demand for Fish. Cambridge, MA: National Bureau of Economic Research. Mimeo.

Angrist, J. D., and A. B. Krueger. 1991. Does Compulsory School Attendance Affect Schooling and Earnings? *Quarterly Journal of Economics* 106:979–1014.

Angrist, J. D., and A. B. Krueger. 1992a. The Effect of Age at School Entry on Educational Attainment: An Application of Instrumental Variables with Moments from Two Samples. *Journal of the American Statistical Association* 87:328–36.

Angrist, J. D., and A. B. Krueger. 1992b. Estimating the Payoff to Schooling Using the Vietnam-Era Draft Lottery. Working Paper no. 4067. Cambridge, MA: National Bureau of Economic Research.

Angrist, J. D., and A. B. Krueger. 1994. Why do World War II Veterans Earn More? *Journal of Labor Economics* 12:74–97.

Ashenfelter, O., and A. Krueger. 1994. Estimates of the Economic Return to Schooling from a New Sample of Twins. *American Economic Review* 84:1157–74.

Barrera, A. 1990a. The Role of Maternal Schooling and Its Interaction with Public Health Programs in Child Health Production. *Journal of Development Economics* 32:69–92.

Barrera, A. 1990b. The Interactive Effects of Mother's Schooling and Unsupplemented Breastfeeding on Child Health. *Journal of Development Economics* 34:81–98.

Barro, R. 1974. Are Government Bonds New Wealth? *Journal of Political Economy* 82:1095–1117.

Becker, G. S. 1965. A Model of the Allocation of Time. *Economic Journal* 75:493–517.

Becker, G. S. 1967. Human Capital and the Personal Distribution of Income: An Analytical Approach. Ann Arbor: University of Michigan, Woytinsky Lecture. Republished in G. S. Becker, *Human Capital*, 2d ed. New York: National Bureau of Economic Research, 1975.

Becker, G. S. 1974. A Theory of Social Interactions. *Journal of Political Economy* 82:1063–93.

Becker, G. S. 1991. *A Treatise on the Family*. 2d ed. Cambridge: Harvard University Press.

Becker, G. S., and C. B. Mulligan. 1993. On the Endogenous Determination of Time Preference. University of Chicago. Mimeo.

Becker, G., and N. Tomes. 1976. Child Endowments and the Quantity and Quality of Children. *Journal of Political Economy* 84:S143–62.

Behrman, J. R. 1988. Intrahousehold Allocation of Nutrients in Rural India: Are Boys Favored? Do Parents Exhibit Inequality Aversion? *Oxford Economic Papers* 40:32–54.

Behrman, J. R. 1994. Intrafamily Distribution in Developing Countries. *Pakistan Development Review* 33:253–96.

Behrman, J. R. 1996. Intrahousehold Distribution and the Family. In *Handbook of Population and Family Economics*. ed. M. R. Rosenzweig and O. Stark. Amsterdam: North-Holland Publishing Company.

Behrman, J. R., and N. Birdsall. 1983. The Quality of Schooling: Quantity Alone is Misleading. *American Economic Review* 73:928–46.

Behrman, J. R., and N. Birdsall. 1988. Implicit Equity-Productivity Tradeoffs in the Distribution of Public School Resources in Brazil. *European Economic Review* 32:1585–1601.

Behrman, J. R., and S. G. Craig. 1987. The Distribution of Public Services: An Exploration of Local Governmental Preferences. *American Economic Review* 77:37–49.

Behrman, J. R., Z. Hrubec, P. Taubman, and T. J. Wales. 1980. *Socioeconomic Success: A Study of the Effects of Genetic Endowments, Family Environment, and Schooling.* Amsterdam: North-Holland Publishing Company.

Behrman, J. R., L. Kletzer, M. McPherson, and M. O. Schapiro. 1995. A Sequential Model of Educational Investment: How Family Background Affects High School Achievement, College Enrollments and Choice of College Quality. University of Pennsylvania. Mimeo.

Behrman, J. R., R. A. Pollak, and P. Taubman. 1982. Parental Preferences and Provision for Progeny. *Journal of Political Economy* 90:52–73.

Behrman, J. R., R. A. Pollak, and P. Taubman. 1986. Do Parents Favor Boys? *International Economic Review* 27:31–52.

Behrman, J. R., R. A. Pollak, and P. Taubman. 1995. The Wealth Model: Efficiency in Education and Equity in the Family. In *From Parent to Child: Inequality and Immobility in the United States*, ed. J. R. Behrman, R. A. Pollak, and P. Taubman. Chicago: University of Chicago Press.

Behrman, J. R., M. R. Rosenzweig, and P. Taubman. 1994. Endowments and the Allocation of Schooling in the Family and in the Marriage Market: The Twins Experiment. *Journal of Political Economy* 102:1131–74.

Behrman, J. R., M. R. Rosenzweig, and P. Taubman. 1996. College Choice and Wages: Estimates Using Data on Female Twins. *Review of Economics and Statistics.*

Behrman, J. R., M. R. Rosenzweig, and P. Vashishtha. 1995. Location-Specific Technical Change, Human Capital and Local Economic Development: The Indian Green Revolution Experience. In *Locational Competition in the World Economy*, ed. H. Siebert. Kiel: Kiel Institute of World Economics.

Behrman, J. R., and R. K. Sah. 1984. What Role Does Equity Play in the International Distribution of Aid? In *Economic Structure and Performance*, ed. M. Syrquin, L. Taylor, and L. E. Westphal. New York: Academic Press.

Behrman, J. R., and P. Taubman. 1976. Intergenerational Transmission of Income and Wealth. *American Economic Review* 66:436–40.

Behrman, J. R., and P. Taubman. 1986. Birth Order, Schooling and Earnings. *Journal of Labor Economics* 4:S121–45.

Behrman, J. R., and P. Taubman. 1989. Is Schooling "Mostly in the Genes"? Nature-Nurture Decomposition with Data on Relatives. *Journal of Political Economy* 97:1425–46.

Behrman, J. R., P. Taubman, and T. J. Wales. 1977. Controlling for and Measuring the Effect of Genetics and Family Environment in Equations for Schooling and Labor Market Success. In *Papers in Kinometrics: Determinants of Socioeconomic Success within and between Families*, ed. P. Taubman. Amsterdam: North-Holland Publishing Company.

Behrman, J. R., and B. L. Wolfe. 1984. The Socioeconomic Impact of Schooling in a Developing Country. *Review of Economics and Statistics* 66:296–303.

Behrman, J. R., and B. L. Wolfe. 1987. How Does Mother's Schooling Affect the Family's Health, Nutrition, Medical Care Usage, and Household Sanitation? *Journal of Econometrics* 36:185–204.

Behrman, J. R., and B. L. Wolfe. 1989. Does More Schooling Make Women Better Nourished and Healthier? Adult Sibling Random and Fixed Effects Estimates for Nicaragua. *Journal of Human Resources* 24:644–63.

Berger, M. C. 1988. Predicted Future Earnings and Choice of College Major. *Industrial and Labor Relations Review* 41:418–29.

Bernheim, B. D., A. Shleifer, and L. Summers. 1985. The Strategic Bequest Motive. *Journal of Political Economy* 93:1045–76.

Betts, J. R. 1995. Is There a Link between School Inputs and Earnings? Fresh Scrutiny of an Old Literature. In *Does Money Matter? The Link between Schools, Student Achievement, and Adult Success*, ed. G. Burtless. Washington, DC: The Brookings Institution.

Bielby, W. T., R. M. Hauser, and D. L. Featherman. 1977. Response Errors of Non-Black Males in Models of the Stratification Process. In *Latent Variables in Socio-Economic Models*, ed. D. A. Aigner and A. S. Goldberger. Amsterdam: North-Holland Publishing Company.

Binswanger, H. P. 1980. Attitudes toward Risk: Experimental Measurement in Rural India. *American Journal of Agricultural Economics* 62:395–407.

Bishop, J. 1976. Reporting Errors and the True Return to Schooling. University of Wisconsin-Madison. Mimeo.

Blackburn, M. L., and D. Neumark. 1995. Are OLS Estimates of the Return to Schooling Biased Downward? Another look. *Review of Economics and Statistics* 77:217–30.

Boissiere, M., J. B. Knight, and R. H. Sabot. 1985. Earnings, Schooling, Ability and Cognitive Skills. *American Economic Review* 75:1016–30.

Boulier, B. L., and M. R. Rosenzweig. 1984. Schooling, Search and Spouse Selection: Testing Economic Theories of Marriage and Household Behavior. *Journal of Political Economy* 92:712–32.

Bound, J., D. A. Jaeger, and R. Baker. 1993. The Cure Can Be Worse than the Disease: A Cautionary Tale regarding Instrumental Variables. Research Technical Paper no. 137. Cambridge, MA: National Bureau of Economic Research.

Bound, J., D. A. Jaeger, and R. M. Baker. 1995. Problems with Instrumental Variables Estimation When the Correlation between the Instruments and the Endogenous Explanatory Variable is Weak. *Journal of the American Statistical Association* 90:443–50.

Bronars, S. G., and J. Grogger. 1994. The Economic Consequences of Unwed Motherhood: Using Twin Births as a Natural Experiment. *American Economic Review* 1141–56.

Burns, T. L., et al. 1987. Mothers Remember Birthweights of Adolescent Children: The Muscatine Ponderosity Family Study. *International Journal of Epidemiology* 16:550–55.

Butcher, K. F., and A. Case. 1994. The Effect of Sibling Sex Composition on Women's Education and Earnings. *Quarterly Journal of Economics* 109:531–64.

Card, D. E. 1993. *Using Geographic Variation in College Proximity to Estimate the Return to Schooling*. Working Paper No. 4,483. Cambridge, MA: National Bureau of Economic Research.

Card, D. E. 1994. Earnings, Schooling, and Ability Revisited. Working Paper No. 4,832. Cambridge, MA: National Bureau of Economic Research.

Card, D. E., and A. B. Krueger. 1992a. School Quality and Black-White Relative Earnings: A Direct Assessment. *Quarterly Journal of Economics* 107:151–200.

Card, D. E., and A. B. Krueger. 1992b. Does School Quality Matter? Returns to Education and the Characteristics of Public Schools in the United States. *Journal of Political Economy* 100:1–40.

Cardell, N. S., and M. M. Hopkins. 1977. Education, Income, and Ability: A Comment. *Journal of Political Economy* 85:211–15.

Cavalli-Sforza, L. L., and W. F. Bodmer. 1971. *The Genetics of Human Populations*. San Francisco: W. H. Freeman and Company.

Chamberlain, G. 1977. Are Brothers as Good as Twins? In *Papers in Kinometrics: The Determinants of Socioeconomic Success within and between Families*, ed. P. Taubman. Amsterdam: North-Holland Publishing Company.

Chamberlain, G. 1982. Multivariate Regression Models for Panel Data. *Journal of Econometrics* 18:5–46.

Chamberlain, G. 1984. Panel Data. In *The Handbook of Econometrics*, ed. Z. Griliches and M. Intrilligator, vol. 2. Amsterdam: North-Holland Publishing Company.

Chamberlain, G., and Z. Griliches. 1975. Unobservables with a Variance Components Structure: Ability, Schooling, and the Economic Success of Brothers. *International Economic Review* 16:442–49.

Chamberlain, G., and Z. Griliches. 1977. More on Brothers. In *Papers in Kinometrics: Determinants of Socioeconomic Success within and between Families*, ed. P. Taubman. Amsterdam: North-Holland Publishing Company.

Cochrane, S. H., J. Leslie and D. J. O'Hara. 1982. Parental Education and Child Health: Intracountry Evidence. *Health Policy and Education* 2:213–50.

Cole, T. J. 1991. Weight-Stature Indices to Measure Underweight, Overweight, and Obesity. In *Anthropometric Assessment of Nutritional Status,* ed. John H. Himes. New York: Wiley-Liss, Inc.

Currie, J., and N. Cole. 1993. Welfare and Child Health: The Link between AFDC Participation and Birth Weight. *American Economic Review* 83:971–85.

Deaton, A. 1995. Data and Econometric Tools for Development Analysis. In *Handbook in Development Economics,* vol. 3A. ed. J. R. Behrman and T. N. Srinivasan. Amsterdam: North-Holland Publishing Company.

Epstein, E., and R. Guttman. 1984. Mate Selection in Man: Evidence, Theory, and Outcome. *Social Biology* 31:243–78.

Fogel, R. W. 1991a. New Sources and New Techniques for the Study of Secular Trends in Nutritional Status, Health, Mortality, and the Process of Aging. Cambridge, MA: National Bureau of Economic Research. Mimeo.

Fogel, R. W. 1991b. New Findings on Secular Trends in Nutrition and Mortality: Some Implications for Population Theory. University of Chicago. Mimeo.

Fortenberry, J. D. 1992. Reliability of Adolescents' Reports of Height and Weight. *Journal of Adolescent Health* 13:114–17.

Foster, A. D., and M. R. Rosenzweig. 1993. Information Flows and Discrimination in Labor Markets in Low-Income Countries. In *World Bank Economic Review and Work Bank Research Observer: Proceedings of the World Bank Annual Conference on Development Economics.* Washington, DC: World Bank.

Foster, A. D., and M. R. Rosenzweig. 1994. Technical Change and Human Resources and Investments: Consequences of the Green Revolution. University of Pennsylvania. Mimeo.

Foster, A. D., and M. R. Rosenzweig. 1995. Learning by Doing and Learning from Others: Human Capital and Technical Change in Agriculture. *Journal of Political Economy* 6:1176–1209.

Fuchs, V. R. 1982. Time Preference and Health: An Exploratory Study. In *Economic Aspects of Health*, ed. V. R. Fuchs. Chicago: University of Chicago Press for the National Bureau of Economic Research.

Gale, D., and L. Shapley. 1962. College Admission and the Stability of Marriage. *American Mathematical Monthly* 69:9–15.

Geronimus, A. J., and S. Korenman. 1992. The Socioeconomic Consequences of Teen Childbearing Reconsidered. *Quarterly Journal of Economics* 107:1187–1214.

Gershberg, A. I., and T. Schuermann. 1994. Education Finance in a Federal System:

Changing Investment Patterns in Mexico. New School for Economic Research and AT&T Bell Laboratories. Mimeo.

Glewwe, P. 1996. The Relevance of Standard Estimates of Rates of Return to Schooling for Education Policy: A Critical Assessment. *Journal of Development Economics*.

Glewwe, P., and H. Jacoby. 1994. Student Achievement and Schooling Choice in Low Income Countries: Evidence from Ghana. *Journal of Human Resources* 29:842–64.

Goldberg, J., W. R. True, S. E. Eisen, and W. G. Henderson. 1990. A Twin Study of the Effects of the Vietnam War on Posttraumatic Stress Disorder. *Journal of the American Medical Association* 263:1227–32.

Griliches, Z. 1977. Estimating the Returns to Schooling: Some Econometric Problems, *Econometrica* 45:1–22.

Griliches, Z. 1979. Sibling Models and Data in Economics: Beginning of a Survey. *Journal of Political Economy* 87:S37–64.

Griliches, Z., and W. M. M. Mason. 1972. Education, Income, and Ability. *Journal of Political Economy* 80:S75–103.

Grossman, M. 1972a. *The Demand for Health: A Theoretical and Empirical Investigation*. New York: Columbia University Press.

Grossman, M. 1972b. On the Concept of Health Capital and the Demand for Health. *Journal of Political Economy* 80:223–55.

Grossman, M., and L. Edwards. 1980. Children's Health and the Family. In *Annual Series of Research in Health Economics*, ed. R. Scheffler, vol. 2. Greenwich, CT: JAI Press.

Grubb, N. W. 1990. The Economic Returns to Postsecondary Education: New Evidence from the National Longitudinal Study of the Class of 1972. University of California-Berkeley. Mimeo.

Grubb, N. W. 1993. The Varied Economic Returns to Postsecondary Education: New Evidence from the Class of 1972. *Journal of Human Resources* 28:365–82.

Halabi, S., et al. 1992. Reliability and Validity of Self and Proxy Reporting of Morbidity Data: A Case Study from Beirut, Lebanon. *International Journal of Epidemiology* 21:607–12.

Hanushek, E. A. 1986. The Economics of Schooling. *Journal of Economic Literature* 24:1141–77.

Hanushek, E. A., J. B. Gomes-Neto, and R. W. Harbison. 1994. Self-Financing Educational Investments: The Quality Imperative in Developing Countries. University of Rochester. Mimeo.

Hanushek, E. A., S. Rivkin, and L. L. Taylor. 1995. Aggregation, Omitted Variables and the Estimation of Education Production Functions. University of Rochester. Mimeo.

Harbison, R. W., and E. A. Hanushek. 1992. *Educational Performance of the Poor: Lessons from Rural Northeast Brazil*. New York: Oxford University Press for the World Bank.

Hauser, R., and T. Daymont. 1977. Schooling, Ability, and Earnings: Cross-Sectional Findings 8 to 14 Years after High School Graduation. *Sociology of Education* 50:182–205.

Haveman, R., and B. L. Wolfe. 1984. Education and Well-Being: The Role of Non-Market Effects. *Journal of Human Resources* 19:408–29.

Haveman, R., and B. L. Wolfe. 1993. Children's Prospects and Children's Policy. *Journal of Economic Perspectives* 7:153–74.

Heckman, J. J., A. Layne-Farrar, and P. Todd. 1994. Does Measured School Quality Really Matter? Understanding the Empirical and Economic Foundations of the Evidence. University of Chicago and the American Bar Foundation. Mimeo.

Heckman, J. J., and T. E. MaCurdy. 1980. A Life Cycle Model of Female Labor Supply. *Review of Economic Studies* 47:47–74.

Herrnstein, R. J., and C. Murray. 1994. *The Bell Curve: Intelligence and Class Structure in American Life*, New York: Free Press.

Horton, S. 1988. Birth Order and Child Nutritional Status: Evidence on the Intra-household Allocation of Resources in the Philippines. *Economic Development and Cultural Change* 36:341–54.

Idler, E. L., and S. Kasl. 1991. Health Perception and Survival: Do Global Evaluations of Health Status Really Predict Mortality? *Journal of Gerontology* 46:S55–65.

Idler, E. L., and S. Kasl. 1995. Self-Ratings of Health: Do They Also Predict Change in Functional Ability? *Journal of Gerontology* 50B:S344–53.

Ilo, I. T., and S. H. Preston. 1992. Effects of Early-Life Conditions on Adult Mortality: A Review. *Population Index* 58:186–212.

King, E. M., and M. A. Hill, eds. 1993. *Women's Education in Developing Countries: Barriers, Benefits, and Policies*. Baltimore and London: Johns Hopkins University Press for the World Bank.

Knight, J. B., and R. H. Sabot. 1990. *Educational Productivity and Inequality: The East African Natural Experiment*. New York: Oxford University Press.

Lam, D. 1988. Assortative Mating with Household Public Goods. *Journal of Human Resources* 23:462–87.

Lillard, L., J. Smith, and F. Welch. 1986. What Do We Really Know about Wages? The Importance of Non-Reporting and Census Imputation. *Journal of Political Economy* 94:489–506.

Loftus, E., and W. Margurger. 1982. Improving the Accuracy of Retrospective Reports with Landmark Events. *Memory and Cognition* 11:114–20.

Lucas, R. E. 1988. On the Mechanics of Economic Development. *Journal of Monetary Economics* 21:3–42.

Lykken, D. T., T. J. Bouchard, M. McGue, A. Tellegen. 1990. The Minnesota Twin Family Registry: Some Initial Findings. *Acta Geneticae Medicae et Gemellologiae* 39:35–70.

Manski, C. F. 1989. Anatomy of the Selection Problem. *Journal of Human Resources* 24:341–60.

Manski, C. F. 1993. Identification of Endogenous Social Effects: The Reflection Problem. *Review of Economic Studies* 60:531–42.

Manski, C. F., G. D. Sandefur, S. McLanahan, and D. Powers. 1992. Alternative Estimates of the Effect of Family Structure during Adolescence on High School Graduation. *Journal of the American Statistical Association* 87:25–37.

Manski, C. F., and D. A. Wise. 1983. *College Choice in America*. Cambridge: Harvard University Press.

Mare, R. D., and W. M. Mason. 1980. Children's Reports of Parental Socioeconomic Status. *Sociological Methods and Research* 9:178–98.

Michael, R. T. 1982. Measuring Non-Monetary Benefits of Education: A Survey. In *Financing Education: Overcoming Inefficiency and Inequality*, ed. V. McMahon and T. Gepke. Urbana: University of Illinois Press.

Miller, P., C. Mulvey, and N. Martin. 1995. What Do Twins Studies Tell Us about the Economic Returns to Education? A Comparison of U.S. and Australian Findings. *American Economic Review* 85:586–99.

Miller, P., C. Mulvey, and N. Martin. 1996. Family Characteristics and the Returns to Schooling: Evidence on Gender Differences from a Sample of Australian Twins, *Economica*.

Nelson, R., and R. Startz. 1990a. The Distribution of the Instrumental Variables Estimator and the T-ratios When the Instrument is a Poor One. *Journal of Business* 63:S125–40.

Nelson, R., and R. Startz. 1990b. Some Further Results on the Exact Small Sample Properties of the Instrumental Variable Estimator. *Econometrica* 58:967–76.

Olneck, M. 1977. On the Use of Sibling Data to Estimate the Effects of Family Background, Cognitive Skills, and Schooling: Results from the Kalamazoo Brothers Study. In *Kinometrics: Determinants of Socioeconomic Success within and between Families*, ed. P. Taubman. Amsterdam: North-Holland Publishing Company.

Pitt, M. M., and M. R. Rosenzweig. 1990. Estimating the Behavioral Consequences of Health in a Family Context: The Intrafamily Incidence of Infant Illness in Indonesia. *International Economic Review* 31:969–89.

Pitt, M. M., M. R. Rosenzweig, and D. M. Gibbons. 1993. The Determinants and Consequences of the Placement of Government Programs in Indonesia. *World Bank Economic Review* 7:319–48.

Pitt, M. M., M. R. Rosenzweig, and M.N. Hassan. 1990. Productivity, Health, and Inequality in the Intrahousehold Distribution of Food in Low-Income Countries. *American Economic Review* 80:1139–56.

Plomin, R., J. C. DeFries, and G. E. McClearn. 1980. *Behavioral Genetics: A Primer*. San Francisco: W. H. Freeman and Company.

Preston, S. H., and C. Campbell. 1993. Differential Fertility and the Distribution of Traits: The Case of IQ. *American Journal of Sociology* 98:997–1019.

Psacharopoulos, G. 1985. Returns to Education: A Further International Update and Implications. *Journal of Human Resources* 20:583–97.

Psacharopoulos, G. 1994. Returns to Investment in Education: A Global Update. *World Development* 22:1325–44.

Rob, R. 1989. The Evolution of Markets under Demand Uncertainty. University of Pennsylvania. Mimeo.

Romer, P. M. 1986. Increasing Returns and Long-Run Growth. *Journal of Political Economy* 94:1002–36.

Rosenzweig, M. R. 1995. Why Are There Returns in Schooling? *American Economic Review* 85:153–58.

Rosenzweig, M. R., and T. P. Schultz. 1981. Education and Household Production of Child Health. In *Proceedings of the American Statistical Association* (Social Statistics Section). Washington, DC: American Statistical Association.

Rosenzweig, M. R., and T. P. Schultz. 1982. Child Mortality and Fertility in Colombia: Individual and Community Effects. *Health Policy and Education*, vol. 2. Amsterdam: Elsevier Scientific Publishing Company.

Rosenzweig, M. R., and T. P. Schultz. 1983. Estimating a Household Production Function: Heterogeneity, the Demand for Health Inputs, and Their Effects on Birth Weight. *Journal of Political Economy* 91:723–46.

Rosenzweig, M. R., and T. P. Schultz. 1987. Fertility and Investments in Human Capital: Estimates of the Consequences of Imperfect Fertility Control in Malaysia. *Journal of Econometrics* 36:163–84.

Rosenzweig, M. R., and T. P. Schultz. 1988. The Stability of Household Production Technology: A Replication. *Journal of Human Resources* 23:535–45.

Rosenzweig, M. R., and T. P. Schultz. 1989. Schooling, Information and Non-Market Productivity: Contraceptive Use and Its Effectiveness. *International Economic Review* 30:457–77.

Rosenzweig, M. R., and K. I. Wolpin. 1980a. Life-Cycle Labor Supply and Fertility: Causal Inferences from Household Models. *Journal of Political Economy* 88:328–48.

Rosenzweig, M. R., and K. I. Wolpin. 1980b. Testing the Quantity-Quality Model of Fertility: Results of a Natural Experiment—Twins. *Econometrica* 48:227–40.

Rosenzweig, M. R., and K. I. Wolpin. 1986. Evaluating the Effects of Optimally Distributed Public Programs. *American Economic Review* 76:470–87.

Rosenzweig, M. R., and K. I. Wolpin. 1988. Heterogeneity, Intrafamily Distribution, and Child Health. *Journal of Human Resources* 23:437–61.

Rosenzweig, M. R., and K. I. Wolpin. 1994a. Are There Increasing Returns to the Intergenerational Production of Human Capital? Maternal Schooling and Child Intellectual Achievement. *Journal of Human Resources* 29:670–93.

Rosenzweig, M. R., and K. I. Wolpin. 1994b. Parental and Public Transfers to Young Women and Their Children. *American Economic Review* 84:1157–73.

Rosenzweig, M. R., and K. I. Wolpin. 1995. Sisters, Siblings and Mothers: The Effects of Teen-Age Childbearing on Birth Outcomes. *Econometrica* 63:303–26.

Schoen, R., and J. Wooldredge. 1980. Who Marries Whom: Marriage Patterns in California.,1970. Mimeo.

Schultz, T. P. 1988. Education Investments and Returns. In *Handbook of Development Economics*, ed. H. Chenery and T. N. Srinivasan. Amsterdam: North-Holland Publishing Company.

Schultz, T. P. 1990. Testing the Neoclassical Model of Family Labor Supply and Fertility. *Journal of Human Resources* 25:599–634.

Schultz, T. P. 1993a. Returns to Women's Education. In *Women's Education in Developing Countries: Barriers, Benefits, and Policies*, ed. E. M. King and M. A. Hill. Baltimore and London: Johns Hopkins University Press for the World Bank.

Schultz, T. P. 1993b. Investments in the Schooling and Health of Women and Men: Quantities and Returns. *Journal of Human Resources* 28:694–734.

Schultz, T. W. 1975. The Value of the Ability to Deal with Disequilibria. *Journal of Economic Literature* 13:827–46.

Seidman, D. S., and R. Gale. 1988. Accuracy of Maternal Recall of Birthweights of Adolescent Children. *International Journal of Epidemiology* 17:688–89.

Sheshinski, E., and Y. Weiss. 1982. Inequality within and between Families. *Journal of Political Economy* 90:105–27.

Stewart, A. 1981. The Reliability and Validity of Self-Reported Weight and Height. *Journal of Chronic Disease* 35:295–309.

Strauss, J. 1990. Households, Communities, and Preschool Children's Nutrition Outcomes: Evidence from Rural Cote d'Ivoire. *Economic Development and Cultural Change* 38:231–62.

Strauss, J., and D. Thomas. 1995. Human Resources: Empirical Modeling of Household and Family Decisions. In *Handbook of Development Economics,* ed. J. R. Behrman and T. N. Srinivasan, vol. 3A. Amsterdam: North-Holland Publishing Company.

Sudman, S., A. Finn, and L. Lannom. 1984. The Use of Bounded Recall Procedures in Single Interviews. *Public Opinion Quarterly* 48:520–24.

Thomas, D. 1990. Intrahousehold Resource Allocation: An Inferential Approach. *Journal of Human Resources* 25:635–64.

Thomas, D. 1993. The Distribution of Income and Expenditure within the Household. *Annales de Economie et de Statistiques* 29:109–36.

Thomas, D. 1994. Like Father, Like Son; Like Mother, Like Daughter: Parental Resources and Child Height. *Journal of Human Resources* 29:950–89.

Thomas, D., and C.-L. Chen. 1994. Income Shares and Share of Income: Empirical Tests of Models of Household Resource Allocations. Rand Corporation. Mimeo.

Thomas, D., J. Strauss, and M. H. Henriques. 1991. How Does Mother's Education Affect Child Height? *Journal of Human Resources* 26:183–211.

Vandenberg, S. G. 1972. Assortative Mating, or Who Marries Whom? *Behavior Genetics* 2:127–57.

Welch, F. 1970. Education in Production. *Journal of Political Economy* 78:35–59.

Weiss, Y. 1993. The Formation and Dissolution of Families: Why Marry? Who Marries Whom? And What Happens upon Marriage and Divorce? Tel-Aviv University, Department of Economics. Mimeo.

Wolfe, B. L., and J. R. Behrman. 1986. Child Quantity and Quality in a Developing Country: The Importance of Family Background, Endogenous Tastes and Biological Supply Factors. *Economic Development Cultural Change* 34:703–20.

Wolfe, B. L., and J. R. Behrman. 1987. Women's Schooling and Children's Health: Are the Effects Robust with Adult Sibling Control for the Women's Childhood Background? *Journal of Health Economics* 6:239–54.

Wolfe, B. L., and J. R. Behrman. 1992. The Synthesis Economic Fertility Model: A Latent Variable Investigation of Some Critical Attributes. *Journal of Population Economics* 5:1–16.

CHAPTER 4

Effects of Education on Health

Michael Grossman and Robert Kaestner

This chapter considers the effects of education in terms of its impacts on end result measures of good health. It also considers these benefits in terms of the effect of education on such proximate determinants of health as cigarette smoking, excessive alcohol use, and nutrition. To be consistent with the theme of this volume, we focus on the indirect or nonmonetary benefits of education (benefits other than those that arise because education raises income, which in turn raises health).[1]

After outlining conceptual foundations in section 4.1, we consider adult, childhood and adolescent, and infant health in sections 4.2, 4.3, and 4.4, respectively. Our focus in these sections is on empirical research, primarily with U.S.

This chapter was presented at a conference entitled "Social Benefits of Education: Can They be Measured?" sponsored by the Office of Research of the U.S. Department of Education and held at the Meridian International Center in Washington, D.C., on 4–5 January 1995. We are grateful to the conference participants for helpful comments, particularly Jere R. Behrman, Mark C. Berger, and Donald S. Kenkel. We also are indebted to J. Paul Leigh for several insightful suggestions. This chapter has not undergone the review accorded official National Bureau of Economic Research publications; in particular, it has not been submitted for approval by the board of directors.

Michael Grossman dedicates this chapter to the memory of Paul Taubman. I was not a close friend or colleague of Paul's, but we shared common research interests and we interacted over a long period of time beginning in the mid-1970s. I was one of a large number of persons who benefited from Paul's extraordinary ability to find extremely rich and novel data sets and his generosity in sharing them with other researchers. In the late 1970s I used the NBER-Thorndike Sample, originally collected by Paul, to undertake a project on the relationship between health and schooling that had a major impact on my professional career. The research resulting from that project and Paul's own work on the effects of schooling on earnings and health form an extremely important component of my chapter in this volume with Robert Kaestner. In my view the measure of a person is whether he or she made a difference in the lives of other persons. Paul Taubman made a difference.

1. If the only reason why more education leads to better health is that income and education are positively related, this is a monetary benefit. It does not differ in any essential way from the increased consumption of goods and services in general by higher-income persons. Note that we do not consider in this chapter the issue of how to translate the improvements in health caused by education into monetary equivalents. For a comprehensive treatment of this topic, see Tolley, Kenkel, and Fabian (1994).

data, especially research that attempts to establish a causal relationship from more schooling to better health. In section 4.5 we raise the issue of the extent to which the effect of education on health reflects externalities that may justify government intervention. Here the emphasis is on externalities associated with health and on the promotion of economic efficiency by increasing education on the one hand or by pursuing a variety of other policies on the other. Finally in section 4.6 we present an agenda for future research.

Before turning to these issues, we summarize trends in the educational attainment and health of the U.S. population since 1960 in tables 4.1 and 4.2,

TABLE 4.1. Educational Attainment, by Race, Selected Years, 1960–90 (percentage of persons aged 25 and older)

Year	All Races	White	Black
	Completed four years of high school or more		
1960	41.0	43.2	20.0
1970	52.4	54.5	31.3
1980	66.6	68.8	51.2
1990	77.6	79.1	66.2
	Completed four years of college or more		
1960	7.8	8.2	3.0
1970	10.8	11.4	4.4
1980	16.4	17.3	8.4
1990	21.4	22.2	11.4

Source: Computed from U.S. Bureau of the Census 1993, table 231.

TABLE 4.2. Infant and Age-Adjusted Mortality Rates, by Race, Selected Years, 1960–90

Year	All Races	White	Black
	Infant mortality rates[a]		
1960	26.0	22.9	44.3
1970	20.0	17.8	32.6
1980	12.6	11.0	21.4
1990	9.2	7.7	17.0
	Age-adjusted death rates[b]		
1960	7.6	7.3	10.7
1970	7.1	6.8	10.4
1980	5.9	5.6	8.4
1990	5.2	4.9	7.9

Source: National Center for Health Statistics 1994, tables 1–3 and 2–1.
[a]Deaths of infants under one year old per 1,000 live births.
[b]Deaths per 1,000 population.

respectively. Due to the substantial racial differences in these outcomes, data for whites and blacks are shown separately. According to the two tables, much progress has been made in raising schooling levels and reducing mortality in the past 30 years. For example, the percentage of whites with at least a high school education approximately doubled between 1960 and 1990, while the percentage of blacks with at least a high school education tripled (see table 4.1). At the same time, the percentage of whites who completed four years of college or more almost tripled, and the corresponding percentage of blacks almost quadrupled.

Equally impressive reductions in infant and age-adjusted mortality are reported in table 4.2. From 1960 through 1990, the white infant mortality rate declined by 66 percent and the black infant mortality rate declined by 62 percent. The corresponding declines in age-adjusted mortality amounted to 33 percent for whites and 26 percent for blacks.

The rapid growth in black schooling has reduced but not eliminated the advantage in this outcome historically enjoyed by whites. In 1960 whites were twice as likely to have completed high school than were blacks and almost three times as likely to have completed college. In 1990 whites were only 20 percent more likely to have completed high school than were blacks and only twice as likely to have completed college.

Despite the reduction in black-white schooling differentials and the sharp decline in mortality, black-white mortality differentials have been very stable during the past 30 years. Black babies were twice as likely to die as white babies were in both 1960 and 1990. The black age-adjusted death rate was 50 percent higher than the white rate in 1960 and 60 percent higher than the white rate in 1990.

Critics of the U.S. health care system frequently point to the excess mortality rate of blacks as one indicator of its shortcomings (see, e.g., National Commission to Prevent Infant Mortality 1992). Other indicators are that the U.S. infant mortality rate remains higher than those of a number of other developed countries and U.S. life expectancy at age 65 remains lower even when the U.S. data are limited to whites (National Center for Health Statistics 1993). Finally, Marks, Buehler, Hogue, Strauss, and Smith (1987, 150) report that in 1980 "differences between the States of the U.S. in infant . . . mortality are greater than those between the U.S. and the countries of Scandinavia [with the lowest infant mortality]."

Clearly, the trends in tables 4.1 and 4.2 suggest an association between educational attainment and good health. If schooling is the causal agent in this association, educational subsidies directed at certain groups could reduce some of the differentials in health just described. We address the issues of causality, the rationale for government intervention in the health outcomes of its citizens, and the nature of optimal interventions in the remainder of this chapter.

4.1. Conceptual Foundations

4.1.1. Household Production Function Model

The household production function model of consumer behavior, developed by Becker (1965) and Lancaster (1966), has served as the point of departure for much of the research by economists dealing with the effects of education, primarily measured by years of formal schooling completed, on health status. According to traditional demand theory, each consumer has a utility or preference function that allows him or her to rank alternative combinations of goods and services purchased in the market. Consumers are assumed to select that combination that maximizes their utility function subject to an income or resource constraint: namely, outlays on goods and services cannot exceed income. While this theory provides a satisfactory explanation of the demand for many goods and services, students of medical economics have long realized that what consumers demand when they purchase medical services is not these services per se but rather "good health." This rather obvious point explains why health economists beginning with Grossman (1972a, 1972b) have adopted the household production function model of consumer behavior.

The household production function model draws a sharp distinction between fundamental objects of choice—called commodities—that enter the utility function and market goods and services. Consumers produce commodities with inputs of market goods and services and their own time. For example, they use sporting equipment and their own time to produce recreation, traveling time and transportation services to produce visits, and part of their Sundays and church services to produce "peace of mind." The concept of a household production function is perfectly analogous to a firm production function. Each relates a specific output or a vector of outputs to a set of inputs. Since goods and services are inputs into the production of commodities, the demand for these goods and services is a derived demand for a factor of production. That is, the demand for medical care and other health inputs is derived from the basic demand for health.[2]

In Grossman's (1972a, 1972b) model, health—defined broadly to include longevity and illness-free days in a given year—is both demanded and produced by consumers. Health is a choice variable because it is a source of utility (satisfaction) and because it determines income or wealth levels. The health production function relates an output of health to such choice variables or health inputs as medical care utilization, diet, exercise, cigarette smoking, and alcohol consumption. In addition, the production function is affected by the efficiency or

---

2. The demand for certain other health inputs, such as cigarette smoking, is derived from the demand for "relaxation" as well as health.

productivity of a given consumer—the amount of health obtained from a given amount of health inputs—as reflected by his or her personal characteristics. Examples include age, race, sex, years of formal schooling completed, and the endowed or initial level of health.

Maximization of the utility function subject to health production and resource constraints generates demand functions for health and endogenous health inputs. These demand functions depend on income, prices, efficiency in production, tastes, and the health endowment. Taste variables influence the choice of different health levels by consumers with identical incomes, prices, efficiency, and endowments.

4.1.2. Empirical Implications

The distinction between health and health inputs, which is embedded in the multivariate production function, is a useful point of departure for research on the effects of education on health because it emphasizes a variety of mechanisms that govern health outcomes. Thus, education can influence health levels by influencing endogenous health inputs or by influencing the amount of health produced or obtained from a given vector of these inputs.

The framework also emphasizes that aspects of joint production are relevant in discussions of the effects of schooling on health. For instance, cigarette consumption has a negative marginal product in the health production function but has a positive marginal product in a production function for smoking satisfaction. To cite another example, some persons may choose a diet with a high fat and cholesterol content because its negative health consequences are outweighed by other factors.

A number of studies in the United States suggest that years of formal schooling completed is the most important correlate of good health (e.g., Auster, Leveson, and Sarachek 1969; Grossman 1972b; Silver 1972; Grossman and Benham 1974; Grossman 1975 and the references he cites; Newhouse and Friedlander 1980; Edwards and Grossman 1981, 1982, 1983; Grossman and Jacobowitz 1981; Shakotko, Edwards, and Grossman 1981; Corman and Grossman 1985; Winkleby, Jatulis, Frank, and Fortmann 1992; and Pappas, Queen, Hadden, and Fisher 1993).[3] This finding emerges whether health levels are measured by mortality rates, morbidity rates, self-evaluation of health status, or physiological indicators of health, and whether the units of observation are individuals or groups. It is notable because the studies suggest that schooling is a more important correlate of health than is occupation or income, the two other components of socioeconomic status. This is particularly true when one controls for reverse causality from poor health to low income. Of course, schooling is

---

3. For other studies, see sections 4.2–4.4.

a causal determinant of occupation and income, so that the gross effect of schooling on health may reflect in part its impact on socioeconomic status. The studies just cited, however, indicate that a significant portion of the gross schooling effect cannot be traced to the relationship between schooling and income or occupation.

In a broad sense, the observed positive correlation between health and schooling may be explained in one of three ways. The first argues that there is a causal relationship that runs from increases in schooling to increases in health. The second holds that the direction of causality runs from better health to more schooling. The third argues that no causal relationship is implied by the correlation; instead, differences in one or more "third variables," such as physical and mental ability and parental characteristics, affect both health and schooling in the same direction.

It should be noted that these three explanations are not mutually exclusive and can be used to rationalize any observed correlation between two variables. But from a public policy perspective it is important to distinguish among them and obtain quantitative estimates of their relative magnitudes. Suppose that a stated goal of public policy is to improve the level of health of the population or of certain groups in the population. Given this goal and the high correlation between health and schooling, it might appear that one method of implementation would be to increase government outlays on schooling. In fact, Auster, Leveson, and Sarachek (1969) suggest that the rate of return on increases in health via higher schooling outlays far exceeds the rate of return on increases in health via higher medical care outlays. This argument assumes that the correlation between health and schooling reflects only the effect of schooling on health. If, however, the causal relationship was the reverse, or if the third-variable hypothesis were relevant, then increased outlays on schooling would not accomplish the goal of improved health.

Causality from schooling to health results when more educated persons are more efficient producers of health. This efficiency effect can take two forms. Productive efficiency pertains to a situation in which the more educated obtain a larger health output from given amounts of endogenous (choice) inputs (Grossman 1972a, 1972b). Allocative efficiency pertains to a situation in which schooling increases information about the true effects of the inputs on health (Rosenzweig and Schultz 1981, 1982, 1983a, 1983b, 1988, 1991). For example, the more educated may have more knowledge about the harmful effects of cigarette smoking or about what constitutes an appropriate diet. Allocative efficiency will improve health to the extent that it leads to the selection of a better input mix.

Causality from schooling to health also results when education changes tastes or preferences in a manner that favors health relative to certain other commodities. In some cases the taste hypothesis cannot be distinguished from the allocative hypothesis, particularly when information has been available for some time. But in a situation in which new knowledge concerning, for example, the harmful effects of smoking on health becomes available, the allocative efficiency hypothesis predicts a more rapid response by the more educated.

Alternatively, the direction of causality may run from better health to more schooling because healthier students may be more efficient producers of additions to the stock of knowledge (or human capital) via formal schooling. Furthermore, this causal path may have lasting effects if past health is an input into current health status. Thus, even for nonstudents, a positive relationship between health and schooling may reflect reverse causality in the absence of controls for past health. Evidence in favor of this proposition is presented by Edwards and Grossman (1979), Shakotko, Edwards, and Grossman (1981), Perri (1984), Wolfe (1985), and Chaikind and Corman (1991).

The "third-variable" explanation is particularly relevant if one thinks that a large unexplained variation in health remains after controlling for schooling and other determinants. To borrow from research results in the related field of investment in human capital and the determinants of earnings (e.g., Mincer 1974), it is clear that the percentage of the variation in health explained by schooling is much smaller than the percentage of the variation in earnings explained by schooling. Yet it also is intuitive that health and illness have larger random components than earnings. The third-variable explanation is relevant only if the unaccounted for factors that affect health are correlated with schooling. Note that both the reverse-causality explanation and the third-variable explanation indicate that the observed relationship between current health and schooling reflects an omitted variable. In the case of reverse causality, the omitted variable is identified as past or endowed health. In econometric terminology, both explanations fall under the general rubric of biases due to unobserved heterogeneity among individuals.

As a prelude to the review of studies of the relationship between schooling and health in sections 4.2–4.4, it is useful to note that the health production function is a structural equation because it shows relationships between an output of health and endogenous health inputs. Ordinary least squares estimates of the parameters of the production function may be biased and inconsistent because the inputs are likely to be correlated with the disturbance term, whose components consist of the effects of all omitted variables (e.g., the health endowment). The output and input demand functions constitute the reduced-form of the model because only predetermined variables appear on their right-hand sides. The health demand function results when the input demand functions are substituted into the production function. Early research in this area assumed that reduced-form health equations could be estimated by ordinary least squares. Later research has questioned this procedure, particularly the assumption that schooling is uncorrelated with the disturbance term in the reduced form.

4.2. Adult Health

4.2.1. Evidence of the Direct Causal Effect of Schooling on Health

We begin our review of the empirical literature dealing with the schooling-health correlation by summarizing studies that attempt to determine whether schooling has a direct causal impact on the health of adults. Thus, these studies primarily focus on the impact of schooling on health, although some of them also treat various mechanisms that explain the observed effect.

Grossman (1975) subjects the alternative explanations of the observed positive correlation between schooling and health to empirical testing and concludes that schooling has a significant and large causal impact on the current self-rated health of middle-aged white males in the NBER-Thorndike Sample.[4] The estimated schooling effect in Grossman's study controls for health in high school, parents' schooling, scores on physical and mental tests taken by the men when they were in their early twenties, current hourly wage rates, property income, and job satisfaction. His finding is particularly notable because all the men graduated from high school. Hence, it suggests that the favorable impact of schooling on health persists even at high levels of schooling. Grossman's decomposition of the schooling effect reveals that a substantial fraction of this effect operates via the impact of schooling on wife's schooling, job satisfaction, and weight difference (the absolute value of actual weight minus ideal weight for a given height). When these variables are included as regressors, they reduce the schooling effect by almost 40 percent.

Grossman's analysis of the mortality experience of the Thorndike sample between 1955 and 1969 confirms the important role of schooling in health outcomes. This analysis is restricted to men who reported positive full-time salaries in 1955. In the fitted logit functions, schooling has a positive and statistically significant effect on the probability of survival. Indeed, schooling is the only variable whose logit coefficient differs from zero in a statistical sense. The schooling effect is independent of the level of median salary in 1955 and suggests that, in the vicinity of the mean death rate, a one-year increase in schooling lowers the probability of death by .4 percentage points. These results must be interpreted with some caution because the men in the Thorndike sample

---

4. In 1955, Robert L. Thorndike and Elizabeth Hagan collected information on earnings, schooling, and occupation for a sample of 9,700 men drawn from a population of 75,000 white males who volunteered for, and were accepted as, candidates for Aviation Cadet status in the Army Air Force in the last half of 1943. Candidates were given 17 specific tests that measured five basic types of ability: general intelligence, numerical ability, visual perception, psychomotor control, and mechanical ability. In 1969, and again in 1971, the National Bureau of Economic Research mailed questionnaires to the members of the Thorndike-Hagan 1955 sample.

were only in their thirties in 1955, and relatively few variables were available for that year.

The importance of schooling as a determinant of self-rated health status and disability of persons in the preretirement years is reinforced in studies by Leigh (1983), Lairson, Lorimor, and Slater (1984), Kemna (1987), Wagstaff (1986), and Desai (1987). Leigh (1983) employs data from the University of Michigan's Quality of Employment Surveys of 1973 and 1977 and considers persons 16 years of age and older who worked for pay for 20 or more hours per week in these two national surveys. He shows that most of the statistically significant positive effect of schooling on health can be explained by decisions with regard to cigarette smoking, exercise, and the choice of less hazardous occupations by the more educated. This finding provides support for the allocative efficiency hypothesis or the taste hypothesis.

Lairson, Lorimor, and Slater (1984) estimate separate demand for health equations for white and black males aged 45 through 59 in the 1966 National Longitudinal Survey. Schooling has a statistically significant positive coefficient in the regression for the self-rated health of white males, but the corresponding coefficient is positive but not significant for black males. Wife's schooling, however, has a positive and significant effect for blacks but not for whites. Given the high correlation between own schooling and wife's schooling and the relatively small sample of blacks ($n = 569$), the results for the latter group may be due to sampling error.

Wagstaff (1986) uses the 1976 Danish Welfare Survey to estimate a sophisticated multiple indicator version of Grossman's (1972a, 1972b) health model by maximum likelihood methods. He performs a principal components analysis of 19 indicators of nonchronic health problems to obtain four health indicators that reflect physical mobility, mental health, respiratory health, and presence of pain. He then treats these four variables as indicators of the unobserved stock of health capital. In his pure investment specification of the demand for health, an increase in schooling leads to an increase in the stock of health.[5]

Kemna (1987) reports significant schooling coefficients in self-rated health equations estimated from the 1980 National Health Interview Survey. His findings are notable because he controls for the initial level of health with a dichotomous variable that indicates activity limitation due to chronic conditions. Unlike Leigh, Kemna reports a large schooling coefficient even when the level of occupational hazards is held constant. His occupational measures, which are based on objective indicators from the *Dictionary of Occupational Titles*, are more refined than the self-reported measures used by Leigh. Moreover, Kemna

---

5. Wagstaff also attempts to fit a pure consumption demand function. This effort is seriously hindered by multicollinearity between education and proxies for the marginal utility of wealth.

utilizes information on both the respondent's current job and longest job, while Leigh lacks this information.

In a study limited to low-income men in the 1974 Health Interview Survey, Desai (1987) finds significant positive impacts of schooling on their self-rated health and significant negative impacts on their work-loss days due to illness. Her results control for such factors as the number of chronic conditions (a measure of the initial level of health), the use of preventive medical care, and housing crowding. Together with Grossman's (1975) results for high-income men, they suggest that the beneficial impacts of schooling on health are observed at all levels of income.

The importance of schooling as a determinant of the self-rated health of older males and the mortality experience of males of all ages is underscored in studies by Rosen and Taubman (1982), Taubman and Rosen (1982), and Sickles and Taubman (1986). The first study is based on the 1973 Exact Match Sample, which was obtained by matching persons in the March 1973 Current Population Survey with their Social Security and Internal Revenue Service records and then tracing their mortality experience through 1977. Rosen and Taubman estimate separate mortality regressions for white males aged 25 through 64 in 1973 and for white males aged 65 and over in that year. For both groups mortality is negatively related to education, with marital status, earnings in 1973, and health status in that year held constant. Rosen and Taubman conclude that " . . . the effect of education does not flow solely or primarily through income effects, does not reflect a combination of differential marriage patterns and the health benefits of having a wife, and . . . those who are disabled or not working because of ill health are not found disproportionately in any one education group" (269).

Taubman and Rosen (1982) use the 1969, 1971, and 1973 Retirement History Survey to study the self-rated health and survival experience of white males who were between the ages of 58 and 63 in the initial year of this panel survey. The dependent variable compares health with that of others the same age and has four categories: better, same, worse, and dead. With health in 1969, income, and marital status held constant, health levels in 1971 and 1973 and changes over time are strongly related to years of formal schooling completed. There also is evidence that own schooling is a more important predictor of health than wife's schooling for married men.

Sickles and Taubman (1986) add the 1975 and 1977 waves to the panel data employed by Taubman and Rosen and include black as well as white males in their analysis. They fit a model with two endogenous variables: health status and retirement status. The model is recursive (health status determines retirement status) and allows for correlated errors between the two equations and heterogeneity, which is treated as a random effect. Since the health equation is an ordered polytomous probit and the retirement equation is a binary probit, full information maximum likelihood estimation methods are employed. As in the Taubman-Rosen study, higher schooling levels are associated with better health. Taken together, the two studies suggest that the schooling effect is not sensitive to very different model specifications and estimation strategies.

The importance of schooling as a determinant of mortality is challenged in studies by Duleep (1986), Behrman, Sickles, Taubman, and Yazbeck (1991), and Menchik (1993). Duleep employs the 1973 Current Population Exact Match Sample, which also was employed by Rosen and Taubman (1982). Duleep's study differs from Rosen and Taubman's because she traces the mortality experience of the sample through 1978 rather than 1977, corrects the undercount of deaths in the Rosen and Taubman study, and limits the analysis to white married males aged 35 to 64 in 1973. With disability status prior to 1973 held constant, dichotomous variables for the two lowest income categories (based on IRS income or Social Security earnings) have positive regression coefficients, with the lowest income category having the largest coefficient. This indicates that the risk of mortality falls up to an income of $6,000 in 1972 dollars but not above that income. The education effect is nonlinear. Those with zero to eight years of formal schooling, nine to 11 years of formal schooling (some high school), or one to three years of college have higher mortality than college graduates do. But high school graduates (those with 12 years of formal schooling) have lower mortality than do those with some college.

Duleep concludes that low income has a significant positive effect on mortality. She also concludes that her results are "not consistent with the theory that more education promotes better health by increasing individual's productivity of health knowledge" (1986, 249). The last conclusion is not obvious. Three of the four education coefficients have signs that are consistent with productive or allocative efficiency. Moreover, persons who attend college but fail to complete it may be less able than persons who complete high school and decide not to attend college. That is, men in the latter group did not make the mistake of attempting to acquire more than the optimal amount of schooling. In addition, Duleep's estimates may be biased since the sample is limited to married men. These men have lower mortality and higher education than their single counterparts do (e.g., Sweet and Bumpass 1987; and Cherlin 1992).

Behrman, Sickles, Taubman, and Yazbeck (1991) examine the mortality experience of white and black males in the Retirement History Survey with the same longitudinal file employed by Sickles and Taubman (1986). They estimate a variety of race-specific continuous-time hazard functions, some of which control for unobserved individual heterogeneity. For both races, pension income and marital status but not education are significant predictors of the conditional probability of death at a given age. An increase in pension income lowers this probability, while married men have lower death rates than never-married or widowed men. Since education may affect both marital status and pension income, it is not clear whether these findings rule out causality from schooling to mortality.

Menchik (1993) examines mortality in the National Longitudinal Survey of Older Men. These men had a median age of 51 when the survey began in 1966. The dependent variable in the estimated logit equations identifies men who died by 1983. Permanent or long-run income is measured by household net worth as of 1966 and the present or discounted value of earnings prior to age 62. Controls for family background include parental education and the number of parents alive in 1966. Menchik finds that net worth and the present value of earnings have statistically significant negative effects on the probability of dying, while education has an insignificant negative effect on this probability. Since he includes marital status in the logit regressions, the lack of a schooling effect may reflect causality from schooling to marital status. Moreover, the inclusion of net worth and the present value of earnings is not fully justified. In particular, net worth in 1966 depends on past decisions with respect to hours of work and savings. Therefore, attempts to sort out the separate effects of human and nonhuman wealth on mortality should consider measures of both at relatively early stages in the life cycle. Finally, Menchik pools white and black males and includes a dichotomous race indicator, whereas most of the studies surveyed in this paper estimate separate health outcome equations for whites and blacks or limit these equations to whites to take account of race differences in the effects of other variables.

4.2.2.   Explanations of the Schooling-Health Correlation

We now turn to studies that attempt to explain the positive correlation between schooling and the health status of adults. Some of these focus on allocative efficiency as reflected by changes in such health inputs as cigarette smoking, excessive alcohol use, exercise, and nutrient intakes caused by schooling. Others consider the extent to which both schooling and health are caused by third variables, most notably differences in time preference among individuals.

Kenkel (1991a) explores the allocative efficiency hypothesis by examining the extent to which schooling helps people choose healthier lifestyles by improving their knowledge of the relationships between health behaviors and health outcomes. He uses direct measures of health knowledge to test this explanation. He does this by estimating the separate effects of schooling and health knowledge on cigarette smoking (the number of cigarettes smoked per day), excessive alcohol use (the number of days in the past year on which the respondent consumed five or more drinks of an alcoholic beverage), and exercise (the number of minutes of exercise in the past two weeks) using data from the Health Promotion/Disease Prevention Supplement to the 1985 National Health Interview Survey. Cigarette knowledge is measured by the number of correct responses to whether smoking causes each of seven illnesses. Drinking knowledge is measured by the number of correct responses to whether heavy drinking causes each of three illnesses. Exercise knowledge is given by correct responses for the amount of exercise required to strengthen the heart and lungs and the required change in heart rate and breathing.

With age, family income, race, marital status, employment status, veteran status (for males only), and self-reported stress levels held constant, an increase in schooling leads to a reduction in smoking and excessive alcohol use and an increase in exercise. Moreover, knowledge of the health consequences of smoking decreases smoking, and similar relationships hold for excessive alcohol consumption and exercise. The results also show that part of the relationship between schooling and health behaviors is due to health knowledge, but the schooling coefficients are significant with health knowledge held constant. Moreover, the reductions in schooling coefficients due to the inclusion of health knowledge are relatively small; they range between 5 and 20 percent. The results are not altered when health knowledge is treated as an endogenous variable.

Kenkel interprets this result as indicating that unobservables, such as individual rates of time preference, are important determinants of health behavior and schooling but acknowledges that other interpretations are possible. One of these is the productive efficiency hypothesis proposed by Grossman (1972a, 1972b) and Michael (1972, 1973). Productive efficiency, as opposed to allocative efficiency, pertains to the amount of output obtained from given amounts of endogenous inputs. According to this hypothesis, schooling raises the marginal products of the endogenous inputs in health and other household production functions. If the income and price elasticities of health exceed one in a Grossman pure consumption model or if the price elasticity of health exceeds one in a Grossman pure investment model, the demand for inputs with positive marginal products in the health production function rises, and the demand for inputs with negative marginal products falls.[6]

The allocative efficiency hypothesis is related to the availability effect in the market for physicians' services—the alleged ability of physicians to manipulate the demand curve for their services in the presence of imperfect

---

6. In Grossman's pure investment model, health does not enter the utility function and is demanded solely because it determines the total amount of time available for market and nonmarket activities. In his pure consumption model the marginal monetary rate of return on an investment in health is assumed to be small enough to be ignored. The statements made in the text pertain to cases in which education changes the marginal products of all health inputs by the same percentage. Other results are possible if, for example, education raises the marginal products of inputs with positive marginal products while having no impact on inputs with negative marginal products. Moreover, the impacts of education in the production function for "smoking pleasure," for example, would have to be considered in a more general treatment.

information by patients. In his penetrating analysis of the availability effect, Pauly (1980) argues that the more educated should be less susceptible to demand manipulation by physicians because they have more information. His demand functions for physician visits conditional on positive visits estimated with the 1970 National Health Interview Survey contain empirical evidence in favor of this proposition.[7] In particular, positive and significant coefficients of physicians per capita in the primary sampling unit of residence are observed only for persons in households in which heads are not high school graduates.

Kenkel (1990) explores the demand manipulation hypothesis in the 1975–76 National Health Survey conducted by the Center for Health Administration Studies and the National Opinion Research Center of the University of Chicago. This survey contains a direct measure of health information because respondents were asked to agree or disagree with a set of statements about the symptoms associated with diabetes, heart disease, cancer, and tuberculosis. Kenkel argues that, if an increase in consumer information decreases demand inducement, the coefficient of the information measure in a demand function for visits conditional on positive visits should be negative. In fact, the coefficient of health knowledge, which is treated as an endogenous variable, is positive but not significant. Kenkel concludes that "the prediction that more informed consumers will use less care because they are subject to less demand inducement is not supported" (590).

This conclusion is subject to the objection that poorly informed consumers may underestimate the marginal product of medical care. This generates two effects that go in opposite directions as the level of information rises.[8] It also is subject to the objection that most discussions of demand manipulation argue that the per capita number of physicians in the respondent's area of residence is the most important determinant of the optimal amount of inducement or misinformation. Therefore, a more complete specification of Kenkel's model would include physician availability, health knowledge, and an interaction between these two variables in the demand function. The theory predicts a negative coefficient associated with the interaction term. Kenkel does not fit this model, probably because he lacked identifiers for area of residence.[9]

---

7. Pauly limits the analysis to persons with positive visits because a physician only can manipulate the demand of a patient who first decides to contact his or her provider of medical care.

8. Kenkel indicates that the effect of information on the probability of a physician visit in the past year should be positive if those with less information underestimate the productivity of medical care. In his estimated probit equation for the probability of positive visits, the endogenous health knowledge measure has a positive and significant coefficient.

9. Dranove (1988) presents a model in which more skilled physicians should be able to induce more visits for a given level of information. Kenkel (1990) finds no support for this prediction. He argues that the skill of the physician should increase with physician age, board certification, and specialty status but decrease with the square of age. When these variables are

Ippolito and Mathios (1990) explore the allocative efficiency hypothesis in the market for ready-to-eat cereal. By the mid-1970s a substantial amount of epidemiological research suggested a negative relationship between the consumption of insoluble dietary fiber and colon cancer (the second-leading cause of cancer deaths in the United States). By 1979 the U.S. surgeon general was recommending an increase in the consumption of fiber as "prudent."

In October 1984 the Kellogg Company, with the cooperation of the National Cancer Institute, began an advertising campaign to highlight the link between fiber and cancer, stressing that their All-Bran cereal was high in fiber. By the end of 1985 Kellogg had extended the campaign to several of its other fiber cereals, and other cereal producers had begun to advertise the health benefits of their fiber cereals. This campaign was in direct violation of Food and Drug Administration (FDA) policy, which created a ban on advertising health claims for food products. This ban was suspended when the Kellogg campaign began in the fall of 1984.

Ippolito and Mathios study the determinants of the amount of fiber per 10 ounces of cereal in the type of cereal consumed by an individual in two independent samples: one taken in the spring of 1985 and the other in the spring of 1986. Both are from the U.S. Department of Agriculture's Continuing Survey of Food Intakes by Individuals for Women between the Ages of 19 and 50 and use information from detailed 24-hour food intake data. In both samples the respondent's years of formal schooling completed had a significant positive effect on fiber intake from cereal, while household income had essentially no effect. In fact, the estimates of the schooling effect were the same across survey years.

Ippolito and Mathios maintain that the schooling coefficient in the 1986 survey regression should be smaller than the coefficient in the 1985 regression if differences in the variable reflect differences in allocative efficiency. Their argument is that the advertising campaign by the cereal companies should have made information concerning the health benefits of fiber more accessible to all segments of the population. But note that the diffusion process may have taken more than the year and a half that elapsed between the beginning of the advertising campaign in the fall of 1984 and the second survey in the spring of 1986.

Suggestive evidence concerning the ability of the more educated to process new information concerning health risks more rapidly than the less educated is contained in the 1990 National Health Interview Survey. In that survey the

---

added to the demand function for visits, all of their coefficients are insignificant. If physicians do not engage in demand manipulation, there is no point in searching for interactions between availability and information in the demand function. A judgment on this undertaking should, however, be based on the full set of demand manipulation variables, including physician density.

more educated were more likely to have heard AIDS called HIV and were more likely to have heard of radon. In addition, they had more information about the causes and effects of AIDS and radon.[10]

The allocative efficiency hypothesis also is related to the large literature on the role of nutrition in health outcomes, primarily in developing countries. Much of this literature employs anthropometric measures of health (height, height for age, weight, weight for age, or weight for height).[11] In a series of related papers, Behrman and Wolfe (Wolfe and Behrman 1983; Behrman and Wolfe 1984, 1987, 1989) study the role of schooling in nutritional, anthropometric, and other health outcomes in a sample of women aged 15 to 45 and their families in Nicaragua, which was collected in 1977–78. They focus on the importance of women's schooling as opposed to family income in the determination of these outcomes and the extent to which the observed schooling effects are causal.

In the first study Wolfe and Behrman (1983) use data for approximately 1,000 households residing in Managua. They measure nutrient intake in terms of calories, protein, iron, and Vitamin A based on information on the number of times each of 15 food groups was served per week. Each nutrient intake is normalized by international standards, given the demographic composition of the households. The regression coefficients of woman's schooling are positive and significant for all four nutrients. Household income coefficients also are positive, but they are significant only for protein and Vitamin A. Based on these results and the small income elasticities (none is larger than .04), they conclude that schooling is a more important determinant of nutrient intake than income. For protein and Vitamin A, Wolfe and Behrman present some evidence in support of allocative efficiency since the schooling coefficients fall when measures of the woman's nutrition knowledge are introduced as regressors. The schooling coefficients, however, retain their significance in these extended specifications.

Using a somewhat larger sample of almost 4,000 households with women aged 15 to 45 (including many who reside outside Managua), Behrman and Wolfe (1984) indicate that the above findings do not change. For each nutrient, the schooling elasticity exceeds the corresponding income elasticity. In both studies schooling retains its significance when proxies for childhood background of the women—primarily whether both parents were present in youth—are included as regressors.

---

10. We are indebted to Donald S. Kenkel for supplying us with unpublished tabulations from the 1990 National Health Interview Survey concerning education and knowledge of AIDS and radon.

11. See Behrman and Deolalikar (1988) for a survey of the economic literature on health and nutrition in developing countries. See Fogel (1994) for a summary of his fascinating research on the contribution of nutrition to secular declines in mortality in the United States and Western Europe over long periods of time.

Behrman and Wolfe argue that the schooling effect is more likely to reflect a taste than an efficiency effect because the schooling effect is not altered when household income is decomposed between women's actual or predicted (conditional on their characteristics) contribution and other income. They state: "This means that for the efficiency interpretation to hold, schooling must be associated with increasing women's efficiency in household production in respects that are not strongly correlated with the impact on market productivity, since the latter are controlled for in these alternative regressions" (1984, 118). A different point of view on this issue is expressed by Michael. He suggests that market and household productivity are much less than perfectly correlated due to "different relative degrees of labor shortage or abundance in different occupations, different degrees of monopoly power or of union strength, different innate ability, . . . different amounts of on-the-job training . . . or other forms of human capital, [and] luck" (1972, 29).

In the last two studies Behrman and Wolfe (1987, 1989) address the extent to which the observed effect of schooling in the Nicaraguan data is causal. Here they consider not only the relationship between schooling and family nutrition but also the relationship between schooling and women's health measured by the number of days too ill to work in the past year and whether the woman ever had four types of diseases: parasitic, medically preventable, therapeutically preventable, and diseases prevented by public policy.[12] The issue in both papers is whether the schooling effects reflect unobserved intergenerational endowments. That is, parents may transmit endowments to their children, which may influence the amount of schooling they obtain, their adulthood health, and the nutritional status of their families. Behrman and Wolfe interpret these endowments broadly. Not only do they include genetic factors but also those associated with the childhood family experiences of adults as reflected by a variety of family background variables.

The approach in the 1987 paper is to estimate a multiple-indicator, multiple-cause model using full information maximum likelihood methods. All the health measures listed previously except diseases prevented by public policy are observed indicators of the woman's latent (unobserved) current health. Caloric and protein intake and the presence of a refrigerator are observed indicators of family nutrition. Finally, the following variables serve as indicators of the woman's unobserved childhood endowment: her own mother's schooling, whether she was raised in an urban area, whether her mother was present in adolescence, whether her father was present in adolescence, and the number of her siblings.

---

12. The first health measure is not considered in their 1989 paper, and the last is not considered in their 1987 paper. The 1987 paper also explores the impact of mother's schooling on child health. This aspect of the paper is discussed in section 4.3.

When the endowment is omitted from the model, a woman's schooling has a positive and significant effect on family nutrition and a positive and insignificant effect on good health. The latter effect emerges from the estimation of a health production function rather than the estimation of a reduced-form health equation. When the endowment is included, it has positive and significant impacts on both outcomes. The schooling coefficient in the nutrition equation becomes negative and significant, and the corresponding coefficient in the health equation becomes negative and insignificant. Behrman and Wolfe write: "From these estimates one could *not* [italics theirs] conclude that . . . schooling has a positive impact on this system of health and nutrition relations" (1987, 202).

They reach a very different conclusion in their 1989 study. Here they use data on the sisters of 500 women in the sample to control for the endowment. They obtain separate reduced-form equations for all health measures except for days of illness and intake of calories and proteins. Behrman and Wolfe estimate Chamberlain's (1980) random-effects model and a fixed-effects model. The former amounts to including sister's schooling as an additional regressor. The true causal schooling effect is then given by the coefficient of a woman's own schooling minus the coefficient of her sister's schooling.[13] In the fixed-effects specification deviations from the means for the adult siblings are the units of observation. This is equivalent to including a dichotomous variable for each childhood family of current adult siblings.

With no controls for sisters, a woman's schooling has negative and significant coefficients in the logit equations for the probabilities of having had three of the four diseases considered (the exception pertains to medically preventable diseases). The schooling coefficients in the regressions for caloric and protein intake are positive and significant. These results are not altered when the random- or fixed-effects estimates are obtained. The findings in this study also differ from the previous one because the basic model (with no controls for sisters) includes specific measures of the indicators for the endowment (parents' schooling, number of siblings, urban childhood, and presence of parents) used in the previous study. Thus, it is not clear whether the results of the 1987 study are due to the methodology and the identification restrictions that must be imposed.

The research by Behrman and Wolfe is unique in that they bring so many different approaches and econometric methodologies to bear in examining relationships between schooling and health and schooling and nutrition in a

---

13. It is somewhat of a misnomer to term Chamberlain's model a random-effects model. In a typical random-effects model, observed and unobserved determinants of the dependent variable are assumed to be uncorrelated. Chamberlain postulates that the disturbance term is an explicit function of the regressors and variables related to them. In the present context this amounts to assuming that own schooling and sister's schooling have equal impacts on the disturbance. Hence, the true effect of own schooling is given by the difference between the coefficients of own and sister's schooling in the health or nutrition regressions.

single but extremely rich sample. The weight of the evidence that they present supports a causal interpretation of the impact of schooling on these outcomes. The evidence has much less to say about the mechanisms at work.

Behrman, Rosenzweig, and Taubman (1994) focus on the anthropometric outcome of body mass (the ratio of weight to the square of height) in the context of a theoretical and empirical methodology that controls for unmeasured endowment effects by using data on twins in the United States. In developing countries low values of body mass are associated with malnutrition and thus poor health. In developed countries high values of body mass are associated with obesity, and thus Behrman, Rosenzweig, and Taubman treat it as an indicator of poor health.

They consider within-twin differences across identical (monozygotic) and nonidentical (dizygotic) twins in two samples. The first is the NAS-NRC twins sample of white male twins who are U.S. veterans born between 1917 and 1927. The second is the Minnesota Twin Registry and consists of male twins born in Minnesota between 1936 and 1955. Their within-twin estimates reveal a negative and significant schooling coefficient in the Minnesota sample but not in the NAS-NRC sample.

It is not clear how sensitive these estimates are to assumptions that are made in order to identify parameters associated with endowments. Moreover, body mass may not be a negative correlate of health over its entire range even in the United States. For example, low values of body mass may be associated with negative differences between actual weight and ideal weight for a given height based on studies of the relationship between weight and mortality. Similarly, high values of body mass may be associated with positive differences between actual and ideal weight. Thus, it would be of interest to reestimate the model with the absolute value of actual weight minus ideal weight for a given height as the dependent variable or to establish categories of deviations.[14]

Fuchs (1982) has challenged the conclusion in most of the studies summarized in this section that schooling has a substantial causal impact on health. He argues that the relationship may be due to an omitted third factor: namely, differences in time preference among individuals. That is, persons who are more future oriented (who have a higher degree of time preference for the future) attend school for longer periods of time and make larger investments in their health.

Fuchs attempts to measure time preference in a telephone survey by asking respondents questions in which they choose between a sum of money now and a larger sum in the future. He includes an index of time preference in a multiple regression in which health status is the dependent variable and schooling is one of the independent variables. Fuchs is not able to demonstrate that the schooling

14. Grossman (1975) employed this measure in the NBER-Thorndike Sample.

effect is due to time preference. The latter variable has a positive regression coefficient, but it is not statistically significant. When time preference and schooling are entered simultaneously, the latter dominates the former. These results must be regarded as preliminary because they are based on one small sample of adults in Long Island and on exploratory measures of time preference.

Farrell and Fuchs (1982) explore the time preference hypothesis in the context of cigarette smoking using interviews conducted in 1979 by the Stanford Heart Disease Prevention Program in four small, agricultural cities in California. They examine smoking behavior of white non-Hispanics who were not students at the time of the survey, had completed 12 to 18 years of schooling, and were at least 24 years old. The presence of retrospective information on cigarette smoking at ages 17 and 24 allows them to relate smoking at these two ages to years of formal schooling completed by 1979 for cohorts who reached age 17 before and after the widespread diffusion of information concerning the harmful effects of cigarette smoking on health.

Farrell and Fuchs find that the negative relationship between schooling and smoking, which rises in absolute value for cohorts born after 1953, does not increase between the ages of 17 and 24. Since the individuals were all in the same school grade at age 17, the additional schooling obtained between that age and age 24 cannot be the cause of differential smoking behavior at age 24. Based on these results, Farrell and Fuchs reject the hypothesis that schooling is a causal factor in smoking behavior in favor of the view that a third variable causes both. Since the strong negative relationship between schooling and smoking developed only after the spread of information concerning the harmful effects of smoking, they argue that the same mechanism may generate the schooling-health relationship.

Farrell and Fuchs indicate two potential third variables that may generate the schooling-smoking relationship: mental ability and time preference for the future. Grossman (1983) reports a negative relationship between smoking and high school achievement test scores, and it is well known that these test results are important predictors of the probability of college attendance. Farrell and Fuchs downplay this explanation because, if the schooling-smoking relationship were due to superior mental ability, it should fall over time as knowledge about the harmful effects of smoking rises. Their analysis by cohort does not provide evidence of a reduction over time. Note, however, that this result is based on a comparison of schooling coefficients for two cohorts: one that reached age 17 between 1953 and 1963 and one that reached age 17 between 1964 and 1972. Since the first Surgeon General's Report on Smoking and Health was not published until 1964, neither of the cohorts reached age 17 after the process of information diffusion was completed.

Farrell and Fuchs conclude that their results are consistent with the time preference hypothesis but are careful to acknowledge that it cannot be tested with their data. In interpreting their findings, one should also keep in mind that they pertain to the residents of four small, agricultural cities in California. Thus, they may not be generalizable to the population of the United States as a whole. Moreover, Farrell and Fuchs fail to uncover a negative effect of parents' schooling on smoking at age 17 even when own schooling is omitted from the set of regressors. Yet it is well known that parents' schooling is a significant predictor of teenage smoking in national data (see, e.g., Lewit, Coate, and Grossman 1981).

Leigh (1985) presents evidence that supports Fuchs's (1982) finding that the positive relationship between schooling and health cannot be explained by time preference. Using the Panel Study of Income Dynamics, a nationally representative panel survey conducted by the University of Michigan's Survey Research Center annually since 1968, Leigh measures health inversely with a dichotomous variable that identifies persons who became disabled (developed conditions that limited the amount or kind of work they could do) in 1971 or 1972. The independent variables in logit equations that explain the probability of becoming disabled pertained to the year prior to the onset of the disability. Schooling has a negative and statistically significant logit coefficient. When a risk preference index, which is highly correlated with a time preference index (Leigh 1986), was introduced into the equation, the schooling coefficient declines by only 10 percent and remains statistically significant (Leigh, personal communication).

Berger and Leigh (1989) have developed an extremely useful methodology for disentangling the schooling effect from the time preference effect. Their methodology amounts to treating schooling as an endogenous variable in the health equation and estimating the equation by a variant of two-stage least squares. If the instrumental variables used to predict schooling in the first stage are uncorrelated with time preference, this technique yields an unbiased estimate of the schooling coefficient. Since the framework generates a recursive model with correlated errors, exogenous variables that are unique to the health equation are not used to predict schooling.

Berger and Leigh apply their methodology to two data sets: the first National Health and Nutrition Examination Survey (NHANES I) and the National Longitudinal Survey of Young Men (NLS). In NHANES I, health is measured by blood pressure, and separate equations are obtained for persons aged 20 through 40 and over age 40 in the period 1971 through 1975. The schooling equation is identified by ancestry and by average real per capita income and average real per capita expenditures on education in the state in which an individual resided from the year of birth to age six. These variables enter the schooling equation but are excluded from the health equation. In the NLS, health is measured by a dichotomous variable that identifies men who in 1976 reported that health limited or prevented them from working and alternatively by a dichotomous variable that identifies the presence of a functional health limitation. The men in the sample were between the ages of 24 and 34 in 1976, had left school by that year, and reported no health limitations in 1966 (the first year of the survey). The schooling equation is identified by IQ, Knowledge of Work test scores, and parents' schooling.

In the NLS, the schooling coefficient rises in absolute value when predicted schooling replaces actual schooling, and health is measured by work limitation. When health is measured by functional limitation, the two-stage least squares schooling coefficient is approximately equal to the ordinary least squares coefficient, although the latter is estimated with more precision. For persons aged 20 through 40 in NHANES I, schooling has a larger impact on blood pressure in absolute value in the two-stage regressions. For persons over age 40, however, the predicted value of schooling has a positive and insignificant regression coefficient. Except for the last finding, these results are inconsistent with the time preference hypothesis and consistent with the hypothesis that schooling causes health.

In another application of the same methodology, Leigh (1990) focuses on the relationship between schooling and the use of seat belts in the Panel Survey of Income Dynamics. The universal adoption of this simple healthy behavior has the potential to decrease the number of serious injuries and deaths in motor vehicle accidents by more than 50 percent. Using father's occupation and parents' wealth to identify the schooling equation, Leigh finds that the positive and significant effect of schooling on the probability of using seat belts falls when schooling is treated as an endogenous variable. Nevertheless, the schooling coefficient remains significant and has a larger t-ratio than any other regressor in the seat belt equation.

Sander (1995a, 1995b) has applied the methodology developed by Berger and Leigh to the relationship between schooling and cigarette smoking studied by Farrell and Fuchs (1982). His data consist of the 1986–91 waves of the National Opinion Research Center's General Social Survey. In the first paper (1995a) the outcome is the probability of quitting smoking, while in the second (1995b) the outcome is the probability of smoking. Separate probit equations are obtained for men and women ages 25 and older. Instruments for schooling include father's schooling, mother's schooling, rural residence at age 16, region of residence at age 16, and number of siblings.

In general schooling has a negative effect on smoking participation and a positive effect on the probability of quitting smoking. These results are not sensitive to the use of predicted as opposed to actual schooling in the probit regressions. Moreover, the application of the Wu-Hausman endogeneity test (Wu 1973; Hausman 1978) in the quit equation suggests that schooling is exogenous in this equation. Thus, Sander's results, like Berger and Leigh's and Leigh's results, are inconsistent with the time preference hypothesis.

The aforementioned conclusion rests on the assumption that the instruments used to predict schooling in the first stage are uncorrelated with time preference. The validity of this assumption is most plausible in the case of measures such as real per capita income and real per capita outlays on education in the state in which an individual resided from birth to age six (used by Berger and Leigh in NHANES I) and rural residence at age 16 and region of residence at that age (used by Sander). The validity of the assumption is less plausible in the case of measures such as parents' schooling (used by Sander and by Berger and Leigh in the NLS and by Leigh in the PSID [Panel Study on Income Dynamics]).

Given this and the inherent difficulty in Fuchs's (1982) attempt to measure time preference directly, definitive evidence with regard to the time preference hypothesis still is lacking. Moreover, Sander (1995a, 1995b) presents national data showing a much larger downward trend in the probability of smoking and a much larger upward trend in the probability of quitting smoking between 1966 and 1987 as the level of education rises. Since information concerning the harmful effects of smoking was widespread by the early 1980s, these results are not consistent with an allocative efficiency argument that the more educated are better able to process new information.[15] Indeed, Viscusi (1992) finds that consumers overestimate, rather than underestimate, the probability of death and illness from lung cancer due to tobacco.

Becker and Murphy's (1988) theoretical model of rational addiction predicts that persons who discount the future heavily are more likely to participate in such addictive behaviors as cigarette smoking. Becker, Grossman, and Murphy (1991) show that the more educated respond more to changes in the harmful future consequences of the consumption of addictive goods because they are more future oriented. Thus, the trends just cited are consistent with a negative relationship between schooling and the rate of time preference for the present.

Using the second National Health and Nutrition Examination Survey, Chaloupka (1991) finds that smoking by the less educated is much more sensitive to changes in cigarette prices than is smoking by the less educated. Townsend (1987) obtains a similar result with British data. Based on Becker and Murphy's (1988) theoretical model of rational addiction, Becker, Grossman, and Murphy (1991) indicate that these differential price responses are consistent with the notion that the more educated discount the future less heavily than the less educated.

Proponents of the time preference hypothesis assume that a reduction in the rate of time preference for the present causes years of formal schooling

---

15. Between the middle 1960s and the early 1970s, smoking participation and quit rates changed more rapidly as the level of education rose. These short-run responses to new information are consistent with the allocative efficiency hypothesis.

to rise. On the other hand, Becker and Mulligan (1994) argue that causality may run in the opposite direction: namely, an increase in schooling may *cause* the rate of time preference for the present to fall (may *cause* the rate of time preference for the future to rise).[16] In most models of optimal consumption over the life cycle, consumers maximize a lifetime utility function defined as the discounted sum or present value of utility in each period or at each age. The discount factor (β) is given by $\beta = 1/(1 + t)$, where t is the rate of time preference for the present. Becker and Mulligan point out that the present value of utility is *higher* the smaller is the rate of time preference for the present. Hence, consumers have incentives to make investments that *lower* the rate of time preference for the present.

Becker and Mulligan then show that the marginal costs of these investments fall and the marginal benefits rise as income or wealth rises. Marginal benefits also are greater when the length of life is greater. Hence, the equilibrium rate of time preference falls as the level of education rises because education raises income and life expectancy. Moreover, the more educated may be more efficient in making investments that lower the rate of time preference for the present—a form of productive efficiency not associated with health production. To quote Becker and Mulligan:

Schooling also determines . . . [investments in time preference] partly through the study of history and other subjects, for schooling focuses students' attention on the future. Schooling can communicate images of the situations and difficulties of adult life, which are the future of childhood and adolescence. In addition, through repeated practice at problem solving, schooling helps children learn the art of scenario simulation. Thus, educated people should be more productive at reducing the remoteness of future pleasures. (10)[17]

---

16. Leigh (1990) points out that schooling may cause time preference but does not present a formal model.

17. Econometrically, the difference between Becker and Mulligan's model of time preference and Fuchs's model can be specified as follows:

$$h = \alpha_1 y + \alpha_2 s + \alpha_3 t$$
$$t = \beta_1 y + \beta_2 s + u$$
$$s = \phi t + w$$
$$y = \gamma s + v.$$

In this system h is health, y is permanent income, s is years of formal schooling completed, t is time preference for the present, and u, v, and w are disturbance terms that are mutually uncorrelated. The first equation is a demand for health function in which the coefficient of s reflects productive or allocative efficiency or both. Fuchs assumes that β_2 equals zero. Hence, the coefficient of s in the

Becker and Mulligan's argument amounts to a third causal mechanism in addition to productive and allocative efficiency in health production via which schooling can cause health. It appears to contain useful insights in considering intergenerational relationships between parents and children. For example, parents can raise their children's future health, including their adulthood health, by making them more future oriented. Note that years of formal schooling completed is a time-invariant variable beyond approximately age 30, while adult health is not time invariant. Thus, parents probably have a more important direct impact on the former than the latter. By making investments that raise their offsprings' schooling, parents also induce them to make investments that lower their rate of time preference for the present and therefore raise their adult health.

4.3. Childhood and Adolescent Health

Evidence that schooling causes health is contained in research by Edwards, Grossman, and Shakotko on the determinants of child and adolescent health (Edwards and Grossman 1981, 1982, 1983; Shakotko, Edwards, and Grossman 1981). They study child and adolescent health in the context of the nature-nurture controversy. Their research uses data primarily on whites from Cycle II of the U.S. Health Examination Survey (children aged six through 11 years in the period 1963 through 1965), Cycle III of the Health Examination Survey (adolescents aged 12 through 17 years in the period 1966 through 1970), and the panel of individuals (one-third of the full Cycle III sample) who were examined in both cycles.

---

first equation is biased if t is omitted. In one version of their model, Becker and Mulligan assume that ϕ equals zero, although in a more general formulation they allow this coefficient to be nonzero. Given that ϕ is zero and substituting the second equation into the first, one obtains

$$h = (\alpha_1 + \beta_1\alpha_3)y + (\alpha_2 + \beta_2\alpha_3)s + \alpha_3 u.$$

If u is not correlated with y and s, the last equation can be estimated by ordinary least squares. The coefficient of y reflects both the direct effect of income on health (α_1) and the indirect effect of income on health through time preference ($\beta_1\alpha_3$). Similarly, the coefficient of s reflects both the direct efficiency effect (α_2) and the indirect effect of schooling on health through time preference ($\beta_2\alpha_3$). Suppose the direct efficiency effect of schooling on health (α_2) is zero. In Fuchs's model, if health is regressed on income and schooling with time preference omitted, the expected value of the schooling coefficient is $\phi^{-1}\alpha_3$. This coefficient reflects causality from time preference to schooling. In Becker and Mulligan's model the schooling coefficient is $\beta_2\alpha_3$. This coefficient reflects causality from schooling to time preference. The equation that expresses income as a function of schooling and a disturbance stresses that schooling has an indirect effect on health via income. Note that Becker and Mulligan would include health as a determinant of time preference in the second equation because greater health lowers mortality, raises future utility levels, and increases incentives to make investments that lower the rate of time preference.

Edwards, Grossman, and Shakotko find that the home environment in general and mother's schooling in particular play an extremely important role in the determination of child and adolescent health. It is not surprising to find that children's home environment has a positive impact on their health with no other variables held constant. Moreover, it is difficult to sort out the effect of nature from that of nurture because it is difficult to measure a child's genetic endowment and genetic differences may induce environmental changes. Nevertheless, Edwards, Grossman, and Shakotko have accumulated a number of suggestive pieces of evidence on the true importance of the home environment. With birth weight, mother's age at birth, congenital abnormalities, other proxies for genetic endowment, and family income held constant, parents' schooling has positive and statistically significant effects on many measures of health in childhood and adolescence. For example, children and teenagers of more-educated mothers have better oral health, are less likely to be obese, and are less likely to have anemia than children of less-educated mothers. Father's schooling plays a much less important role in the determination of oral health, obesity, and anemia than mother's schooling does. The latter findings are important because equal effects would be expected if the schooling variables were simply proxies for unmeasured genetic endowments. On the other hand, if the effect of schooling is primarily environmental, one would expect the impact of mother's schooling to be larger because she was the family member most involved with children's health care in the late 1960s and early 1970s.

Several additional pieces of evidence underscore the robustness of the above finding. When oral health is examined in a longitudinal context, mother's schooling dominates father's schooling in the determination of the periodontal index in adolescence, with the periodontal index in childhood held constant. Similar comments apply to the effect of mother's schooling on school absence due to illness in adolescence (with school absence due to illness in childhood held constant) and to the effect of mother's schooling on obesity in adolescence (with obesity in childhood held constant).

Edwards and Grossman (1979) document a variety of positive associations between good health and cognitive development, measured by IQ and school achievement, in Cycle II of the Health Examination Survey. As part of the longitudinal study just described, Shakotko, Edwards, and Grossman (1981) investigate the direction of causation implied by these associations. They apply the notion of causality introduced by Granger (1969) by estimating two multivariate equations. One relates adolescent health to childhood health, childhood cognitive development, and family background measures. The second relates adolescent cognitive development to childhood cognitive development, childhood health, and family background. They find feedback both from good health to cognitive development and from cognitive development to good health, but the latter of these relationships is stronger. Since an individual's cognitive development is an important determinant of the number of years of formal schooling that he or she ultimately receives, this finding may be viewed as the forerunner of the positive impact of schooling on good health for adults that we discussed previously.

The study by Shakotko, Edwards, and Grossman (1981) is unique in several respects. First, it exploits time-varying measures of health and school achievement in panel data to investigate the causal priorness of these measures. The authors assume that the processes governing these outcomes are Markov and can be estimated by a simple first-order autoregressive model. They show that, if the genetic impact on these outcomes is restricted to the determination of initial conditions, then the estimates of the time paths will be free of genetic bias and will reflect the true environmental effects of family background, childhood health, and childhood cognitive development variables. Second, indicators of education generally are fixed over time in panel studies of adult health, but these indicators are not fixed in the panel employed by Shakotko, Edwards, and Grossman. Finally, most of the studies summarized in this paper measure education by years of formal schooling completed and ignore the quality of schooling. The school achievement variable employed by Shakotko, Edwards, and Grossman reflects in part school quality.

Research by Wilcox-Gök (1983) calls into question some of the findings of the studies just described. She studies the determinants of child health in a sample of natural and adopted sibling pairs. The children in her sample were between the ages of five and 14 in 1978 and were all members of the Medical Care Group of Washington University (a prepaid, comprehensive, medical care plan) in St. Louis, Missouri. Health is measured by the number of days a child had missed his or her usual activities due to illness or injury in a five-month period as reported by parents. The results for natural siblings reveal that the proportion of the variation in health explained by unmeasured sources of common family background is much greater than the proportion explained by measured variables. Moreover, the correlation between natural siblings' health is significantly higher than for sibling pairs in which one child was adopted (was not the natural child of at least one parent). These results point to the importance of genetic endowment.

Clearly, Wilcox-Gök's findings are not generalizable to the population of the United States. Not only are they specific to the residents of one city, but the families in the sample had a higher mean income and a larger number of children (the prepaid group practice offered special family membership rates) than the typical U.S. family has. In addition, one parental reported health indicator is employed in contrast to the variety of measures, many of which come from physical examinations, used by Edwards, Grossman, and Shakotko.

Behrman and Wolfe (1987) and Wolfe and Behrman (1987) examine the effect of mother's schooling on the health of children under the age of five in the Nicaraguan sample described in section 4.2.2. The child health equation estimated in the first study is one component of their multiple-indicator model. Three anthropometric measures (standardized by age and gender) serve as indicators of latent child health: weight, height, and biceps circumference. Mother's schooling has a positive and significant impact on the health indicator in an estimate of the model that omits her endowment. When the endowment is included, the schooling coefficient becomes insignificant.

Wolfe and Behrman (1987) examine the three anthropometric measures as separate dependent variables using the fixed-effects methodology for adult siblings employed in Behrman and Wolfe (1989) and outlined in section 4.2.2. Since children's health is being investigated, this amounts to using differences between cousins as the units of observation. In the standard reduced-form estimates (no controls for the endowment), mother's schooling is positively associated with child height. This relationship disappears in the fixed-effects model. These results are based on women and children from a small number (263) of families.

Strauss (1990) and Thomas, Strauss, and Henriques (1990) present evidence challenging Behrman and Wolfe's conclusion that the effect of mother's schooling on child health in developing countries is due to unmeasured genetic and family background variables. Strauss (1990) investigates the determinants of height for age and weight for height in a sample of approximately 650 children under the age of six who reside in households in Côte d'Ivoire. These data were collected as part of the World Bank's Living Standards Measurement Studies in 1985. Strauss includes mother's height as a regressor and argues that it "helps to capture not only genetic effects but also unobserved family background characteristics such as Wolfe and Behrman are worried about" (234). He also tests a fixed-effects model (which can be estimated since there is more than one child per household in the sample) against a standard random-effects (variance components) model. He cannot reject the latter, which assumes that the disturbance term is not correlated with the regressors. With mother's height held constant, her education has positive coefficients in the height for age and weight for height regressions. Mother's and father's education are significant as a set in the last equation.

Thomas, Strauss, and Henriques (1990) present more definitive evidence from a much larger sample: the 1974–75 Estudo Nacional da Despesa Familiar survey of over 50,000 households in Brazil. Their outcome is height for age of children under age eight. Schooling and height of both parents are included as regressors. In all specifications the schooling coefficients are positive and significant. They decline by between 20 and 40 percent when parental height is held constant. This suggests that part, but by no means all, of the gross schooling effect is due to genetic and family background factors. They also report that the education effects are only slightly reduced when family income is added to the regressors.

In a study based on approximately 1,300 children aged five or less in the 1986 Brazilian Demographic and Health Survey, Thomas, Strauss, and Henriques (1991) focus on the source of the positive effect of mother's schooling on child height standardized for age and sex in this sample. They find that practically all of the effect is due to information as measured by whether the woman reads newspapers, watches television, and listens to the radio. These three variables are treated as endogenous. Thus, they find much more support for the allocative efficiency hypothesis than Kenkel does (1990, 1991a). This may be traced to the more general and "less noisy" information variables that they employ. Of course, Thomas, Strauss, and Henriques's study pertains to a developing country. They do, however, conduct separate analyses for children who reside in rural and urban areas. Despite the larger values of schooling and information in the urban areas, they report the same results for both areas.

Chernichovsky and Coate (1980, 1983) are the only two economists who have conducted studies of the general determinants of children's anthropometric development and nutritional intake with fairly recent U.S. data. The first study is based on 500 children less than three years of age in the Ten State Nutrition Survey, conducted in low-income enumeration districts in the period 1968 through 1970. The second is based on approximately 2,500 children aged one to five years in the first National Health and Nutrition Examination Survey (NHANES I), conducted between 1971 and 1975, with some oversampling of low-income families. In the first study (1980), mother's education has insignificant negative coefficients in structural input demand functions for calories and proteins estimated by two-stage least squares. These demand functions are not reduced form equations because they are conditional on weight. Production functions for height, weight, and head circumference also are estimated, but mother's schooling is excluded from these equations. Chernichovsky and Coate report, however, that children in this predominantly low-income sample have calorie and protein intakes that are at least as large as the recommended dietary allowances (RDAs) specified by the U.S. Department of Agriculture. Moreover, the average of the ratios of height, weight, and head growth to the relevant age- and sex-specific national norms is near unity in each case.

In the second study, Chernichovsky and Coate (1983) present reduced form as well as structural estimates and consider Vitamin C intakes and the number of colds in the past six months as additional outcomes. In the reduced form the mother's schooling coefficients are rarely significant. These equations include mother's weight and mother's and father's height. They also include birth weight, which has very significant impacts on child weight, child height, and child head circumference with t-ratios ranging from 9.5 to 12.5 (the largest of any variable in the reduced form). Since birth weight depends on mother's schooling (see sec. 4.4), these results may be quite different if birth weight is omitted. Chernichovsky and Coate omit schooling from the growth (measured by height, weight, or head circumference) production functions, but schooling has a negative effect in the health (measured inversely by colds) production function. In the structural nutrient intake demand functions, which are conditional on weight, the schooling coefficients generally are positive and significant. It is not clear why these results differ from the corresponding coefficients in the reduced form.

In addition to the problematic treatment of birth weight, Chernichovsky and Coate (1983) pool whites and blacks with a race dummy entered in some but not all of the equations. On the other hand, most of the studies surveyed in this paper either estimate separate health outcome equations for whites and blacks or limit these equations to whites to take account of race differences in the effects of other variables. In NHANES I the elasticities of child growth with respect to nutrients are substantial. The elasticities of height and head circumference with respect to protein are 0.05 and 0.25, respectively. The elasticity of weight with respect to calories is 0.20. Chernichovsky and Coate point out that these findings are important because "although children in poor households consumed nutrients in excess of dietary standards, their growth could be accelerated by increasing nutrient intakes" (1983, 121). Perhaps a different treatment of birth weight would have led to different conclusions with regard to the role of mother's schooling.

Researchers have not focused on children's growth and nutrition in the United States because of substantial evidence that these outcomes in the developing world fall far short of the corresponding outcomes in the developed world. Chernichovsky and Coate's findings with respect to the elasticity of growth with respect to intakes of calories and proteins indicate that these measures may have some utility as health indicators in the United States. Currie and Thomas (1995) reach a similar conclusion in a recent analysis of the impact of participation in Head Start on height for age. Using the National Longitudinal Survey of Youth, they study children of NLS mothers who attended Head Start and their siblings who did not. Black children aged five and older who attended Head Start are taller than their siblings who did not attend the program. These differentials are not observed for white or Hispanic children or for children aged eight and older regardless of race and ethnicity. When similar comparisons are made for NLS mothers who attended Head Start as preschoolers, compared with their siblings who did not, long-run height differentials are observed for whites but not blacks. The latter findings are based on a small number of observations.

Currie and Thomas do not examine the effects of schooling on health. Indeed, given the fixed-effects model for height differences between young children of the same mother, variations in mother's schooling are eliminated. But their study does suggest that it may be worthwhile to formulate and estimate models of the production and demand for health and nutrition with U.S. data.

4.4. Infant Health

Since 1980, Grossman and his associates (Grossman and Jacobowitz 1981; Corman and Grossman 1985; Corman, Joyce, and Grossman 1987; Joyce 1987a, 1987b, 1994; Grossman and Joyce 1990) as well as other economists (Rosenzweig and Schultz 1981, 1982, 1983a, 1983b, 1988, 1991; Harris 1982) have devoted a considerable amount of attention to infant health in the United States. In part this is because birth outcomes are objectively measured by birth weight and survival to age one and because the infant death rate is approximately equal to the mortality rate of persons between the ages of 55 and 64 and much greater than age-specific death rates of persons between the ages of one and 54. Moreover, data bases have become available or have been constructed that contain information on the use of a variety of infant health inputs such as prenatal care, neonatal intensive care, nutrition, maternal cigarette and alcohol consumption, abortion, and contraception.

These data bases have facilitated attempts to fit infant health production functions in which the inputs are treated as endogenous or choice variables and such simultaneous equations estimation methods as two-stage least squares are employed. In particular, women with poor genetically determined birth outcomes, or their physicians, have incentives to offset these unfavorable prospects by selecting a different mix of inputs than other women do. Consequently, ordinary least squares estimates of the parameters of the production function may be biased and inconsistent because the inputs are likely to be correlated with the disturbance term, which reflects the infant's unobserved biological endowment. Put differently, the observed correlation between an infant health outcome and an input reflects causality not only from an increase in input use to a better outcome but also from a reduction in the level of health to an increase in input use.

A number of the studies mentioned contain complete estimates of the components of models of the production of and demand for infant health. Not only are production functions fitted, but health output and input demand equations also are obtained. The demand functions constitute the reduced form of the model because only exogenous variables appear on their right-hand sides. The infant health demand function results when the input demand functions are substituted into the production function. This generates an equation in which birth weight or infant survival depends on a vector of input prices, whose direct and indirect cost components are negatively related to input availability, and socioeconomic characteristics that reflect command over resources, productive and allocative efficiency, and tastes.

Estimation of the reduced form is useful in assessing the importance of mother's schooling in infant health outcomes. This is particularly true if one wants to explain the trend in infant mortality documented in table 4.2 and evaluate the contribution of education relative to trends in other exogenous determinants. Corman and Grossman (1985) fit this equation using large counties of the United States (counties with a population of at least 50,000 persons in 1970) as the units of observation and a three-year average of the neonatal mortality rate (deaths of infants within the first 27 days of life per 1,000 live births) centered on 1977 as the dependent variable. Separate regressions are obtained for whites and blacks. The independent variables are as follows: the race-specific percentage of women with family income less than 200 percent of the poverty level; the race-specific percentage of women aged 15 to 49 with at least a high school education; the number of hospitals with neonatal intensive care units per 1,000 women aged 15 to 44; the number of abortion providers per 1,000 women aged 15 to 44; the number of organized family planning clinics per 1,000 women aged 15 to 44 with family income less than 200 percent of the poverty level; the sum of the number of maternal and infant care projects and community health centers per 1,000 women aged 15 to 44 with family income less than 200 percent of the poverty level; the percentage of eligible pregnant women served by the Special Supplemental Food Program for Women, Infants, and Children (the WIC program); categorical variables pertaining to Medicaid coverage of prenatal care for first-time pregnancies and the likelihood of obtaining Medicaid financing of newborn care; and the average annual Medicaid payment per adult recipient in the Aid to Families with Dependent Children (AFDC) program.

To examine the relative contributions of schooling, poverty, and public program measures to the recent U.S. neonatal mortality experience, Corman and Grossman (1985) apply the estimated regression coefficients to trends in the exogenous variables between 1964 and 1977. The extrapolations start in 1964 because that year marked the beginning of the acceleration in the downward trend in neonatal mortality. They end in 1977 because the regressions pertain to that year. In the period at issue the white neonatal mortality rate declined by 7.5 deaths per 1,000 live births, from 16.2 to 8.7. The black neonatal mortality rate declined by 11.5 deaths per 1,000 live births, from 27.6 to 16.1. The statistical analysis "explains" approximately 28 percent of the white decline and 33 percent of the black decline on average. The increase in white female schooling makes the largest contribution to the decline in white neonatal mortality. The reduction due to schooling amounts to approximately .5 death per 1,000 live births. The increase in black female schooling ranks second to the increase in abortion availability as a contributing factor to the reduction in black neonatal mortality. The estimated abortion effect amounts to a decline of about 1 death per 1,000 live births, while the schooling trend produces a decline of about .7 death per 1,000 live births.

Rosenzweig and Schultz (1981, 1982, 1983a, 1983b, 1988, 1991) examine birth weight and infant survival outcomes (not race specific) in the 1967–69 and 1980 National Natality Followback Surveys (NNFS). They estimate production functions in the context of a model in which mother's age at birth, birth interval, prenatal care, and mother's cigarette smoking are endogenous inputs. Rosenzweig and Schultz stress the allocative efficiency, as opposed to the productive efficiency, role of mother's schooling in the production process. To be specific, they argue that an increase in mother's schooling may improve the household's information about the true nature of the production function. Given such a model, schooling is a relevant regressor in the reduced-form demand functions for the health inputs and outputs, but it is not a relevant regressor in the structural production functions. The same conclusion emerges from a model in which schooling influences the parents' preferences for healthy offspring or in which it influences the rate of time preference.

Rosenzweig and Schultz (1981) test the implication of the allocative model by estimating birth weight production functions by two-stage least squares with and without mother's schooling. They find that schooling has a positive and statistically significant effect on birth weight (a continuous variable), but the inclusion of the schooling variable increases the sum of squared errors. (This is possible only in the context of an estimation method other than ordinary least squares.) Rosenzweig and Schultz conclude that they cannot reject the hypothesis that schooling should be omitted from the production function. This exclusion restriction is adopted but not tested in structural production functions obtained by Corman, Joyce, and Grossman (1987) and by Joyce (1987a, 1987b) with the county data base used in the 1985 Corman-Grossman study.

The conclusion that mother's schooling does not belong in the infant health production function should be interpreted with caution for several reasons. First, the overidentification test employed by Rosenzweig and Schultz is not correct. The correct test is given by Hwang (1980). When the exclusion of only one exogenous variable (in this case education) is at issue, it amounts to testing the significance of education in the production function via an F-test. Since Rosenzweig and Schultz report a significant education coefficient, they should have retained education in the production function. The significance of education in the structural model is consistent with the productive efficiency hypothesis.

Second, and more generally, the use of two-stage least squares rather than ordinary least squares frequently involves a tradeoff between a reduction in simultaneous equations bias and increases in specification or omitted variables bias and multicollinearity. Specification bias becomes a problem because certain variables must be omitted from the production function to satisfy identification restrictions. To be sure, income and input prices are natural identifying variables in a situation in which data on all inputs are present. But if some inputs are missing or imperfectly measured, a case can be made for including income, for example, in the production function.[18] The degree of multicollinearity in the data rises because the predicted values of the inputs tend to be more highly correlated than the actual values are.

Even if the hypothesis that mother's schooling should be omitted from the infant health production function is accepted, Rosenzweig and Schultz (1988, 1991) present evidence of the importance of schooling in birth outcomes. Their estimated input demand functions reveal that more educated mothers are much less likely to smoke cigarettes or delay the initiation of prenatal care. These same mothers are much more likely to have a smaller number of previous births, to deliver when they are older, to receive an X ray while pregnant, and to deliver by caesarean section. The results in their 1991 study include a control for the infant's health endowment (essentially, the residual from the birth weight production function). Hence, the schooling coefficients in the input demand functions are unlikely to reflect correlations between unobserved genetic characteristics of parents and their infants.[19] Moreover, Joyce's (1987a) county-level abortion demand functions reveal that an increase in the fraction of black women aged 15 through 49 with at least a high school education leads to an increase in the abortion rate. Similarly, Leibowitz, Eisen, and Chow (1986) report that unmarried pregnant teenagers in a California sample were more likely to have an abortion if they were high school graduates as opposed to dropouts and if they had higher self-reported grade point averages. These findings are relevant because Grossman and Jacobowitz (1981), Joyce (1987b), and Corman, Joyce, and Grossman (1987) show that an increase in the abortion rate lowers the neonatal mortality rate.

Harris (1982) finds a significant productive efficiency effect of mother's schooling for black birth outcomes in Massachusetts in 1974–75, and Grossman and Joyce (1990) indicate a similar finding for black birth outcomes in New York City in 1984. Neither study employs two-stage least squares estimation. Instead, Harris controls for the unobserved health endowment by making specific assumptions about the nature of the correlation between the disturbance term in the production function and the corresponding term in the demand function for pre-

18. If the price of medical care has no effect on the quantity of the missing input demanded (e.g., nutrition in the case of infant health), a consistent estimate of the medical care parameter in the production function can still be obtained by two-stage least squares. For a more detailed discussion of this issue, see Panis and Lillard (1994).

19. In estimating the birth weight production function Rosenzweig and Schultz (1991) do not use maternal schooling and father's income as instruments because endowments may be correlated across generations and maternal schooling may be correlated with her endowment.

natal care. Grossman and Joyce control for a variety of unobservables governing pregnancy resolutions and birth weight by pooling data on births and abortions. They then estimate a three-equation model. The first equation is a probit for the probability of giving birth, given that a woman is pregnant. With this as the criterion equation, they test for self-selection (correlations between unobserved variables and observed outcomes) in the birth weight production function and in the prenatal care demand function using Heckman's (1979) methodology.[20]

Harris's result pertains to gestation, while Grossman and Joyce's pertains to birth weight. The latter authors report that black women who completed at least one year of college gave birth to infants who weighed 69 grams more than the infants of women who completed at least eight but no more than 11 years of schooling. This amounts to a 2 percent increase relative to a mean of 3,132 grams for the latter group.

4.5. Health Externalities and Government Intervention

4.5.1. General Discussion

The upshot of most of the studies summarized in sections 4.2 through 4.4 is that education has a positive causal effect on good health. This is the case despite a number of issues that should be resolved in future research and are highlighted in section 4.6. In the present section we take the causal effect as given and ask whether it justifies government intervention with the education decisions of its citizens. As Behrman (1996) emphasizes in his excellent discussion of this question, the general answer is no. Government intervention is justified only to correct for externalities and capital market imperfections and possibility to promote a more equal distribution of health outcomes. We focus on externalities—broadly defined to include distribution issues—because they are most closely related to the education effects in the studies reviewed.

To some extent, we emphasize externalities associated with cigarette smoking, alcohol abuse, and lack of exercise. Cigarette smoking has been labeled as the largest preventable cause of death in the United States by the last three annual Surgeon General's Report on Smoking and Health. Motor vehicle accident mortality is the leading cause of death of persons under the age of 35, and alcohol is involved in more than half these fatal accidents (National Highway Traffic Safety Administration 1986). Regular exercise, which promotes weight control, plays a very prominent role in the 1991 Public Health Service Report entitled *Healthy People 2000: National Health Promotion and Disease*

---

20. Based on Wu's (1973) test, Grossman and Joyce (1990) accept the consistency of birth weight production functions obtained by ordinary least squares once these functions are corrected for self-selection.

Prevention Objectives. The difficulties that arise in defining the externalities of cigarette smoking, alcohol abuse, and weight control illustrate the general problems of distinguishing between external and internal costs or benefits. Moreover, by focusing on these behaviors, we highlight issues involved in comparing the effectiveness of policies to increase schooling and health knowledge on the one hand with policies to increase excise taxes on cigarettes and alcohol or impose stiff fines and penalties for drunken driving and raise the probability of conviction on the other.

Externalities arise when one person imposes costs or benefits on others, costs or benefits that the decision maker ignores. We include in this definition costs or benefits that the decision maker imposes on himself or herself and neglects due to imperfect information. Three basic types of externalities have been identified in the literature: production externalities, consumption externalities, and moral hazard externalities. Production externalities refer to situations in which the health of some persons depends on the health or health inputs of others. Consumption externalities refer to situations in which the utility, rather than the health, of some persons depends on the health of others. Moral hazard externalities, which are particularly relevant for cigarette smoking and alcohol abuse, arise when premiums paid for health or life insurance do not fully reflect the insured's expected use of medical care services or probability of death.

Health-related consumption externalities, treated in detail by Pauly (1971), make health a "merit good" in the literature on public finance and explain why society may not be satisfied with the distribution of health outcomes determined by market forces that shape household decisions. Given the multivariate health production function, the optimal public policy involves reductions in the prices of all health inputs used by persons who choose health levels that are less than optimal from society's point of view. This involves lowering the price of education if the effect of that variable on health is due to productive efficiency. But, as demonstrated by Pauly (1971), the optimal price cuts should not be the same for everyone. For example, suppose that the private demand for health rises with education, while the marginal benefit that the community at large derives from a given member's health falls as his or her health rises. Then the optimal price reductions should fall with education. Beyond some education level, no price reductions are required.

Perhaps the most common example of a health production externality pertains to immunizations against contagious diseases. As Behrman (1996) notes, if the more educated are more likely to immunize themselves and their families against these diseases and these actions lower the probabilities that other members of the community contract these diseases, the total returns to education exceed the private returns. But this does not necessarily justify subsidies to education. Since education is not an input in this example, the least-cost way to reach the socially optimal output is to subsidize the money price of an immunization. This improves welfare by an area that is approximately equal to one-half of the difference between private and social marginal cost multiplied by the difference between private and social equilibrium output.[21] On the other hand, if the optimal output is reached by raising the level of education, welfare increases by this area less the cost of the additional education.[22]

In the preceding example, we assume that the education differences in immunization are not due to imperfect information. If the less educated lack information about the private returns to immunization, provision of this information by the government may be an alternative to lowering the money price of an immunization.[23] Since schools are attractive and effective settings to provide information, subsidies aimed at schools attended by the children of the less educated may be appropriate. But note that an education subsidy to correct for imperfect information will not lower the difference between private and social marginal cost unless this difference falls as the level of immunization rises.

The studies reviewed in sections 4.3 and 4.4 highlight the positive impact of parents' schooling on their children's health. If parents ignore these effects when they determine their schooling levels, they will acquire less than the optimal amount of education. Lazear (1983) has conducted an extremely interesting analysis of the importance of this type of externality in the context of the positive effect of father's education on his son's wage rate. He shows that, if white fathers ignore all of this effect, they will underinvest in their own education by at most one-third of a year. For black fathers, the amount of underinvestment is much larger. It equals 2.3 years, and a subsidy of approximately $28,000 in 1993 dollars would be required to reach the optimal level of education.

It is reasonable to assume that most parents take account of the impact of their current decisions on their children (see sec. 4.6 and chap. 5 for some examples). But Lazear certainly has a valid point in stating that schooling decisions, which frequently precede the birth of children by a fairly long period, may not be characterized in this manner. An extension of his analysis to health would be useful but difficult unless health returns are limited to those arising because improvements in health raise earnings.

4.5.2. Cigarette Smoking, Alcohol Abuse, and Fitness

Having examined health externalities and education in a fairly general setting, we now turn to these externalities in the context of cigarette smoking, alcohol abuse, and lack of exercise. Much of our discussion is based on recent studies

---

21. We treat the externality as a subtraction from private marginal cost. The same result emerges if it is treated as an addition to private marginal benefit.

22. If the positive difference between private and social marginal cost falls as the quantity of immunizations rises, the optimal price cut is a negative function of education and may fall to zero at some level of education.

23. The inability of private firms to capture all of the returns from the provision of information justifies the undertaking of this activity by the government.

by Manning, Keeler, Newhouse, Sloss, and Wasserman (1991), Grossman, Sindelar, Mullahy, and Anderson (1993), and Grossman, Chaloupka, Saffer, and Laixuthai (1994). The reader should consult these references for more details, including summaries of the detailed research by Grossman and his colleagues pertaining to the price sensitivity of cigarette smoking, alcohol use and abuse, and motor vehicle accident mortality.

4.5.2.1. Smoking

Various external costs of smoking are controversial. Consider those associated with imperfect information. In response to the first Surgeon General's Report on Smoking and Health in 1964, smoking participation rates of more educated consumers declined rapidly in the late 1960s and early 1970s. In this period educated consumers were more likely to quit smoking and less likely to begin than less-educated consumers were. These data imply differential ability to process new information as a function of education and possibly some government action. But it is still true today after 30 years of providing information that the more educated are less likely to smoke than the less educated are, despite the massive antismoking campaigns mounted by federal and state governments.

We attribute the recent data to more future-oriented behavior by the more educated rather than to differences in information. Indeed, a survey taken by Viscusi (1992) shows that both smokers and nonsmokers overestimate, rather than underestimate, the probability of death and illness from lung cancer due to tobacco. Teenagers, who have less information and are less future oriented than adults, actually attach much higher risks to smoking than does the rest of the population.

Becker, Grossman, and Murphy (1994) report that smokers are farsighted in the sense that they anticipate the expected future consequences of their current actions. Smokers who behave in this manner reduce their current consumption of cigarettes in response to a reduction in expected future consumption due to an increase in future price. This is exactly what they find.

Given the Becker, Grossman, and Murphy study, the results of Viscusi's survey, and the widespread diffusion of information concerning the harmful effects of smoking, the case for government intervention in the cigarette market because people have imperfect information is weak. Even if some teenagers ignore the health costs of smoking, it is naive to assume that the government is better able to internalize these costs than their parents are. The latter have natural incentives to invest in their children in a variety of ways, including ways that make them more future oriented.[24]

---

24. In light of Becker and Mulligan's (1994) model of the endogenous determination of time preference, and hence the degree of future orientation, government intervention would be

Some parents behave in ways that harm their children's health, and the health of unrelated persons can be worsened by the actions of smokers. The best example of these external costs is the harm done to their fetuses by pregnant women who smoke. Numerous studies show that these women are more likely to miscarry and to give birth to low-weight infants. Many of these babies require neonatal intensive care.[25] It is not clear, however, whether maternal smoking during pregnancy should be treated as a cost imposed on one person by another and ignored by the smoker because pregnant women may already have taken into account the impacts of their behavior on their infants. Since they still choose to smoke, the benefits to them outweigh the potential costs. Still, programs to modify the behavior of some pregnant women who smoke may well be justified, and they are alternatives to a broad-based cigarette tax. As in the immunization example, school-based programs in poor areas may be effective vehicles, especially since maternal smoking is one of many problems associated with teenage pregnancies (see Maynard 1995 for a more detailed discussion of this issue).

Scientific evidence with regard to the detrimental health effects suffered by nonsmokers from secondhand smoke is much weaker than that pertaining to smoking during pregnancy. The U.S. Environmental Protection Agency (1992) estimates that these effects include annually roughly 3,000 additional lung cancer deaths as well as a host of other respiratory illnesses. But Barro (1994) and Sullum (1994) raise serious questions about the standards for statistical significance used by the EPA to reach these conclusions. Even using standards that in effect double the odds of being wrong, only one of 11 studies analyzed by the EPA found a statistically significant relationship between secondhand smoke and lung cancer.

According to Manning et al. (1991), the principal external cost of smoking arises because the premiums paid by smokers for health and life insurance do not fully reflect their excess use of medical care services and their higher probability of premature death. This moral hazard external cost takes account of smokers' smaller pension benefits, including Social Security payments. It amounts to 28 cents on a pack of cigarettes in 1993. This figure excludes the costs of low birth weight, fetal death, and passive smoking, which might be measured by the cost of neonatal intensive care and the cost of premature death. If these costs are treated as externalities, the optimal tax on a pack of cigarettes (the tax that equals the external cost per pack) is 68 cents. This upper-bound figure exceeds

---

justified if some parents lacked information about the investment process described by Becker and Mulligan. But, since their work is so new, more research is required before it can be used as the basis for public policy.

25. The moral hazard externality that this behavior imposes is discussed later when the issue of insurance is considered.

the average federal and state tax of 52 cents on a pack of cigarettes in 1993. Since the current federal tax rate is 24 cents per pack, these estimates justify a federal tax hike of 16 cents (a federal tax rate of 40 cents) if one accepts the EPA's evidence with regard to passive smoking and assumes that all pregnant women ignore the impact of their behavior on their fetuses. But, if the external costs of smoking are limited to those that are not controversial, the average federal and state tax exceeds the optimal tax.

Hay (1991) criticizes Manning et al. for excluding the long-term intellectual and physical developmental consequences of low birth weight. He estimates that the inclusion of these costs raises the optimal tax to more than $4.80 a pack. Hay, however, is not nearly as careful as Manning et al. in controlling for factors correlated with smoking in making this estimate.

Clearly, the range of choice here is considerable, particularly since educational programs to modify the behavior of pregnant women who smoke are alternatives to a broad-based cigarette tax.

To expand on this point, suppose that all the external costs of smoking were attributable to these women. Then an excise tax on cigarettes or an increase in the excise tax would impose welfare costs in terms of losses in consumer surplus minus revenues generated by the tax on smokers who are not pregnant women. The optimal excise tax is the one that sets the reduction in the external cost of smoking caused by a small increase in the tax equal to the increase in the welfare cost of the tax. Clearly it would be much smaller than $4.80 a pack since Hay ignores the welfare costs of the tax. Moreover, an education program aimed at pregnant women who smoke might have a more favorable cost ratio than a tax hike would. This would depend on the impacts of these alternative policies on smoking and on the resource cost of the education program compared with the welfare cost of the tax program.[26]

4.5.2.2.   Alcohol

According to Manning et al. (1991), the principal external cost of alcohol abuse is the loss of life associated with drunk driving. Even here, controversies arise. Consider, for example, a sober passenger who knowingly agrees to ride in a motor vehicle operated by an intoxicated driver. If the driver causes a crash in which the passenger is killed, is this premature death an external cost of alcohol abuse or was the risk taken voluntarily (and thus internalized) by the passenger? Or suppose that the driver is killed. If he or she had complete information about the risk involved, the monetary value of this loss of life is not an external cost of alcohol abuse. But it is an external cost if the driver

---

26. It is well known that the first-best solution would be to costlessly tax only pregnant women who smoke. We assume that this is not feasible.

has no information about the risk involved. In intermediate cases some fraction of the number of drunk drivers killed in motor vehicle accidents should be counted as external costs.

Despite the controversies just mentioned, the story with respect to the optimal tax on alcohol is somewhat different than that with respect to cigarettes. Although they examine differing estimates of the costs of alcohol abuse, Pogue and Sgontz (1989), Blumberg (1992), Kenkel (1996), and Saffer and Chaloupka (1994) conclude that the optimal tax on alcohol is at least twice as large as the current average federal and state tax of approximately $35 per gallon of pure alcohol. All these studies take into account the welfare losses suffered by consumers who do not abuse alcohol when the tax rate rises.

Kenkel (1993) performs a cost-effectiveness analysis of alternative policies to reduce drunk driving that has implications with regard to the use of health education as a policy instrument. His analysis is based on the Health Promotion/Disease Prevention Supplement to the 1985 National Health Interview Survey. He focuses on two outcomes: the number of days in the previous year on which a respondent had five or more drinks in a row (heavy drinking) and the reported number of occasions of drunk driving in the previous year. He estimates a two-equation recursive model with correlated errors. In the first equation heavy drinking depends on the price of alcohol in the respondent's city of residence,[27] state-specific laws that attempt to deter drunk driving by increasing the probability that a drunk driver will be apprehended and convicted and by raising the penalty if convicted, drinking knowledge (the number of correct responses to whether heavy drinking causes each of three illnesses), years of formal schooling completed, and other personal characteristics. In the second equation, drunk driving depends on heavy drinking (treated as endogenous), the drunk driving laws, schooling, and other personal characteristics. Identification is achieved by assuming that the price of alcohol and drinking knowledge have no impact on drunk driving with heavy drinking held constant.

Kenkel finds that heavy drinking is negatively related to deterrence, the price of alcohol, drinking knowledge, and schooling. He also finds that drunk driving is positively related to heavy drinking and negatively related to deterrence. Simulations suggest that a tax hike that raises the price of alcohol by 23 percent has the same impact on drunk driving as a policy under which half the population of the United States lives in states with the deterrence laws in place. But the cost of the tax policy is smaller than the cost of the deterrence policy, indicating that the former is more cost effective.

Although Kenkel reports a negative and significant effect of drinking knowledge on heavy drinking and a negative drinking knowledge coefficient

---

27. The price used is a weighted average of the prices of beer, wine, and distilled spirits. Most of the variation in this price is due to the very different rates at which states tax alcoholic beverages.

in the reduced form for drunk driving, he does not consider a policy to increase health knowledge as an alternative to the two just mentioned. This is because his empirical work "does not provide evidence on the link between the provision of health education by the government and its acquisition by consumers" (1993, 897). Another consideration may be traced to his 1991 study with the same data, described in section 4.2. Here the negative effect of schooling on heavy drinking is reduced by 20 percent at most when drinking knowledge is included as a regressor.

The more educated, however, may have more accurate information about the probability of being apprehended for drunk driving and about the risks that they impose on themselves when they engage in this activity. In the first instance, health education complements stiffer deterrence. The combination of the two may be more cost effective than the tax policy.[28] In the second instance, an education program, while aimed solely at an ignored internal cost, will lower the difference between the social and private marginal cost of drunk driving if this difference falls as the level of drunk driving falls. This seems likely: the probability that an innocent victim is harmed by a drunk driver should decline as the per capita number of drunk drivers decreases.

4.5.2.3. Fitness

With regard to lack of exercise, Manning et al. (1991) report that the external cost of a "mile-not-walked" is 37 cents in 1993 dollars. This cost is driven almost entirely by the difference between the medical care costs incurred by those with a sedentary life style and the health insurance premiums that they pay. Manning et al. also point out that excise taxes cannot be used to remedy this externality. To quote them:

> Lack of exercise differs from smoking and drinking as sins of omission differ from sins of commission. From the standpoint of taxes, society can tax people for "wrongful consumption"—per unit of substance consumed. It is hard to imagine how they can be taxed for not doing the "right" thing. They could, however, be "rewarded" for doing it (23).

To correct for this externality, the authors propose encouraging and rewarding exercise through educational efforts, benefits to people who exercise, and subsidies to facilities and programs that promote exercise. Part of the benefits might take the form of reduced life and health insurance premiums for persons

---

28. Kenkel (1996) reports that excise tax hikes may complement policies to raise health knowledge since the price elasticity of demand for the frequency of heavy drinking appears to rise in absolute value as health knowledge rises. The source of this interaction has not been fully identified.

who demonstrate that they are fit. Indeed, differential premiums as a function of cigarette smoking, alcohol abuse, and amount of exercise constitute another general policy tool in addition to taxes, education programs, and deterrence through the legal system.[29]

Kenkel (1991b) is pessimistic about the effectiveness of health education programs to promote exercise and discourage alcohol abuse and cigarette smoking. Recall that in his study, described in section 4.2.2 (Kenkel 1991a), he found that more knowledgeable people smoke less, engage in less heavy drinking, and exercise more. Kenkel (1991b) estimates that large increases in health knowledge are required to meet Public Health Service (1991) objectives for the year 2000. These objectives translate into a 15 percent increase in smoking knowledge, a 50 percent increase in drinking knowledge, and a 120 percent increase in exercise knowledge. But these large increases in health knowledge translate into modest changes in the behaviors at issue. For example, Kenkel predicts that the number of male exercisers would increase from 68 to between 69 and 80 percent. The number of female exercisers would rise from 64 to between 66 and 72 percent. Based on the midpoints of these ranges, a 120 percent expansion in exercise knowledge would be required to increase the number of exercisers in the population by 10 percent.

Kenkel's results are based on very specific measures of health knowledge. In the case of exercise, they are the correct responses to three questions pertaining to the amount of exercise required to strengthen the heart and lungs in terms of days a week, minutes a day, and increase in heart rate. An analysis based on more general measures might lead to different conclusions. Interactions among the addictive nature of the health behaviors at issue, the formation of time preference, and peer pressure—discussed in the next section—also must be considered to fully evaluate health education programs.

4.6. Implications for Future Research

We raised two questions in this chapter. First, does schooling have a positive causal impact on good health? Second, if the answer to the first question is yes, does this justify additional government intervention in the schooling market? Our interpretation of the extensive literature dealing with the first issue is that the weight of the evidence suggests that more schooling does in fact cause better health. But because the mechanisms through which schooling affects health have not been fully identified, more research is required before the second

29. Health care reform proposals pending in Congress in 1994 contained provisions for community-rated as opposed to experience-rated premiums. They also prohibited insurance companies from denying or limiting coverage to any group or individual because of a preexisting condition. These provisions are inconsistent with a program to correct for externalities by rewarding consumers for healthy behaviors and punishing them for unhealthy behaviors.

question can be answered and the nature of new government programs, if any, can be described.

In providing a positive response to the first question, we are sensitive to the difficulties of establishing causality in the social sciences where natural experiments rarely can be performed. Our affirmative answer is based on the numerous studies in the United States and developing countries that we have summarized. These studies employ a variety of adult, child, and infant health measures, many different estimation techniques, and controls for a host of third variables.

One can always argue that an observed schooling coefficient is biased due to heterogeneity among individuals and associate this heterogeneity with unobserved genetic and home environmental endowments. But in our view too much emphasis has been given to this argument in the literature. No one would deny that own schooling is a predetermined endogenous variable in an equation in which own health is the dependent variable or that parents' schooling is a predetermined endogenous variable in an equation in which infant or child health is the dependent variable. One cannot rule out, however, a recursive model with uncorrelated errors. Indeed, the evidence presented by Berger and Leigh (1989), Leigh (1990), and Sander (1995a, 1995b) is consistent with this type of model.

By analogy, consider the relationship between earnings on the one hand and schooling and ability on the other. Much ink has been spilled on the bias that arises when an earnings function is estimated with ability omitted. But it is possible to formulate a model in which ability should be omitted from the reduced-form earnings function even though it enters the structural production function and has a causal impact on schooling. As an identity, the earnings (e_i) of the ith person can be written

$$\ell n\ e_i \equiv \ell n\ e_{0i} + \phi_i s_i, \tag{1}$$

where e_{0i} is his or her raw earnings, s_i is years of formal schooling completed, ϕ_i is the average internal rate of return to schooling, and ℓn stands for natural logarithm. Let the human capital production function or the structural earnings function be

$$\ell n\ e_i = f(s_i, a_i), \tag{2}$$

where a_i is ability (assumed to be exogenous). The marginal rate of return to schooling (ρ_i) is defined as

$$\rho_i \equiv (\partial \ell n\ e_i / \partial s_i) \equiv \phi_i + s_i(\partial \phi_i / \partial s_i). \tag{3}$$

If schooling is selected to maximize wealth, then in equilibrium

$$\rho_i = r_i, \tag{4}$$

where r_i is the marginal rate of interest.

Suppose that the structural earnings function has the following form (subscripts for individuals deleted from now on):

$$\ell n\ e = \ell n\ e_0 + as^{1-\alpha}, 0 < \alpha < 1. \tag{5}$$

Given this function,

$$\phi = as^{-\alpha}. \tag{6}$$

From the first-order condition for optimal s:

$$s = r^{-1/\alpha}(1 - \alpha)^{1/\alpha}a^{1/\alpha}, \tag{7}$$

where we assume that the rate of interest does not depend on s or other variables. Using equations 1, 6, and 7, Mincer's (1974) semilogarithmic earnings function emerges:

$$\ell n\ e = \ell n\ e_0 + [r/(1 - \alpha)]\ s. \tag{8}$$

Note that the coefficient of s in equation 8 is the equilibrium average internal rate of return. This is the same for everyone because each person faces the same market rate of interest and because the elasticity of the average rate of return with respect to $s(-\alpha)$ has the same constant value for each person. Note also that ability (a) does not appear in equation 8 unless e_0 depends on a. Note finally that equation 8 can be estimated by ordinary least squares even though s is endogenous.[30] This would be true even if the structural earnings function were rewritten as

$$\ell n\ e = \ell n\ e_0 + as^{1-\alpha}u,$$

---

30. The natural logarithm of raw earnings ($\ell n\ e_0$) is the disturbance term in equation 8. From equation 7, this variable is not correlated with schooling. Thus, ordinary least squares estimation of equation 8 is appropriate. Technically, that natural logarithm of raw earnings of the ith person can be written as

$$\ell n\ e_{0i} \equiv \ell n\ e_0 + \epsilon_i.$$

In this form, $\ell n\ e_0$ becomes the intercept and ϵ_i is the disturbance term. Incorporation of an intercept does not alter the conclusion that the disturbance term is uncorrelated with schooling.

where u is not observed. Of course, if raw earnings also depends on u, s and the disturbance term in equation 8 would be correlated.[31]

Our point here is not that unobserved heterogeneity can be ignored in estimating the effect of schooling on health. Rather, this bias may be nonexistent in certain instances and small in others. Moreover, the methods used to eliminate heterogeneity bias are not without cost. For example, several papers use samples of identical twins to control for the unobserved endowment, but these samples are not representative of the population at large, contain limited measures of health, and are characterized by limited variation in schooling. The variance in schooling is further reduced by a within-twin estimator, and the schooling coefficient obtained with that estimator can be seriously biased due to measurement error (see Behrman 1996 for more details). Finally, time preference for the present, which has been labeled as a key unobservable by a number of investigators, may actually be caused by schooling—a point emphasized by Becker and Mulligan (1994).

We heartily endorse more research dealing with the impact of schooling on health because, as indicated previously, the mechanisms via which schooling alters health have not been fully identified. Until this is done, behavioral changes required to correct for externalities will be difficult and costly to achieve. Future research will be particularly useful if it is based on national data with a variety of health outputs, a complete set of health and schooling inputs, and a panel component. We conclude by identifying some key issues to address.

1. With data that are rich enough to identify health production functions, one can compare the productive efficiency hypothesis to the allocative efficiency hypothesis using the appropriate overidentification tests. Evidence in support of the latter would justify health education programs, possibly in a school setting, to encourage or discourage the use of certain inputs. Evidence in support of the former has less clear-cut policy implications. It does suggest that expansions in schooling, at least for some segments of the population, should not be neglected if increases in the health of those segments are desired. The content of the schooling should be more general than the specific expansions in health knowledge suggested by allocative efficiency.

2. New panel data on the health and school achievement of children and adolescents would shed additional light on those dimensions of education other than years of formal schooling completed that impact on health and interactions between these variables and parents' schooling. Here we have in mind a national panel like the longitudinal component of the 1966–70 Health Examination Survey (HES) used by Shakotko, Edwards, and Grossman (1981). Unfortunately, the most recent waves of this data collection effort—the

---

31. Part of the above model is outlined verbally by Mincer (1974, 137–40). The conclusion that the rate of return to schooling is not biased by the omission of ability is supported by Ashenfelter and Krueger (1994) but not by Behrman, Rosenzweig, and Taubman (1994).

first three National Health and Nutrition Examination Surveys (NHANES)—have not obtained cognitive development measures. The National Longitudinal Survey of Youth has this information, but its health measures are rather limited and are based on self-reports or parental-reports. On the other hand, the members of HES and NHANES were given physical examinations. If the new data collection effort also obtained more detailed health knowledge measures than those used by Kenkel (1991a, 1991b), relationships among schooling, cognitive development, health knowledge, and health outcomes could be subjected to further testing and evaluation.

3. Further investigations of relationships among health, schooling, and nutrition with U.S. data may be worthwhile for a number of reasons. Nutrient intakes are intermediate outputs of household production and direct inputs into the production of health. Given detailed data on food consumption, one could examine one aspect of the efficiency of education in household production. Namely, do the more educated obtain more nutrient intakes per dollar of food purchased?[32] The U.S. Department of Agriculture's Continuing Survey of Food Intakes by Individuals and NHANES appear to have the information to conduct this research. As is stressed by Silberberg (1985), this research must recognize that food is demanded for reasons other than pure nutrition.

In the previous section we summarized the important externalities associated with exercise. Appropriate nutrition and exercise are likely to be complementary inputs in the production of ideal weight for a given height. Thus, the estimation of a model that includes nutrient intake and ideal weight production functions and demand functions for nutrient intakes and exercise may further inform the debate concerning the mechanisms via which schooling affects health.

4. The work by Becker and Mulligan (1994) suggests a more definitive and concrete way to measure time preference and incorporate it into estimates of health demand functions. They point out that the natural logarithm of the ratio of consumption between consecutive time periods ($\ell n\ R$) is approximately equal to $\sigma[\ell n(1 + r) - \ell n(1 + t)]$, where σ is the intertemporal elasticity of substitution in consumption, r is the market rate of interest, and t is the rate of time preference for the present. If σ and r do not vary among individuals, variations in $\ell n\ R$ capture variations in time preference. With panel data, $\ell n\ R$ can be included as a regressor in the health demand function. Since Becker and Mulligan stress the endogeneity of time preference and its dependence on schooling, simultaneous equations techniques appear to be required. Identification of this model will not be easy, but success in this area has the potential to greatly inform public policy.

5. If most of the effect of schooling on health operates through time preference, the school-based programs to promote health knowledge described

---

32. For one unpublished effort along these lines, see Michael (1967).

in the previous section may have much smaller payoffs than those that encourage the investments in time preference made by the more educated. Indeed, in an ever-changing world in which new information constantly becomes available, general interventions that encourage future-oriented behavior may have much larger rates of return in the long run than do specific interventions designed, for example, to discourage smoking.

6. There appear to be important interactions between Becker and Mulligan's theory of the endogenous determination of time preference and Becker and Murphy's (1988) theory of rational addiction. Such addictive behaviors as cigarette smoking, excessive alcohol use, and the consumption of illegal drugs have demonstrated adverse health effects. Increased consumption of these goods raise present utility but lower future utility. According to Becker and Mulligan: "Since a decline in future utility reduces the benefits from a lower discount on future utilities, greater consumption of harmful substances would lead to higher rates of time preference by discouraging investments in lowering these rates" (1994, 28–29). This is the converse of Becker and Murphy's result that people who discount the future more heavily are more likely to become addicted. Thus, "harmful addictions induce even rational persons to discount the future more heavily, which in turn may lead them to become more addicted" (Becker and Mulligan 1994, 29).

It is well known that cigarette smoking and excessive alcohol abuse begin early in life (e.g., Grossman, Sindelar, Mullahy, and Anderson 1993). Moreover, bandwagon or peer effects are much more important in the case of youth smoking or alcohol consumption than in the case of adult smoking or alcohol consumption. The two-way causality between addiction and time preference and the importance of peer pressure explain why parents who care about the welfare of their children have large incentives to make investments that make their children more future oriented. These forces may also account for the relatively large impact of schooling on health with health knowledge held constant reported by Kenkel (1991a).

Some parents may ignore or be unaware of the benefits of investments in time preference. Given society's concern with the welfare of its children, subsidies to school-based programs that make children more future oriented may be warranted. But much more research dealing with the determinants of time preference and its relationship with schooling and health is required before these programs can be formulated and implemented in a cost-effective manner.

REFERENCES

Ashenfelter, O., and A. Krueger. 1994. Estimates of the Economic Return to Schooling from a New Sample of Twins. *American Economic Review* 84:1157–73.

Auster, R., I. Leveson, and D. Sarachek. 1969. The Production of Health: An Exploratory Study. *Journal of Human Resources* 4:411–36.

Barro, R. J. 1994. Send Regulations up in Smoke. *Wall Street Journal,* 3 June, A12.

Becker, G. S. 1965. A Theory of the Allocation of Time. *Economic Journal* 75:493–517.

Becker, G. S., M. Grossman, and K. M. Murphy. 1991. Rational Addiction and the Effect of Price on Consumption. *American Economic Review* 81:237–41.

Becker, G. S., M. Grossman, and K. M. Murphy. 1994. An Empirical Analysis of Cigarette Addiction. *American Economic Review* 84:396–418.

Becker, G. S., and C. B. Mulligan. 1994. On the Endogenous Determination of Time Preference. Discussion Paper no. 94–2, Economics Research Center/National Opinion Research Center, July. Mimeo.

Becker, G. S., and K. M. Murphy. 1988. A Theory of Rational Addiction. *Journal of Political Economy* 96:675–700.

Behrman, J. R. 1996. Conceptual and Measurement Issues. Paper presented at a conference entitled "Social Benefits of Education: Can They Be Measured?" sponsored by the Office of Research of the U.S. Department of Education at the Meridian International Center, Washington, DC, January. Revised version is chapter 3 in present volume.

Behrman, J. R., and A. B. Deolalikar. 1988. Health and Nutrition. In *Handbook of Development Economics,* ed. H. Chenery and T. N. Srinivasan, vol. 1. Amsterdam: Elsevier Science Publishers. Pp. 633–711.

Behrman, J. R., M. R. Rosenzweig, and P. Taubman. 1994. Endowments and the Allocation of Schooling in the Family and in the Marriage Market: The Twin Experiment. *Journal of Political Economy* 102:1131–74.

Behrman, J. R., R. Sickles, P. Taubman, and A. Yazbeck. 1991. Black-White Mortality Inequalities. *Journal of Econometrics* 50:183–203.

Behrman, J. R., and B. L. Wolfe. 1984. More Evidence on Nutrition Demand: Income Seems Overrated and Women's Schooling Underemphasized. *Journal of Developmental Economics* 14:105–28.

Behrman, J. R., and B. L. Wolfe. 1987. How Does Mother's Schooling Affect Family Health, Nutrition, Medical Care Usage, and Household Sanitation? *Journal of Econometrics* 36:185–204.

Behrman, J. R., and B. L. Wolfe. 1989. Does Schooling Make a Woman Better Nourished and Healthier? Adult Sibling Random and Fixed Effects Estimates for Nicaragua. *Journal of Human Resources* 24:644–63.

Berger, M. C., and J. P. Leigh. 1989. Schooling, Self-Selection, and Health. *Journal of Human Resources* 24:433–55.

Blumberg, L. J. 1992. Second-Best Alcohol Taxation: Balancing Appropriate Incentives with Deadweight Loss. Ph.D. diss., University of Michigan.

Chaikind, S., and H. Corman. 1991. The Impact of Low Birthweight on Special Education Costs. *Journal of Health Economics* 10:291–311.

Chaloupka, F. J. 1991. Rational Addictive Behavior and Cigarette Smoking. *Journal of Political Economy* 99:722–42.

Chamberlain, G. 1980. Analysis of Covariance with Qualitative Data. *Review of Economic Studies* 47:225–38.

Cherlin, A. J. 1992. *Marriage, Divorce, Remarriage.* Cambridge, MA: Harvard University Press.

Chernichovsky, D., and D. Coate. 1980. The Choice of Diet for Young Children and Its Relation to Children's Growth. *Journal of Human Resources* 15:255–63.

Chernichovsky, D., and D. Coate. 1983. An Economic Analysis of the Diet, Growth, and Health of Young Children in the United States. In *Human Capital and Development,* ed. D. Salkever, I. Sirageldin, and A. Sorkin, vol. 3. Greenwich, CT: JAI Press Inc. Pp. 111–25.

Corman, H., and M. Grossman. 1985. Determinants of Neonatal Mortality Rates in the United States: A Reduced Form Model. *Journal of Health Economics* 4:213–36.

Corman, H., T. J. Joyce, and M. Grossman. 1987. Birth Outcome Production Functions in the U.S. *Journal of Human Resources* 22:339–60.

Currie, J., and D. Thomas. 1995. Does Head Start Make a Difference? *American Economic Review* 85:341–64.

Desai, S. 1987. The Estimation of the Health Production Function for Low-Income Working Men. *Medical Care* 25:604–15.

Dranove, D. 1988. Demand Inducement and the Physician/Patient Relationship. *Economic Inquiry* 26:281–98.

Duleep, H. O. 1986. Measuring the Effect of Income on Adult Mortality Using Longitudinal Administrative Record Data. *Journal of Human Resources* 21:238–51.

Edwards, L. N., and M. Grossman. 1979. The Relationship between Children's Health and Intellectual Development. In *Health: What Is It Worth?,* ed. S. J. Mushkin and D. W. Dunlop, Elmsford: Pergamon Press. Pp. 273–314.

Edwards, L. N., and M. Grossman. 1981. Children's Health and the Family. In *Advances in Health Economics and Health Services Research,* ed. R. M. Scheffler, vol. 2. Greenwich, CT: JAI Press. Pp. 35–84.

Edwards, L. N., and M. Grossman. 1982. Income and Race Differences in Children's Health in the Mid-1960's. *Medical Care* 20:915–30.

Edwards, L. N., and M. Grossman. 1983. Adolescent Health, Family Background, and Preventive Medical Care. In *Research in Human Capital and Development,* ed. D. S. Salkever, I. Sirageldin, and A. Sorkin, vol. 3. Greenwich, CT: JAI Press. Pp. 77–109.

Farrell, P., and V. R. Fuchs. 1982. Schooling and Health: The Cigarette Connection. *Journal of Health Economics* 1:217–30.

Fogel, R. W. 1994. Economic Growth, Population Theory, and Physiology: The Bearing of Long-Term Processes on the Making of Economic Policy. *American Economic Review* 84:369–95.

Fuchs, V. R. 1982. Time Preference and Health: An Exploratory Study. In *Economic Aspects of Health,* ed. V. R. Fuchs. Chicago: University of Chicago Press for the National Bureau of Economic Research. Pp. 93–120.

Granger, C. W. J. 1969. Investigating Causal Relations by Econometric Models and Cross-Spectral Methods. *Econometrica* 37:424–38.

Grossman, M. 1972a. On the Concept of Health Capital and the Demand for Health. *Journal of Political Economy* 80:223–55.

Grossman, M. 1972b. *The Demand for Health: A Theoretical and Empirical Investiga-*

tion. New York: Columbia University Press for the National Bureau of Economic Research.

Grossman, M. 1975. The Correlation between Health and Schooling. In *Household Production and Consumption,* ed. N. E. Terleckyj, Studies in Income and Wealth, Vol. 40, Conference on Research in Income and Wealth. New York: Columbia University Press for the National Bureau of Economic Research. Pp. 147–211.

Grossman, M. 1983. Economic and Other Factors in Youth Smoking. Final Report, Grant Number SES–8014959, National Science Foundation (December).

Grossman, M., and L. Benham. 1974. Health, Hours, and Wages. In *The Economics of Health and Medical Care,* ed. M. Perlman. Proceedings of a conference sponsored by the International Economics Association, Tokyo. New York: Wiley. Pp. 205–33.

Grossman, M., F. J. Chaloupka, H. Saffer, and A. Laixuthai. 1994. Effects of Alcohol Price Policy on Youth: A Summary of Economic Research. *Journal of Research on Adolescence* 4:347–64.

Grossman, M., and S. Jacobowitz. 1981. Variations in Infant Mortality Rates among Counties of the United States: The Roles of Public Policies and Programs. *Demography* 18:695–713.

Grossman, M., and T. J. Joyce. 1990. Unobservables, Pregnancy Resolutions, and Birth Weight Production Functions in New York City. *Journal of Political Economy* 98:983–1007.

Grossman, M., J. L. Sindelar, J. Mullahy, and R. Anderson. 1993. Policy Watch: Alcohol and Cigarette Taxes. *Journal of Economic Perspectives* 7:211–22.

Harris, J. E. 1982. Prenatal Medical Care and Infant Mortality. In *Economic Aspects of Health,* ed. V. R. Fuchs. Chicago: University of Chicago Press for the National Bureau of Economic Research. Pp. 15–52.

Hausman, J. A. 1978. Specification Tests in Econometrics. *Econometrica* 46:1251–71.

Hay, J. W. 1991. The Harm They Do to Others: A Primer on the External Costs of Drug Abuse. In *Searching for Alternatives: Drug-Control Policy in the United States,* ed. M. B. Krauss and E. P. Lazear. Stanford: Hoover Institution Press. Pp. 200–225.

Heckman, J. J. 1979. Sample Selection Bias as a Specification Error. *Econometrica* 47:153–61.

Hwang, H.-S. 1980. A Comparison of Overidentifying Restrictions. *Econometrica* 48:1821–25.

Ippolito, P. M., and A. D. Mathios. 1990. Information, Advertising and Health Choices: A Study of the Cereal Market. *Rand Journal of Economics* 21:459–80.

Joyce, T. J. 1987a. The Demand for Health Inputs and Their Impact on the Black Neonatal Mortality Rate in the U.S. *Social Science and Medicine* 24:911–18.

Joyce, T. J. 1987b. The Impact of Induced Abortion on Black and White Birth Outcomes in the United States. *Demography* 24:229–44.

Joyce, T. J. 1994. Self-Selection, Prenatal Care, and Birthweight among Blacks, Whites, and Hispanics in New York City. *Journal of Human Resources* 29:762–94.

Kemna, H. J. M. I. 1987. Working Conditions and the Relationship between Schooling and Health. *Journal of Health Economics* 6:189–210.

Kenkel, D. S. 1990. Consumer Health Information and the Demand for Medical Care. *Review of Economics and Statistics* 72:587–95.

Kenkel, D. S. 1991a. Health Behavior, Health Knowledge, and Schooling. *Journal of Political Economy* 99:287–305.

Kenkel, D. S. 1991b. What You Don't Know Really Won't Hurt You. *Journal of Policy Analysis and Management* 10:304–9.

Kenkel, D. S. 1993. Drinking, Driving, and Deterrence: The Effectiveness and Social Costs of Alternative Policies. *Journal of Law and Economics* 36:877–913.

Kenkel, D. S. 1996. New Estimates of the Optimal Tax on Alcohol. *Economic Inquiry* 34:296–319.

Lancaster, K. J. 1966. A New Approach to Consumer Theory. *Journal of Political Economy* 74:132–57.

Lairson, D., R. Lorimor, and C. Slater. 1984. Estimates of the Demand for Health: Males in the Pre-Retirement Years. *Social Science and Medicine* 19:741–47.

Lazear, E. P. 1983. Intergenerational Externalities. *Canadian Journal of Economics* 16:212–28.

Leibowitz, A., M. Eisen, and W. K. Chow. 1986. An Economic Model of Teenage Pregnancy Decision-Making. *Demography* 23:67–77.

Leigh, J. P. 1983. Direct and Indirect Effects of Education on Health. *Social Science and Medicine* 17:227–34.

Leigh, J. P. 1985. An Empirical Analysis of Self-Reported, Work-Limiting Disability. *Medical Care* 23:310–19.

Leigh, J. P. 1986. Accounting for Tastes: Correlates of Risk and Time Preferences. *Journal of Post Keynesian Economics* 9:17–31.

Leigh, J. P. 1990. Schooling and Seat Belt Use. *Southern Economic Journal* 57:195–207.

Lewit, E. M., D. Coate, and M. Grossman. 1981. The Effects of Government Regulation on Teenage Smoking. *Journal of Law and Economics* 24:545–69.

Manning, W. G., E. B. Keeler, J. P. Newhouse, E. M. Sloss, and J. Wasserman. 1991. *The Costs of Poor Health Habits,* Cambridge: Harvard University Press.

Marks, J. S., J. W. Buehler, L. T. Strauss, C. J. R. Hogue, and J. C. Smith. 1987. Variations in State-Specific Infant Mortality Risks. *Public Health Reports* 102:146–50.

Maynard, R. 1995. Social Benefits of Education: Family Formation, Parenting, and Child Welfare. Paper presented at a conference entitled "Social Benefits of Education: Can They be Measured?" sponsored by the Office of Research of the U.S. Department of Education at the Meridian International Center, Washington, DC, January. Mimeo.

Menchik, P. L. 1993. Economic Status as a Determinant of Mortality among Black and White Older Men: Does Poverty Kill? *Population Studies* 47:427–36.

Michael, R. T. 1967. The Effect of Education on Efficiency in Nutrition Consumption. Working Paper, Department of Economics, Columbia University (February). Mimeo.

Michael, R. T. 1972. *The Effect of Education on Efficiency in Consumption.* New York: Columbia University Press for the National Bureau of Economic Research.

Michael, R. T. 1973. Education in Nonmarket Production. *Journal of Political Economy* 81:306–27.

Mincer, J. 1974. *Schooling, Experience, and Earnings.* New York: Columbia University Press for the National Bureau of Economic Research.

National Center for Health Statistics, U.S. Department of Health and Human Services. 1993. *Health, United States, 1992,* Washington, DC: Government Printing Office.

National Center for Health Statistics, U.S. Department of Health and Human Services, 1994. *Vital Statistics of the United States, 1990,* vol. 2. Mortality, Part A. Washington, DC: Government Printing Office.

National Commission to Prevent Infant Mortality. 1992. *Troubling Trends Persist: Shortchanging America's Next Generation,* Washington, DC: National Commission to Prevent Infant Mortality.

National Highway Traffic Safety Administration, U.S. Department of Transportation. 1986. *Fatal Accident Reporting System, 1984.* DOT HS 806 919 (February). U.S. Department of Transportation, Washington, DC.

Newhouse, J. P., and L. J. Friedlander. 1980. The Relationship between Medical Resources and Measures of Health: Some Additional Evidence. *Journal of Human Resources* 15:200–218.

Panis, C. W. A., and L. A. Lillard. 1994. Health Inputs and Child Mortality: Malaysia. *Journal of Health Economics* 13:455–89.

Pappas, G., S. Queen, W. Hadden, and G. Fisher. 1993. The Increasing Disparity in Mortality between Socioeconomic Groups in the United States, 1960 and 1986. *New England Journal of Medicine* 329:103–8.

Pauly, M. V. 1971. *Medical Care at Public Expense.* New York: Praeger.

Pauly, M. V. 1980. *Doctors and Their Workshops: Economic Models of Physician Behavior.* Chicago: University of Chicago Press for National Bureau of Economic Research.

Perri, T. J. 1984. Health Status and Schooling Decisions of Young Men. *Economics of Education Review* 3:207–13.

Pogue, T. F., and L. G. Sgontz. 1989. Taxing to Control Social Costs: The Case of Alcohol. *American Economic Review* 79:235–43.

Public Health Service, U.S. Department of Health and Human Services. 1991. *Healthy People 2000: National Health Promotion and Disease Prevention Objectives.* DHHS Publication no. (PHS) 91–50212, Washington, DC: Government Printing Office.

Rosen, S., and P. Taubman. 1982. Some Socioeconomic Determinants of Mortality. In *Economics of Health Care,* ed. J. van der Gaag, W. B. Neenan, and T. Tsukahara Jr. New York: Praeger. Pp. 255–71.

Rosenzweig, M. R., and T. P. Schultz. 1981. Education and Household Production of Child Health. In *Proceedings of the American Statistical Association* (Social Statistics Section) Washington, DC: American Statistical Association. Pp. 382–87.

Rosenzweig, M. R., and T. P. Schultz. 1982. The Behavior of Mothers as Inputs to Child Health: The Determinants of Birth Weight, Gestation, and Rate of Fetal Growth. In *Economic Aspects of Health,* ed. V. R. Fuchs. Chicago: University of Chicago Press for the National Bureau of Economic Research. Pp. 53–92.

Rosenzweig, M. R., and T. P. Schultz. 1983a. Consumer Demand and Household

Production: The Relationship between Fertility and Child Mortality. *American Economic Review* 73:38–42.

Rosenzweig, M. R., and T. P. Schultz. 1983b. Estimating a Household Production Function: Heterogeneity, the Demand for Health Inputs, and Their Effects on Birth Weight. *Journal of Political Economy* 91:723–46.

Rosenzweig, M. R., and T. P. Schultz. 1988. The Stability of Household Production Technology: A Replication. *Journal of Human Resources* 23:535–49.

Rosenzweig, M. R., and T. P. Schultz. 1991. Who Receives Medical Care? Income, Implicit Prices, and the Distribution of Medical Services among Pregnant Women in the United States. *Journal of Human Resources* 26:473–508.

Saffer, H., and F. J. Chaloupka. 1994. Alcohol Tax Equalization and Social Costs. *Eastern Economic Journal* 20:33–43.

Sander, W. 1995a. Schooling and Quitting Smoking. *Review of Economics and Statistics* 77:191–99.

Sander, W. 1995b. Schooling and Smoking. *Economics of Education Review* 14:23–33.

Shakotko, R. A., L. N. Edwards, and M. Grossman. 1981. An Exploration of the Dynamic Relationship between Health and Cognitive Development in Adolescence. In *Contributions to Economic Analysis: Health, Economics, and Health Economics*, ed. J. van der Gaag and M. Perlman. Amsterdam: North-Holland Publishing Company. Pp. 305–25.

Sickles, R. C., and P. Taubman. 1986. An Analysis of the Health and Retirement Status of the Elderly. *Econometrica* 54:1339–56.

Silberberg, E. 1985. Nutrition and the Demand for Tastes. *Journal of Political Economy* 93:881–900.

Silver, M. 1972. An Econometric Analysis of Spatial Variations in Mortality Rates by Race and Sex. In *Essays in the Economics of Health and Medical Care*, ed. V. R. Fuchs. New York: Columbia University Press for the National Bureau of Economic Research. Pp. 161–227.

Strauss, J. 1990. Households, Communities, and Preschool Children's Nutrition Outcomes: Evidence from Rural Côte d'Ivoire. *Economic Development and Cultural Change* 38:231–62.

Sullum, J. 1994. Smoke and Mirrors: EPA Wages War on Cigarettes. *Wall Street Journal*, 24 March, A12.

Sweet, J. A., and L. L. Bumpass. 1987. *American Families and Households*. New York: Russell Sage Foundation.

Taubman, P., and S. Rosen. 1982. Healthiness, Education, and Marital Status. In *Economic Aspects of Health*, ed. V. R. Fuchs. Chicago: University of Chicago Press for the National Bureau of Economic Research. Pp. 121–40.

Thomas, D., J. Strauss, and M.-H. Henriques. 1990. Child Survival, Height for Age and Household Characteristics in Brazil. *Journal of Developmental Economics* 33:197–234.

Thomas, D., J. Strauss, and M.-H. Henriques. 1991. How Does Mother's Education Affect Child Height? *Journal of Human Resources* 26:183–211.

Tolley, G., D. S. Kenkel, and R. Fabian, eds. 1994. *Valuing Health for Policy: An Economic Approach*. Chicago: University of Chicago Press.

Townsend, J. L. 1987. Cigarette Tax, Economic Welfare and Social Class Patterns of Smoking. *Applied Economics* 19:355–65.

U.S. Bureau of the Census, U.S. Department of Commerce. 1993. *Statistical Abstract of the United States: 1993*, 113th edition, Washington, DC: Government Printing Office.

U.S. Environmental Protection Agency. 1992. *Respiratory Health Effects of Passive Smoking: Lung Cancers and Other Disorders*. Publication EPA/600/6–90/006F (December). U.S. Environmental Protection Agency, Washington, DC.

Viscusi, W. K. 1992. *Smoking: Making the Risky Decision*. New York: Oxford University Press.

Wagstaff, A. 1986. The Demand for Health: Some New Empirical Evidence. *Journal of Health Economics* 5:195–233.

Wilcox-Gök, V. L. 1983. The Determination of Child Health: An Application of Sibling and Adoption Data. *Review of Economics and Statistics* 65:266–73.

Winkelby, M. A., D. E. Jatulis, E. Frank, and S. P. Fortmann. 1992. Socioeconomic Status and Health: How Education, Income, and Occupation Contribute to Risk Factors for Cardiovascular Disease. *American Journal of Public Health* 82:816–20.

Wolfe, B. L. 1985. The Influence of Health on School Outcomes: A Multivariate Approach. *Medical Care* 23:1127–38.

Wolfe, B. L., and J. R. Behrman. 1983. Is Income Overrated in Determining Adequate Nutrition? *Economic Development and Cultural Change* 31:525–49.

Wolfe, B. L., and J. R. Behrman. 1987. Women's Schooling and Children's Health. *Journal of Health Economics* 6:239–54.

Wu, D.-M. 1973. Alternative Tests of Independence between Stochastic Regressors and Disturbances. *Econometrica* 41:733–50.

CHAPTER 5

Family Structure, Fertility, and Child Welfare

Rebecca A. Maynard and Daniel J. McGrath

Much of the argument for *public* education derives from recognition that education provides not only economic rewards to individual students but also a variety of benefits that are shared by society at large. These social benefits include a more-educated and better-informed electorate, lower rates of crime and violence, lower rates of poverty, better health and nutrition, and, generally, a more smoothly functioning society. Some of these benefits, such as higher personal incomes and improved health status, accrue to individuals. Others, such as the benefits of a more efficient and productive economy and lower crime rates, are shared by society at large. In recent years, public concern with our schools has heightened as the overall performance of schools in their central mission of preparing youths for higher education and the labor market has leveled off or, in central cities, declined quite dramatically. This concern has been fueled as much by our schools' failure to preserve the social fabric of the nation as by their failure to promote strong educational outcomes for all children.

The public school system, together with the family, is the main institution for socializing American children. Moreover, for a variety of reasons, in recent years, schools have shouldered an increasing share of responsibility for children's social development and welfare *in addition* to their educational achievement. On average, children begin school at earlier ages than they did 20 years ago—with many children in poverty stricken urban areas beginning school as young as age three. With the rising labor-force participation of women, including mothers of preschool and school-age children, and the growing incidence of families headed by a single parent, more children are spending significant amounts of time in out-of-home care. Relatedly, increasing numbers

This chapter was presented at a conference sponsored by the U.S. Department of Education entitled "The Social Benefits of Education" held in Washington, D.C., 3–5 January 1995. Research assistance was provided by Meredith Kelsey. The authors are grateful to Jere Behrman, David Crawford, Anita Summers, Paul Glewwe, Nevzer Stacey, and conference participants for helpful comments on a draft of this essay.

of children now begin their school day before breakfast and remain in after-school programs or activities into the early evening hours.

One consequence of these socioeconomic trends is that schools are spending more per pupil and yet marching in place or losing ground in terms of their efficacy in promoting their intended social outcomes (Hanushek 1994). The reasons for this are complex and not well understood by social scientists. What we do know is that there is an important interplay between education and national trends in family formation patterns, fertility patterns and parenting, and child welfare.

> *Education* per se *has not* caused *the weakening of the American family structure, the rise in teenage and single parenthood, or the rise in child abuse and neglect.* These adverse social trends have occurred in the face of an educational system that, by aggregate measures of achievement and attainment, has been holding its own or improving.

> *Failings of the American education system do, nonetheless, contribute in a major way to the adverse consequences of these other social trends.* The consequences of single parenthood and teenage childbearing are indeed significantly heightened by the social and economic consequences of poor school performance and limited educational attainment. Furthermore, child abuse and neglect are much more prevalent among those whose social and economic prospects have been limited by low educational attainment and performance.

> *There are social benefits and costs associated with the interplay of education with family formation, parenting, and child welfare.* An important social benefit of education is the resilience it imparts to youths and adults who encounter divorce or single parenthood or who are victims of child or sexual abuse. A hidden cost of the current educational system's failures is the foregone opportunity of *not* preparing youths to address, if not avoid, these challenging social consequences.

> *We have limited evidence as to effective policies or programs for preventing the occurrence of educational failure among youths or for mitigating the social consequences of failures where they do occur.* Neither the school reform and enrichment efforts that have proliferated in the past decade nor a wide array of social policies and programs to improve the economic and social welfare of disadvantaged youths and young adults have had substantial impact on the problems. At best, we are amassing a body of evidence regarding strategies that are effective in addressing only specific aspects of these problems.

Below, we first outline a behavioral model that highlights education's role in various aspects of social welfare and vice versa. We then discuss trends in education and these key social outcomes in the context of this model. The third section summarizes the state of knowledge regarding the effectiveness of various social policy interventions designed to prevent or mitigate the consequences of these social outcomes. Finally, we reflect on promising future demonstrations, evaluations, and policy initiatives.

5.1. The Links between Education and Trends in Social Outcomes

Concern over the social benefits of education is prompted in large part by the strong observed relationships between school performance and educational outcomes and the socioeconomic well-being of families. However, concern also arises from strong correlations between the social well-being of families and the educational success of their children. Thus, there are intergenerational consequences of negative educational outcomes for youth, regardless of whether poor educational outcomes are attributable to the school, family, or community.

It is increasingly clear that numerous factors contribute to the disappointing life prospects for many of today's youth and that these factors interact in complex ways. Figure 5.1 illustrates the linkages as they have been identified through measuring the various policy-relevant influences on and consequences of educational outcomes.[1] We will first consider the literature dealing with the direct social costs of poor school outcomes for the most disadvantaged youths (fig. 5.1, panel A). This literature suggests that students' educational outcomes have strong direct impacts on their later socioeconomic outcomes. That is, the educational investments of youths, their school performance, their educational attainment, and their social behaviors (including involvement in crime and teenage childbearing) directly affect their future earnings prospects and family formation patterns.

We then look at the implications of these direct benefits on outcomes for the next generation (fig. 5.1, panel B). The socioeconomic status and family formation patterns resulting from educational outcomes of youths impact on the educational outcomes of their children through an array of influences: quality of the home environment, residential location and school choices, and resources families can bring to school. These, in turn, affect the quality of education offered to students and the nature of the community forces influencing student decisions about academic, economic, and other time uses. The net results of these school, community, and family formation patterns condition the educational outcomes of subsequent generations.

---

1. Haveman and Wolfe (1994) present an excellent review of this literature.

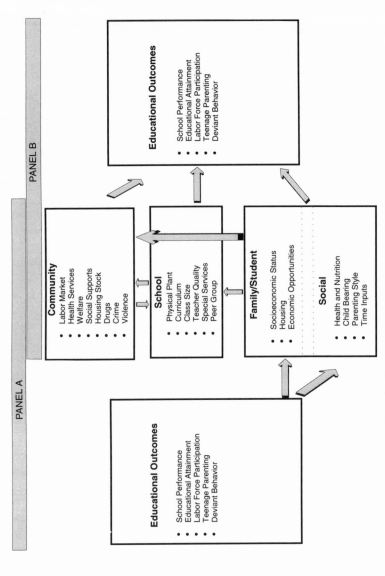

Fig. 5.1. An illustrative model of the social benefits of education

5.1.1.   The Research Data Base for Understanding Causal
Relationships and Assessing Interventions

Throughout this discussion and the interpretive discussions that follow, we rely on a variety of types of evidence, each with its own strengths and limitations. At the most basic level, we rely on aggregate descriptive statistics to paint the overall picture of relationships between educational inputs, outcomes, and social benefits. However, as noted by Behrman (1996), these measures cannot be interpreted as indications of causality or opportunities for effective policy intervention. Therefore, to glean insights into underlying behavioral (causal) models and, more important, into the likely effectiveness of various types of policy options, we resort to the large body of analytic work by economists, sociologists, and demographers. Moreover, we have selected our "causal" evidence from among those studies that use the strongest data sets and methodologies available on a particular issue. In general, this means that the studies are based on relatively large samples, rich (usually longitudinal) data sets, and carefully specified analytic models. Where possible, we focus on experimental evaluations, since they provide the clearest evidence of causal relationships. However, in most areas of inquiry relevant to this chapter, experimental evaluations either have not been conducted or address only a narrow set of the issues of interest. In essence, the conclusions of the chapter should be viewed as a synthesis of the "best available evidence" to guide future policy initiatives and research agendas aimed at improving the social benefits of education in terms of family structure, fertility, and child outcomes.

5.1.2.   The Effects of Education on Adult Opportunities
and Behaviors

The most obvious link between educational outcomes and adult opportunities and behaviors (fig. 5.1, panel A) is through employment opportunities and earnings potential. Increased levels of education are associated with higher employment rates, higher wage rates among those who are employed, and significantly higher family incomes (table 5.1). Median earnings of high school graduates are more than 25 percent higher than earnings of dropouts, while college graduates earn nearly 50 percent more than high school graduates do. Over the past 20 years, the "payoff" to both high school and college educations also has increased. Moreover, marriage patterns result in even greater disparities in family incomes by education levels.

In part, as a result of the economic consequences of higher education levels and in part because of the educational impacts themselves, there are many positive social outcomes associated with higher levels of school completion and related higher earnings. For example, the rates of poverty, out-of-wedlock

TABLE 5.1. Median Earnings by Educational Level (full-time, year-round workers 25 years or older)

| | Earnings (1990 dollars) | | | % Increase |
	1970	1980	1990	1970–90
Men				
Less than high school	$28,680	$25,539	$20,902	−27
High school	$32,227	$30,881	$26,653	−17
College	$44,681	$38,561	$39,238	−12
High school premium	12%	21%	28%	122
College premium	39%	25%	47%	22
Women				
Less than high school	$15,681	$15,348	$14,429	−8
High school	$18,797	$18,300	$18,319	−3
College	$27,474	$24,019	$28,017	2
High school premium	19.9%	19.2%	27.0%	35.7
College premium	46.2%	31.3%	52.9%	14.7

Sources: All data are from *Digest of Educational Statistics, 1993*, 93–292, table 369.
Note: Earnings were adjusted using the Historical Consumer Price Index for All Urban Consumers (CPI—U), annual average.

childbearing, early family formation, and child abuse and neglect are all substantially lower among high school graduates than among school dropouts (Moore 1994; Zill 1994; Wolfner and Gelles 1993).

The incidence of teenage childbearing is 12 percentage points higher among teenage girls whose parents have less than a high school diploma than among those who have completed high school but no college (30 versus 18 percent); the difference among blacks is only five percentage points but on a much larger base (40 versus 45 percent [Zill 1994]). Among young girls whose parents have completed college, the teenage pregnancy rate is only 10 percent among blacks and 5 percent among whites. Similarly large differences are observed between those living with only their mother and those living with both parents.

Teenage parents have elevated probabilities of dropping out of school, demonstrate lower parenting skills, and experience higher rates of poverty, especially if they have given birth out of wedlock (Hayes et al. 1990; Zill 1994; Zill and Nord 1994). Each of these adverse outcomes tends to hurt the life chances of children born to teenagers (Krein and Beller 1988; Mott and Marsiglio 1985; Zill and Nord 1994).

Child abuse and neglect are also associated with parental education levels and, relatedly, economic status (Finkelhor 1994; Roper and Weeks 1993; Boyer and Fine 1992; Lewitt 1994; Wolfner and Gelles 1993). While the rates of reported minor violence against children vary little by parental income or education, the incidence of reported severe abuse is 1.5 times higher among children from poor families as compared with their more affluent counterparts—a difference replicated between children whose fathers have less than a high school education and those whose fathers have more education (Wolfner and Gelles 1993).[2]

Dual-earner families with higher levels of education are more likely than others to provide high-quality child care for their children, in large part because of their greater ability to pay (Kisker et al. 1989; Willer et al. 1991). Additionally, increased levels of parental education are associated with markers of good parenting, including greater school involvement (Zill and Nord 1994). Finally, the higher earnings capacity of individuals with more education enables them to live in communities that offer a wider array of social services and can devote more resources to education in relation to local need (Kantor and Brenzel 1993). Such communities also tend to offer more positive peer influences and lower crime rates, including less crime against persons (Crane 1991).

5.1.3.   Intergenerational Effects of Education

These direct effects of education have fairly significant implications for the educational prospects of the next generation (fig. 5.1, panel B) that should be factored into any inventory of the social benefits of education. Not only does the socioeconomic status of the family have a significant influence on the educational success of children, but so does the family's choice of school and community. In reviewing these influences on children's outcomes, we should note that the literature clearly demonstrates that most of the variation in child outcomes is *unexplained* by specific, measurable attributes of families, schools, or communities (McLanahan and Sandefur 1994; Swanson and Spencer 1991). Most of the variation in child outcomes seem to be due to behavioral patterns of the children and their individual endowments or predispositions independent of measurable community and family factors (Behrman, Rosenzweig, and Taubman 1994, 1996; Haveman and Wolfe 1984, 1994; Werner and Smith 1992; Haveman, Wolfe, and Spaulding 1991).[3] However, a large body of research points to strong family influences on student outcomes and opens possible avenues for program and policy initiatives that could improve outcomes for future generations of youth.

Some intergenerational influences are direct and enduring—for example, those resulting directly from the socioeconomic status of the family and the

---

2. Although the rate of reported incidents has increased substantially over time, there is some evidence that much of the increase is attributable to higher rates of reporting (Lewitt 1994).

3. Recent findings indicate a tendency among families to actually reinforce differences in siblings through schooling allocations (Behrman, Rosenzweig, and Taubman 1994, 1996).

physical environment of the home (Maynard 1977; Murnane et al. 1981; Ramey and Ramey 1992; Currie 1994). Others are more episodic—factors such as the amount and quality of time parents spend with their children, the number and spacing of children, changes in family status, and residential mobility (Leibowitz 1974; Wolfe 1994; Haveman and Wolfe 1994; McLanahan and Sandefur 1994).

5.1.4. The Mediating Role of Education and Earnings for Social Outcomes

Especially noteworthy in these relationships are the strong mediating roles of education and income vis à vis many of the commonly cited negative consequences of school failure. For example, the adverse impacts of single parenthood are significantly greater for those who do not complete their high school education compared with those who do. In large part, this is because of the income effect of higher levels of education (McLanahan and Sandefur 1994; Krein and Beller 1988; Mulkey et al. 1992; Haveman and Wolfe 1994).

Similarly, the consequences of single parenthood are largely concentrated among those with low levels of education and, thus, low earning power. In the case of divorce, youths raised in families that experience divorce, as compared with those reared in intact families, have 9 percent higher probabilities of dropping out of school, 7 percent higher probabilities of teenage childbirth, and 7 percent higher probabilities of "idleness" (neither working nor going to school). Yet, more than half of these observed differences in outcomes are attributable to the drop in family income that often results from divorce (McLanahan and Sandefur 1994).

In essence, the loss of economic resources as a result of divorce substantially lowers children's resilience, regardless of their parents' education levels. Although children of divorced parents are less likely to complete high school or attend college and more likely to be idle (neither working nor in school) as young adults, initiate sex earlier, and express discontent with their lives, it is the income loss associated with divorce that explains much of these differences (Furstenberg and Teitler 1994; McLanahan and Sandefur 1994). Moreover, divorced parents with low levels of education are at a severe disadvantage when they attempt to earn back some of the lost resources. It is for this reason that education and earnings serve as important mediators, helping to provide resilience for children in the face of trying circumstances.

5.2. National Trends: Causal and Mediating Forces

Contrasts of national trends in educational, family, and student inputs to education with student outcomes highlight the enormous challenge in devising effective policies to improve educational and social outcomes. Indeed, as noted previously, while we have witnessed a number of alarming trends indicating a significant deterioration of the social fabric of the nation, our investments in education have been increasing and aggregate student outcomes are holding constant or improving slightly.

5.2.1. Trends in Educational Inputs

By many standards, schools have improved over the past 20 years while family and community resources have deteriorated, especially among some population subgroups. On average, schools have much higher levels of resources per pupil today than they did 20 years ago (table 5.2; NCES 1994). Indeed, average per pupil expenditures on elementary and secondary education have increased 80 percent in real terms between 1970 and 1990 (from $3,079 to $5,570 per pupil). A part of this increase has been devoted to increasing the salaries of teachers, both to attract more highly qualified teachers and encourage longer tenure in education. However, major portions of the increased expenditures

TABLE 5.2.   Trends in Educational Inputs and Student Outcomes

	1970	1980	1990	% Change 1970–90
Educational Inputs				
Expenditure per pupil (1992–93 dollars) (165)	$3,079	$4,171	$5,570	80.9
Average pupil-teacher ratio in public elementary and secondary schools (63)	22	19	17	−22.7
Average teacher salary ($1,000 1992–93 dollars) (76)	$33	$29	$35	6.1
Ratio of students to one special education teacher	n.a.	18	15	−16.7[a]
Student Inputs				
Racial/ethnic composition of schools				
All schools				
Percent black	15	16	18	20.0
Percent Hispanic	6	9	12	100.0
Urban schools				
Percent black	33	35	33	0.0
Percent Hispanic	11	17	20	81.8
Percentage of children in programs for students with disabilities	n.a.	9.8	11.3	15.3[a]
Percentage of children from low-income families				
Elementary school	n.a.	13.1	18.4	40.5[a]
High school	n.a.	10.5	14.7	40.0[a]
Percent of students speaking English with difficulty	n.a.	4.2	5.3	26.2[a]

Source: All data are from *Digest of Educational Statistics, 1993,* 93–292, table 369.

Note: n.a. = Figures not available.

[a] These figures are the percentage changes from 1980 to 1990.

Numbers in parentheses indicate the table number from which the data were obtained that come from other tables.

have been devoted to reducing class size, from 22 to 17 pupils per teacher, and increasing the number of special education teachers per pupil. The research is not clear, however, about whether increased funding for education alone will improve student outcomes. On the one hand, there is evidence that class size and teacher salary are related to student outcomes (Hedges et al. 1994; Ferguson 1991). On the other hand, school production functions explain relatively little of the variance in student outcomes and certainly do not provide convincing evidence that marginal changes in spending will significantly affect outcomes (Hanushek 1994).

5.2.2. Trends in Family and Student Inputs

In contrast to positive trends in school inputs over the past 20 years, the characteristics of students and their family support capacity have changed significantly in ways that pose greater challenges for schools. For example, the proportion of minority students has increased substantially over the past 10 years, particularly the representation of Hispanics, which increased from 9 to 12 percent of all school-age children (table 5.2). Together, African Americans and Hispanics now constitute the student majority in center city schools. By most measures of educational and life outcomes, inner city minority youth fare poorly due to their low socioeconomic status and less supportive family and neighborhood circumstances. However, a substantial portion of their lower performance is attributable to other factors that are *correlated* with race/ethnicity (Haveman and Wolfe 1994).

As a result of cultural differences between minority groups, especially language-minority groups, and the dominant culture as represented in most schools, parenting styles of many minorities are sometimes at odds with the cultural norms in schools. In addition, many minority children, especially those in minority groups with long histories of economic and social hardship in the United States, are likely to see few economic prospects in their future and so little reason to strive for academic success. Ethnographers suggest that cultural differences and perceptions of poor economic prospects account for some of the residual performance differences between some minority groups and white youth after controlling for easily measurable socioeconomic factors (Erickson 1987; Ogbu 1987).

Shifts in immigration patterns have led to a rising proportion of youth speaking a language other than English at home. In 1990, nearly one in seven school-age children spoke another language in the home. Half of these children (5 percent) have difficulty speaking English—an increase of 27 percent from a decade earlier (table 5.2). In addition to difficulty learning the language, differences in parenting and educational values among various racial/ethnic groups work to the disadvantage of children from minority racial/ethnic groups (Ogbu 1987; Anderson 1994; Natriello 1987).

Following national poverty trends, schools are serving increasing numbers of poor children. In the last 10 years alone the percentage of public school children from low-income families increased by 40 percent (table 5.2). Accompanying the rising poverty rates are modest (15 percent) increases in the incidence of children who have diagnosed learning disabilities warranting special services.

Missing from this aggregate picture of improvements and declines in school climate and resources are the widening disparities in resources and problems faced by schools in this country. Over the past 20 years, there has been an increasing concentration of minority children and poor children in center city schools. In five of the top 20 cities in this country in terms of concentration of poverty, more than 90 percent of the student population is minority (table 5.3). In all of the largest cities, the minority student population is more than 30 percent above the national average of 33 percent minority students. Relative to their suburban school counterparts, these schools have higher rates of reported school violence, increasing rates of children with diagnosed learning disabilities, average or below-average levels of resources per pupil, and, not

TABLE 5.3. Selected Characteristics of the 20 Top Cities in Terms of Concentrations of Persons Living in Distressed Neighborhoods

City	Population (1,000s)	% in Distressed Neighborhoods	% Minority Students	Per Pupil Expenditures ($1,000)	Pupil-Teacher Ratio
Detroit	486	47	92	4.7	n.a.
Flint	53	39	70	5.1	n.a.
Buffalo	107	33	60	n.a.	16
Cleveland	157	31	77	6.6	20
New Orleans	142	29	93	3.8	18
Newark	78	28	90	8.4	14
Shreveport	53	27	n.a.	n.a.	n.a.
St. Louis	101	25	80	5.0	13
Dayton	45	25	64	6.5	16
Baton Rouge	53	24	56	3.7	16
Atlanta	92	23	n.a.	6.0	15
Jacksonville	45	23	n.a.	n.a.	n.a.
Syracuse	37	22	44	7.3	12
Gary	26	22	99	4.7	20
Memphis	133	22	80	3.4	20
Milwaukee	136	22	70	6.6	17
Birmingham	52	19	90	3.6	17
Baltimore	138	19	83	4.7	19
Cincinnati	65	18	65	6.0	17
Chicago	472	17	88	4.9	18
U.S. average	n.a.	n.a.	33	4.5	17

Sources: *Statistical Abstract of the United States* 1992, table 38; Kasarda, 1993, 253–302; *Digest of Educational Statistics, 1993*, tables 47, 63, 91.
Note: n.a. = Figures not available.

surprisingly, much worse student outcomes. Dropout rates often exceed 50 percent, absenteeism is high, and test scores are low relative to those in schools serving more affluent families.

There are some trends in family inputs that work to the advantage of children and many that work against them. On the positive side, parents today have higher levels of education than was the case 20 years ago. Moreover, blacks have gained relative to whites in this dimension. The size of the American family also has decreased from an average of just over three children to just under two—a change that has been most pronounced among low-income families. And families have been increasing the average spacing between children. Each of these factors has shown evidence of impacting positively on child outcomes even after controlling for a wide range of family, school, and community characteristics (Haveman and Wolfe 1994).

Other trends have more ambiguous impacts for children. One is the rapid increase in the labor force participation of mothers (Zill and Nord 1994; Hayes et al. 1990; Blau 1991). Currently, a majority of children have mothers in the labor force, including more than half of all preschool-age children. As a result, many families—notably two-parent families—enjoy higher standards of living. However, these trends in labor force participation of women also mean that children must spend substantial amounts of time in child care.[4] The best available evidence suggests that, on balance, child outcomes either are not affected or are improved slightly by this trend (Stafford 1986; Haveman and Wolfe 1994; Murnane, Maynard, and Ohls 1981).

Several trends in the conditions of American families are clearly associated with negative outcomes for children—for example, rising divorce rates, an increasing proportion of out-of-wedlock births, rising teenage birth rates, higher child poverty rates, and higher rates of domestic violence. Whereas in 1970, only 1.2 percent of children experienced a divorce by their parents each year (double the rate in 1950), by 1988, this rate had increased by 50 percent to 1.8 percent (NCES 1993b). Indeed, half of all children today can expect to live part of their childhood in a single-parent household (Zill and Nord 1994; Haveman and Wolfe 1994).

Longitudinal studies have demonstrated some adverse consequences for children of growing up with a single parent. However, as noted previously, even more significant than the loss of a parent from the household is the lower income that generally accompanies single parenthood. Indeed, the drop in income that frequently accompanies divorce has been found to account for the majority of

---

4. Less than one-fourth of children whose mothers are in the labor force are cared for by a parent during the time the mother works. A small fraction accompany their mothers to work or have mothers who work at home. The larger portion have two parents who work different shifts (U.S. Department of Commerce 1987; Hayes et al. 1990). Among poor and single-parent families, the proportion of children of working mothers cared for by a parent is very small (Kisker et al. 1989).

the difference in educational and social outcomes between children in divorced and intact families (Haveman and Wolfe 1994; McLanahan and Sandefur 1994).

Compounding the adverse consequences for children of divorce is the fact that the number of children being born to single parents is increasing rapidly. Currently, 30 percent of all children in this country are born out of wedlock, more than triple the rate in 1970. Indeed, more than two out of three minority women and teenagers giving birth are unmarried. Similarly, more than half of all births in 11 of our largest cities were to unmarried women.[5] If current trends persist, more than half of the children born out of wedlock to teens will grow up in poverty and have high probabilities of experiencing these adverse educational and social outcomes.

Although average family income has increased by about 6 percent (in real terms) over the past 20 years, these gains have been disproportionately enjoyed by two-parent families in which both parents are employed. The combined effect of the rising out-of-wedlock birthrate and the rising divorce rate is that more than one-fourth of all children and more than half of black children today live in single-parent households. These households are at high risk of poverty. More than half of all children in single-parent families (and more than two-thirds of African American and Hispanic children in single-parent families) live in poverty, compared with only about 20 percent of those in two-parent families.[6]

One factor contributing to the high poverty rate is a lack of support from absent parents. Over half of single mothers receive no financial support from absent fathers, and most who receive payments receive relatively small amounts (NCES 1993b).

Another factor is the decline in real wages, especially among low-skilled workers (Murnane 1993). For example, between 1979 and 1991, real wages of men declined by 36 percent for high school dropouts, 24 percent for high school graduates, and 18 percent for those with some college. Only college graduate men held their own. Young women with low levels of education suffered small real wage losses, while those with some college or a college degree enjoyed real wage gains (7 and 18 percent, respectively). Under the resulting current wage structure, a sizable proportion of single parents (who are disproportionately low skilled) cannot escape poverty even through full-time work (Ellwood 1988; U.S. House of Representatives 1993).[7]

---

5. These cities are Atlanta (64 percent), Baltimore (62 percent), Chicago (54 percent), Cleveland (64 percent), Detroit (71 percent), Miami (51 percent), Newark (65 percent), Philadelphia (59 percent), Pittsburgh (52 percent), St. Louis (66 percent), and Washington, D.C. (66 percent).

6. The poverty rate among single-parent families has remained fairly stable since 1970 (NCES 1993b, 48).

7. Labor force participation rates are higher among single parents than among women in two-parent-families (Hayes et al. 1990). Moreover, rates among minority women have consistently been substantially higher than among white women.

A third factor contributing to the high child poverty rate is the decline of the youth job market after 1959, which has weakened the ability of teenagers to contribute to family income (Wilson 1987; Stern 1993). And a fourth factor that is particular to single-parent families is the 23 percent decline in real welfare benefits per recipient since 1970 (NCES 1993b). Single-parent families not only have significantly higher probabilities of being poor than do other families, but they have only about half the amount of parental time to devote to child rearing. They also have less choice about whether or not to use child care than do parents living together. For the vast majority of single parents, their only hope of escaping poverty is through employment.[8] This requires them to rely on nonparental (and indeed generally nonrelative) child care for significant amounts of time.[9]

5.2.3. Community Trends

In many respects trends in communities mirror those in families. What is striking about community trends is how much more homogeneous communities have become in terms of both their strengths and their problems. For example, poverty rates outside of central cities have been falling, while those inside have been rising. As a result, the proportion of the poor population residing in central cities has nearly doubled (Kantor and Brenzel 1993). Within cities, the population is further segregated by neighborhood (Wilson 1987; Kasarda 1993; Lynn and McGeary 1990). There also has been a trend toward higher rates of private school attendance by children from higher-income families relative to low-income families (NCES 1993b).

Together these trends have led to a situation in which, in close to half of inner city schools, the majority of students come from low-income families (Kantor and Brenzel 1993), a factor that has strong negative association with educational outcomes even after controlling for other factors (Chubb and Moe 1990; Coleman and Hoffer 1987). While the student population has become increasingly needy, the fiscal capacity of inner city schools to raise funds for education has declined (Kantor and Brenzel 1993).

These trends are compounded by other communitywide trends—increases in crime rates, particularly in inner city areas; high rates of drug use and, in some communities, employment opportunities in the drug industry; and decreasing job opportunities for those without postsecondary educations, again particularly in the inner city. These trends go hand in hand with high rates of

---

8. As previously mentioned, the current wage structure makes escaping poverty difficult for many low-skilled single mothers and their children, even through the mother's full-time work (Ellwood 1988; U.S. House of Representatives 1993).

9. With the rise in labor force participation rates among women, relative care is generally (and increasingly less often) a realistic option (Hayes et al. 1990; Willer et al. 1991).

teenage parenting, single-parent households, and school failure (Wilson 1987; Haveman and Wolfe 1994; Walker and Sutherland 1993; Datcher 1982; Crane 1991; Corcoran and Datcher 1981).

Even at the state level, children are raised in substantially different community contexts. Personal income per capita ranges from $11,000 in the poorest state, Mississippi, to more than $23,000 in Connecticut. State child poverty rates range from 33 percent in Mississippi to 7 percent in New Hampshire, and the percentage of all adults who have completed high school ranges from 64 percent in Mississippi to 86 percent in Alaska. These characteristics tend to move together and follow per pupil expenditures and local tax efforts. For example, per pupil expenditures range from a low of $3,187 in Mississippi to a high of $8,645 in New Jersey. Moreover, the gap in per pupil expenditures has widened dramatically over the past 20 years, as is illustrated by the fact that expenditures in the lowest-spending state (Mississippi) only doubled in nominal terms since 1970, while those in the highest-spending state (New Jersey) increased more than eightfold (NCES 1993a).

5.2.4. Student Outcomes

In the aggregate, schools have continued to improve over the past 20 years on some key performance objectives—enrolling more children in school, keeping youths in school through the full 12 years of program study, and preparing them for post-secondary education and training options (table 5.4).

The school system has succeeded in beginning the formal education process at younger ages for increasing numbers of children. Whereas in 1970 only 38 percent of three to five year olds were enrolled in preschool programs, by 1990 this figure had increased to nearly 60 percent (table 5.4). In part, this trend is accounted for by the rapid rise in labor force participation of women with young children (Hayes et al. 1990; Zill and Nord 1994). However, it also reflects expansions in Head Start and pre-K programs intended as "jump-start" initiatives for children from disadvantaged backgrounds.

Over this same period, the proportion of 14 to 17 year olds enrolled in school has remained fairly stable (90 to 94 percent). However, increasing proportions of young people are completing high school by the time they reach young adulthood. In 1990, 12 percent of all 16 to 24 year olds had dropped out of school prior to attaining a high school degree, down from 15 percent in 1970. Notably, the large disparity in school dropout rates between white and black youth was reduced by 73 percent over this period. The proportion of black youth who failed to complete high school fell by more than 50 percent, or 15 percentage points (from 28 to 13 percent), while the proportion of white youth aged 16 to 24 who neither were attending nor had completed school declined only 30 percent or four percentage points (from 13 to 9 percent). In part, this trend toward higher high school completion rates reflects the institution of alternative educational opportunities within the regular secondary education system and through alternative credentialing options (most notably, the General Educational Development [GED] certificate).[10]

By one set of measures, the educational *achievement* of young people has been constant over the past 20 years. For example, performance on the National Assessment of Educational Progress has been fairly stable among all age groups. Moreover, there has been some improvement in the performance

TABLE 5.4.   Trends in Student Outcomes

	1970	1980	1990	% Change 1970–90
Percentage of 3 to 5 year olds in preschool (48)	38	53	59	55.2
Percentage of 14 to 17 year olds in school (55)	92	90	94	2.2
Percentage of 17 year olds graduated from high school (98)	77	71	72	−6.5
Percentage of dropouts among persons 16 to 24 years old (101)	15	14	12	−2
White, Non-Hispanics	13	11	9	−30.8
Black, Non-Hispanics	28	19	13	−53.6
Hispanics	n.a.	35	32	−8.6[a]
SAT verbal scores (125 and 126)	455	424	422	−7.3
Whites	n.a.	442	442	0[a]
Blacks	n.a.	330	353	7[a]
Mexican Americans	n.a.	372	380	2.2[a]
Percentage of high school graduates enrolled in college (178)	52	49	60	15.4
Percentage of students taking SAT	34.1	32.6	39.7	16.4
Percentage minority	n.a.	17.9	26.6	48.6[a]
Births per 1,000 school-age women	68.3	53	59.9	−12.3
Unmarried young women	22.4	27.6	42.5	89.7
Minority young women	133	94.9	96.3	−27.8
Percentage of high school students employed	31.5	35.1	32.1	1.9
Percentage of seniors using drugs	n.a.	37.2	17.1	−54[a]
Percentage using alcohol	n.a.	72.1	57.1	−20.8[a]

Source: All data are from *Digest of Educational Statistics, 1993,* 93–292, table 369.
Note: n.a. = Figures not available.
[a] These figures are the percentage changes from 1980 to 1990.
Numbers in parentheses indicate the table number from which the data that come from other tables were obtained.

10. In 1990, 287,000 youths under the age of 24 earned a GED, compared with only 182,000 youths in 1970 (NCES 1993a, table 100).

in math and science of children from lower socioeconomic groups relative to other students (NCES 1994, tables 12–18).[11]

While there has been considerable concern raised through reports of the declining *average* performance on the Scholastic Aptitude Test (SAT) scores (Haveman and Wolfe 1994), average performance has remained stable or increased slightly among all racial/ethnic groups except whites (table 5.4). What has driven the time trends in the averages is primarily a shift in the composition of the population taking the test. Over the past 20 years, increasing proportions of youth from minority racial/ethnic groups and low-income whites who have substantially lower average scores than middle- and upper-middle-class white youth have entered the pool of test takers. Indeed, the proportion of minorities taking the SAT increased by nearly 50 percent in the last decade alone (from 17 to 27 percent).

Perhaps the most encouraging trends have been the increasing rates of participation in postsecondary education, particularly in the last 10 years. Between 1970 and 1990, the percentage of high school graduates enrolling in college (including two-year colleges and vocational schools) increased by 19 percent from 52 to 60 percent (table 5.4).

Trends in other student outcomes have been less favorable. For example, after years of decline in teenage pregnancy and birthrates following the introduction of oral contraceptives, these are again on the rise (Zill and Nord 1994; Alan Guttmacher Institute 1994). In 1990, there were 60 births per 1,000 women aged 15 to 17 in this country, a 13 percent increase from the 1980 level (table 5.4). Even more problematic, the birthrate among *unmarried* young women has increased by 50 percent over that same period, a trend that parallels the dramatic rise in out-of-wedlock births among all age groups. Teenage motherhood increases drastically the likelihood that a young woman will drop out of school or exhibit poor performance if she remains in school (Congressional Budget Office 1990; Geronimus and Korenman 1993; Moore et al. 1993; Nord et al. 1992).

The recent upturn in the incidence of early family formation has been stimulated by both a rise in the incidence of single-parent households and rising child poverty rates (Nord et al. 1992; Moore et al. 1993; Zill 1994). Teenage childbearing has numerous adverse consequences for both the educational outcomes of the teenagers who are giving birth and their children. The teenagers themselves have significantly elevated probabilities of dropping out of school and entering a life of dependency, particularly if they give birth out of wedlock (Moore et al. 1993; Congressional Budget Office 1990; Ahn 1994; Geronimus and Korenman 1993; Horwitz et al. 1991; Hoffman et al. 1993). Moreover, these

---

11. Average proficiency scores of children whose parents did not complete high school lagged 10 to 15 percent below those of children whose parents completed more than high school (NCES 1994).

outcomes for the mother tend to result in less supportive home environments for their children (Haveman and Wolfe 1994; Zill and Nord 1994).

Schools are also turning out youths who have high rates of alcohol and drug use. More than half of all seniors in 1990 reported using alcohol within the past 30 days, and 17 percent had used drugs, including 9 percent who had used drugs other than marijuana (table 5.4). On the bright side, these figures represent a substantial (53 percent) decline in drug use and a 20 percent decrease in alcohol use compared with the class of 1980.

5.3. Effectiveness of Policies and Programs to Improve Outcomes

Over the past 20 years, this country has witnessed a proliferation of policies and programs aimed at improving school outcomes or mitigating the consequences of adverse socioeconomic outcomes that are often attributed to weaknesses in our educational system. The most general of these are various income support and supplementation programs. Others focus on improving the school system itself or supplementing educational services offered by the schools. These include schoolwide programs such as Chapter I and myriad school reform and improvement initiatives. They also include programs focused on the preparation of children for school—such as Head Start, Even Start, and the Comprehensive Child Development Programs—and programs intended to provide a comprehensive set of supports and opportunities throughout the high school years for at-risk youth—for example, the Quantum Opportunities Program (QOP). Another class of programs has been directed toward second-chance efforts to compensate for poor student outcomes, including adverse social outcomes such as early childbearing and single-parent family formation and poor performance in the labor market. These have included alternative schools, job training programs, and special teen parent initiatives.

The designs of these various initiatives have been based on observed strong correlations between educational outcomes and the social or economic problem being addressed. For example, as noted previously, family income is the single strongest predictor of educational outcomes for children and thus indirectly predicts their socioeconomic status in adulthood. As a result, one rationale for income support and welfare policies is that they will open doors for children from disadvantaged backgrounds, thereby preventing the intergenerational transfer of poverty.

The strong correlations between years of school completed and employment and earnings have led to the suggestion that providing youths who drop out of school with alternative certification programs (such as the GED) might compensate for their lack of a high school diploma. Similarly, the strong association with early childbearing and long-term poverty has prompted the emergence of programs to upgrade the academic and job skills of teenage mothers.

The fact that children of teenage parents are observed to experience a host of social and educational disadvantages—increased probabilities of dropping out of school, of doing poorly in school, and of becoming parents at an early age themselves—has led to the development of programs aimed at improving the parenting skills of teenage parents and enriching community and educational supports for their children. National employment and welfare policies also incorporate special initiatives to boost or compensate for the educational deficiencies of young people who enter adulthood at significant social and economic disadvantage. The most prominent examples are the national Job Training Partnership Act (JTPA) programs supported by the U.S. Department of Labor and the Job Opportunities and Basic Skills Training (JOBS) programs created as part of the federal welfare system.

The hard reality is, however, that none of these initiatives has made a real dent in the poverty and underclass problems that are so strongly associated with educational outcomes. Although there are examples in each domain of programs that have enjoyed some level of success, by and large their abilities to mitigate the consequences of either school failure or related and compounding adverse social outcomes have been extremely limited. In the following pages, we discuss briefly the range of evidence regarding the effectiveness of three types of intervention and policy strategies: (1) income support policies, (2) school improvement efforts, and (3) second-chance initiatives. Throughout this discussion, we pay particular attention to those efforts that have been evaluated through experimental evaluations. However, where the experimental evidence is lacking, we provide some discussion of the "best available" evidence.

5.3.1. Income Support Programs

Among the earliest social intervention experiments in this country were the negative income tax experiments. These experiments were intended to alter the economic welfare and employment incentives of families rather than intervening directly in educational programs. Negative income tax programs provided a minimum income guarantee regardless of earnings and imposed variable tax rates on earnings, so that total income rose with additional work effort while the income subsidy declined. The experiments were designed so that no family would be made worse off financially through their random assignment to the experimental welfare program.

The primary goal of the experiments was to test the work incentive effects of negative income tax plans as contrasted with the local welfare policy. However, the architects of the demonstrations also recognized that by changing family income levels and work incentives the negative income tax could have other socially important impacts on families, particularly impacts on incentives for family formation and dissolution, social well-being, nutrition, and school performance of children. In each case, there is well-documented evidence of strong correlations between income and outcomes.

Indeed, the research on the negative income tax experiments confirmed that income transfer programs can increase educational outcomes for children, apparently through a combination of income enhancing effects and labor force disincentive effects. For example, positive school performance impacts were estimated for students in three of the four experiments that included studies of educational outcomes (see app. A, table A.5.1). In one of the two rural negative income tax experiment sites (North Carolina) and in one of the two urban sites where school performance impacts of elementary school children were assessed (Gary, Indiana), children whose parents were in the experimental welfare programs, and so were experiencing substantial income gains, improved their performance on standardized tests by 20 to 30 percent (Maynard 1977; Maynard and Murnane 1979).

In the only site that systematically investigated school completion and college enrollment effects of older children (New Jersey), the income support programs were found to have substantial benefits even though none of the studies found notable impacts on measures of in-school performance for older youths (see table A.5.2 and Mallar and Maynard 1981). Youths whose parents were enrolled in the New Jersey Negative Income Tax Experiments were 20 to 90 percent more likely to have completed school than were their control group counterparts. Moreover, by age 19 to 20, the youths in the experimental group had completed an average of between one-third and one-half year more school.

The income transfer programs were found to have significant impacts on several other aspects of family structure and consumption patterns that have been linked to educational outcomes. For example, the experiments reduced labor force participation among men and women, thus providing more time input for children but also diminishing the income effect of the new welfare policy (Robins 1985). They also were found to improve child nutrition among families in poorer communities (O'Connor, Madden, and Pringle 1976). On the other hand, there is some controversial research suggesting that the more generous income support programs also resulted in higher rates of marital dissolution—an outcome that has been found in the nonexperimental literature to correlate strongly with poor school outcomes for children (Hannan et al. 1977; Munnell 1986; Cain and Wissoker 1990).

5.3.2. School Improvement Efforts

Nationwide, efforts to improve outcomes for at-risk youths and dropouts include hundreds of special programs, few of which have been rigorously evaluated for their effectiveness (U.S. General Accounting Office 1987). These include alternative schools, school restructuring efforts, preschool readiness programs, and integrated and school-linked services. With the exception of the preschool readiness programs, we do not yet have the benefit of the results of rigorous, large-scale evaluations. Nonetheless, evidence indicating the strengths and limitations of various types of school improvement intervention strategies is accumulating.

Preschool programs in general, and Head Start, in particular, are among the most popular interventions aimed at improving outcomes for disadvantaged children. In large part, this popularity derives from research that documents through experimental interventions the potential of early intervention programs to change developmental outcomes for seriously at-risk children. However, few of these studies provide any evidence that the short-term gains for children in preschool programs persist beyond the early elementary years.

The most widely cited of these evaluations, a study of the Perry Preschool Project, which provided a rich preschool intervention to at-risk children in Yp-silanti, Michigan, shows positive long-term benefits to children but also raises serious questions about the robustness and generalizability of the findings. The Perry Preschool Project was an intensive preschool and home visiting program for three and four year olds. Children in the program group attended preschool 2.5 hours a day, five days a week, and received weekly home visits intended to help their parents improve their parenting skills. As compared with a randomly selected control group of children, those offered the preschool intervention and home visiting services scored better on both IQ and achievement tests. They also had significantly higher rates of high school completion and higher employment rates and earnings as young adults (Barnett 1991; Berrueta-Clement et al. 1984; Barnett 1985). By age eight, however, the 12-point IQ gains from program participation had disappeared, even though measured achievement test scores continued to be higher among the program group throughout the 12-year study period.

While encouraging, these results have been criticized on three counts—the small sample size (123 children), adjustments in the experimental and control groups to accommodate working mothers who could not participate in the parenting portions of the interventions, and the inability of the researchers to link the strong longer-term results in employment and crime reduction to the modest (and more typical) short-term results on IQ and achievement measures (McGroder 1990; Gramlich 1986). Moreover, these favorable long-term results have not been replicated in any of the few other evaluations of early intervention programs, including evaluations of Head Start.

More typically, the research shows that patterns of improved developmental outcomes during the intervention period fade out over time (McKey et al. 1985; Layzer et al. 1982). Even programs specifically designed to extend the intervention into the elementary school years as a means of preventing fade-out have had disappointing results (U.S. General Accounting Office 1993; Barnett 1991).

Combining academic, community service, and developmental activities with financial incentives, the Quantum Opportunities Project Demonstration presents a promising opportunity for improving the chances of success for disadvantaged youth and increasing our knowledge base of what works. QOP was designed to use community-based organizations to help provide educational opportunities and support for at-risk youth through mentoring and financial rewards for positive behaviors. Results of pilot programs in five cities suggest that the consistent presence of a caring adult appears to contribute toward improved outcomes in school attainment and continuance with higher education (Hahn et al. 1994; U.S. Department of Labor 1995). However, implementation was inconsistent across sites, and the samples were very small. As a result, the study does not provide clear evidence of the efficacy of the program cornerstones—financial incentives for participants; programs; and staff and academic, community, and developmental activities within a supportive group atmosphere (Hahn et al. 1994).

Evidence on the effectiveness of alternative schools or classroom settings for at-risk youths is largely anecdotal and descriptive at this point, focusing on the theoretical rationale for alternative learning environments and the attitudes of those who have had the benefit of an alternative school option (Young 1990; Orr 1989). The one random assignment evaluation of an alternative school model—the Career Beginnings Demonstration—provides some evidence that alternatives to the traditional high school model may have modest impacts on school outcomes for some youths (Cave et al. 1993; Stern et al. 1992). However, there is clearly room for improvement in the intervention. Ongoing studies being supported by the U.S. Departments of Labor and Education will enrich our understanding of the role of such programs in our national and local education policies. The preliminary evidence indicates that these programs may be useful complements to our educational options but that they are unlikely to solve the majority of the problems.

A third education reform strategy entails total restructuring of elementary and secondary schools to promote school-based management, teacher profes- sionalization, and curricular reform (Raywid and Shaheen 1994). Here, not only is experimental evidence lacking but the very nature of these efforts makes it impractical to design rigorous experimental evaluations since the unit of inter- vention is the school not the individual. We do know, however, that restructuring initiatives have had limited operational success (Summers and Johnson 1994; Hershey et al., 1995). From this we can infer that they have had limited to no impact on student outcomes. Reasons for the limited implementation success range from lack of organizational commitment to physical and time constraints.

Nonetheless, there are emerging lessons from these efforts regarding alternative models of teaching and learning that are more and less effective with various groups of students and in varying educational settings.

A fourth school-oriented strategy for improving educational outcomes is the provision of integrated or school-linked social services and community schools that afford at-risk children the compensatory services they need to perform on a par with other children. These services are designed to address a variety of social and economic needs related to educational outcomes—particularly health care (physical and mental), nutrition, and family planning. As with restructuring initiatives, there are no rigorous experimental evaluations of integrated services interventions. However, there is a large body of research based on comparison group and before-and-after evaluation methods (U.S. General Accounting Office 1992; Dryfoos 1994; Kirst 1992; Swanson and Spencer 1991; Whelage et al. 1989).

On balance, the evidence suggests that these types of services do improve the immediate outcomes of interest (particularly increased use of preventive health care and use of lower-cost providers). However, these types of services have not been proven to induce reductions in teenage pregnancy or behaviors with significant health or safety risks (Kirby et al. 1994; Kisker et al. 1994). Moreover, there are hosts of challenges to effective implementation of integrated services programs (Stephens et al. 1994; University of Pennsylvania 1994).

To sum up, the research as to the *effectiveness* of these various school improvements is weak at best. Estimated benefits of Head Start have varied from study to study and even in the most favorable studies have shown only modest impacts that generally fade over time (McGroder 1990). Evidence on school reform consistently points to major implementation problems (Urbanski 1993; Summers and Johnson 1994; Fuhrman 1993; Fuhrman et al. 1993; Cohen 1991). The latest evidence on school-linked health services suggests that there are modest to no health-related gains and no substantial benefits in terms of delayed sexual activity or reduced teenage childbearing (Kirby et al. 1994). And the emerging research on the effectiveness of special demonstration initiatives designed to enrich or provide alternative educational environments within the public schools for at-risk youths is showing modest to no effects.

5.3.3. Second-Chance Programs

We have tested a wide range of second-chance programs designed to "pick up the pieces" after youths fail to successfully make the transition from the public schools to adulthood. Brief discussions of the results of several of the programs evaluated using experimental designs will illustrate the lessons from this body of research.

Supported employment programs are relatively high-cost programs designed to provide structured and heavily supportive employment experiences with gradual withdrawal of support as youths make the transition to the unsubsidized work force. The results of large-scale experiments with such programs suggest that they are moderately effective for the most severely disadvantaged (particularly those with borderline retardation) but that they make no difference in the social or economic well-being of most youths (Maynard 1980; Hollister et al. 1984; Kerachsky et al. 1985). For example, the young school dropouts in the national Supported Work Demonstration experienced short-term, but not long-run, earnings gains from their program participation (based on comparisons with a randomly selected control group).

In contrast, young, mentally retarded youths experienced substantial earnings gains from participation in supported employment, particularly if they had moderate as opposed to borderline retardation. Based on a modest sized experimental evaluation, researchers found that those who would have had the greatest difficulty securing employment on their own benefited substantially from this demonstration program by increasing their rates of employment. The program did not, however, affect significantly the wage rates of those who would have found work on their own (Kerachsky et al. 1985).

Adult education programs are designed to provide youths and young adult dropouts with the basic skills necessary to succeed in the work force and to be better parents. The programs do indeed generate short-run gains in measured basic skills and issue alternative educational degrees (the GED) to high fractions of participants (see table A.5.3). However, there is mounting evidence that the true knowledge gains of participants (as opposed to test scores) may be minimal and, for the most part, insufficient to affect significantly employment and earnings outcomes. One body of research based on nonexperimental methods suggests that the benefits of a GED are modest or nonexistent (Murnane et al. 1994; Cameron and Heckman 1993).

Complementing this research are the results of experimental studies of employment and training programs designed to promote employment through human capital development (Cohen et al. 1994). Many of these programs have been successful in increasing significantly the probability that welfare recipients or other low-wage workers will attain their GED. However, these same studies show no consistent pattern of improving measured basic skills or employment outcomes as a result of their success in promoting GED attainment. For example, in the experimental evaluation results from California's welfare-to-work program (GAIN), GED attainment impacts of the intervention did not translate into improved earnings and generally were not even related to program-induced impacts on measured basic skills. The only site in this program evaluation with significant increases in both school completion (primarily GED attainment effects) and measured basic skills witnessed no earnings gains (see table A.5.4). Moreover, the only site with statistically significant earnings gains among program participants, compared with a no-treatment control group, showed no evidence of increasing GED attainment and evidence of significantly lower measured skills among the program group relative to the control group.

A similar pattern of nonconcurrence of program-induced impacts on GED attainment, basic skills attainment, and earnings also has been observed in a large-scale demonstration of a comprehensive service model for teenage parents who have dropped out of school—New Chance. The New Chance demonstration evaluation, which was based on large samples drawn from multiple sites and relied on an experimental design, produced large measured impacts on GED attainment. However, the program had no measured effects on basic skills and significant negative impacts on the earnings of program participants (see tables A.5.5 and A.5.6). More notably, there was no consistent pattern of program-induced impacts on these outcomes within sites. The few sites with significant earnings gains for teenagers, for example, were not those that succeeded in increasing the incidence of GED attainment and/or completion of regular high school (Quint et al. 1994; Maynard 1994).

Job training programs are designed to prepare disadvantaged youths and adults for employment through classroom and/or on-the-job instruction and learning. Sometimes the programs include a remedial education component concurrent with vocational training. However, most programs establish basic skills requirements for participation. These programs have been widely evaluated for their impacts on social and economic outcomes with quite disappointing results (see tables A.5.3 through A.5.9). The most favorable results have been for those programs that have integrated basic skills and job training, most notably the Center for Employment Training (CET) employment and training model and Job Corps, both of which offer basic and job skills training concurrently (Cave et al. 1993, Burghardt and Gordon 1990; Mallar et al. 1982). In the discussion that follows, we address in particular the findings of several of these programs (see table B.5.1 for a listing of key employment and training program evaluations and table B.5.2 for sources of more information on all the programs).

Although not evaluated using experimental methods, the Job Corps evaluation conducted in the 1980s has undergone careful scrutiny for the rigor with which it addressed the issues of selection bias in its comparison group methodology and been judged to yield reasonably reliable results. Credence in these nonexperimental results has been strengthened by corroborative evidence from the other two evaluations of concurrent basic and job skills training, which used experimental evaluation methods—the evaluations of the Minority Female Single Parent Demonstration and the Job Start Evaluation. Although the Minority Female Single Parent Demonstration focused on adult women and the Job Start demonstration focused on youth, both were programs offering basic skills, employment, and job training services provided by community-based organizations. Moreover, both studies independently found evidence of significant program-induced gains in earnings in only those sites that followed a particular service delivery model—an open entry, open exit program offering basic skills and job skills training concurrently. The CET program, which participated in both studies, was similarly successful with adult women and youth (see tables A.5.6 and A.5.7). None of the other three sites in the Minority Female Single Parent Demonstration succeeded in improving long-term earnings of participants relative to their control group counterparts. Similarly, the few other Job Start sites that showed signs of promising earnings impacts were nonresidential Job Corps sites, thus offering concurrent basic and job skills training.

These favorable research findings for the Job Corps and the CET program stand in sharp contrast to those for the National Job Training Partnership Act programs, which form the core of our national employment and training services for school dropouts and other disadvantaged groups (see tables A.5.6 through A.5.8). A large-scale experimental evaluation of JTPA programs indicated that these second-chance programs are not effective in improving (and may reduce) the long-run employment and earnings prospects of participating youths. Indeed, the national evaluation indicated that the programs in the study sites actually lowered the short-run earnings of young males significantly (table A.5.6), while it left the earnings of *young* females and adult males unchanged (tables A.5.6 and A.5.8). The program proved to be somewhat more effective (but still only modestly so) with adult women (Table A.5.7; Bloom et al. 1994). Still, the overall earnings gains for adult women are less than $1,000 a year on average.

Comprehensive programs for teenage parents have arisen in response to the rise in teenage parenting and out-of-wedlock birth, in large part because of the substantial public expenditures for welfare and related social services associated with early childbearing.[12] The response has been the emergence of a variety of programs directed specifically at promoting improved outcomes for this population. The most widespread such initiatives are reflected in the adolescent parent provisions of the JOBS programs created under the Family Support Act of 1988. These programs require teenage parents on welfare to remain in school until graduation or face a reduction in their welfare benefits. Welfare, in turn, provides a modest level of child care and other support services to help young mothers meet these program participation requirements.

Research on these programs suggests that they will induce increased levels of educational participation and degree attainment as well as promote higher earnings (Maynard 1993, 1994; Bloom et al. 1993; Quint et al. 1994; Long

---

12. One set of estimates puts the cost of teenage childbearing at $20 billion annually (Advocates for Youth 1994).

et al. 1996). However, they have fallen far short of solving the economic problems of these young mothers. Educational gains have been primarily in GED attainment, which, as noted previously, is of questionable value. And earnings and welfare effects have been modest and nearly offsetting, resulting in no net impact on poverty.

Other programs that have provided a richer array of support and services, without the financial incentives to participate, have had a similar level of success in promoting attainment of the GED, but they have been less successful in promoting improved economic outcomes (Quint et al. 1994; Maynard 1994).[13] None of these programs has succeeded in helping the young women delay repeat pregnancies and births (see table A.5.9), an outcome that is critical to mitigating the long-run consequences of early childbearing (Moore et al. 1993).

Current welfare reform deliberations have attracted considerable attention to the seeming perversity of providing substantial resources in the form of "special" programs for teenage parents and other seriously at-risk youths and young adults. One argument is that our public resources should reward "good" behavior not bad. However, another argument builds on the weak record of our myriad demonstration and policy efforts to prevent and mitigate the consequences of school failure.

5.4. Future Policy Directions

The history of well-intentioned efforts to improve outcomes for youths is discouraging at best. Nonetheless, there is strong evidence that education is key to the future welfare of our young people and the nation as a whole. The benefits to individuals are clear. The personal earnings gains are large (see table 5.1). But, more importantly, this income advantage offers strong protection against serious consequences of otherwise adverse social outcomes such as early childbearing and single parenthood. Much of the adverse social and economic disadvantage normally associated with early childbearing can be traced to the limited education and lower socioeconomic status of the families of teenage parents. Indeed, one study that contrasts outcomes for early childbearers with those for pregnant teens who experience spontaneous abortions finds no sizable differences in long-term social and economic outcomes (Hotz et al. 1994). Other studies suggest that the advantages of delayed childbearing are significant only if the birth can be delayed well into early adulthood (Moore et al. 1993).

Similarly strong protective forces of education have been observed for single-parent families. Whereas, on average, child outcomes are significantly worse for children of divorce than for those in two-parent families, careful

---

13. The array of comprehensive teenage parent programs embedded within school systems has not been rigorously evaluated.

analysis traces large shares of the differences to the lower incomes of divorced and never-married families and to the lower incomes of those families headed by school dropouts (McLanahan and Sandefur 1994). For example, nearly 40 percent of persons in female-headed families have incomes below the poverty line, compared with only 13 percent of all persons in families—a difference of 27 percentage points. This difference contrasts with only 11 points (14 versus 3 percent) for those with a high school degree and less than three points for those with some college (McLanahan and Sandefur 1994, fig. 9). Similarly, large portions of the observed differences between children reared in single-parent families compared with those reared in two-parent families can be traced to economic disadvantages associated with low levels of education.

Results like these provide the stimulation for us to persist in our efforts to improve the educational outcomes of our young people. Education is not the cause of these adverse social outcomes. However, it is key to promoting resilience among young people to succeed despite the odds. It is critical for the economic and social health of the nation that we break the cycle of poverty and social ills that plague our inner cities and rural areas in particular. In the short run, benefits may not appear in the form of lower teenage birth rates, higher rates of family formation, or even lower rates of child abuse and neglect. However, the compound intergenerational effects may indeed justify the investment.

TABLE A.5.1. Estimated Program Impacts of the Negative Income Tax Experiments on Education-Related Outcomes of Elementary School Students

Performance Measure	Rural Sites		Urban Sites		
	North Carolina[a]	Iowa[a]	Gary[b]	Seattle[c]	Denver[c]
Estimated program impact (percentage of control group mean)					
Social/behavioral outcomes					
Absenteeism	−30.5**	−19.7	7.5	−1.3	−2.1
Comportment grade point average	6.7**	−0.4	n.a.	n.a.	n.a.
Cognitive outcomes					
Academic grade point average	6.2*	−4.6	−0.5	n.a.	−0.0
Reading test score[d]	n.a.	n.a.	22.3***	n.a.	n.a.
Deviation from expected grade equivalent score on standard achievement test	18.9**	−188.4	n.a.	n.a.	n.a.
Standardized verbal achievement test	1.6	−14.8	n.a.	−4.8	7.1
Participant group mean					
Social/behavioral outcomes					
Absenteeism (days per school year)	9.1	7.5	12.0	12.8	11.4
Comportment grade point average	233.4	229.4	n.a.	n.a.	n.a.
Cognitive outcomes					
Academic grade point average	225.9	249.9	81.6	n.a.	77.8
Reading test score[d]	n.a.	n.a.	0.0	n.a.	n.a.
Deviation from expected grade equivalent score on standard achievement test	−14.4	−1.2	n.a.	n.a.	n.a.
Standardized achievement test (percentile)	25.8	44.7	n.a.	33.2	30.0

Sources: Maynard, 1977, 373; Maynard and Murnane, 1979, 369; Manheim and Minchella, 1978, 16–17.

Note: n.a. = Figures not available.

[a] Grades 2–8; total sample size for North Carolina and Iowa, grades 2–12, 847 (Maynard 1977, 373).

[b] Grades 4–6; sample size for absenteeism = 608; academic GPA = 619; reading test score = 575 (Maynard and Murnane, 1979, 369).

[c] Seattle sample size for absenteeism data = 451; verbal test = 261; Denver sample size for absenteeism = 335; academic GPA = 711; and for verbal = 85 (Manheim and Minchella, 1978, 16–17).

[d] Impacts and means for North Carolina and Iowa are standardized raw scores from the Iowa Test of Basic Skills.

* Statistically significant at the 10 percent level.

** Statistically significant at the 5 percent level.

*** Statistically significant at the 1 percent level.

TABLE A.5.2. Estimated Program Impacts of the Negative Income Tax Experiments on Education-Related Outcomes of High School Students

Performance Measure	Rural Sites		Urban Sites			
	North Carolina[a]	Iowa[a]	Gary[b]	New Jersey[c]	Seattle[d]	Denver
Estimated program impact (percentage of control group mean)						
Social/behavioral						
Absenteeism (days)	3.2	−17.0	4.7	n.a.	−0.23	n.a.
Cognitive						
Academic grade point average	4.3	−4.6	−2.0***	n.a.	1.41*	0.3
Reading test scores[e]	n.a.	n.a.	−12.5	n.a.	n.a.	n.a.
Attainment						
Probability of completing high school	n.a.	n.a.	n.a.	−26.9 to 90.4	n.a.	n.a.
Years of schooling	n.a.	n.a.	n.a.	−0.3 to 13.7	n.a.	n.a.
Probability of attending college for high school graduates	n.a.	n.a.	n.a.	69.5 to 430.5	n.a.	n.a.
Unconditional probability of attending college[f]	n.a.	n.a.	n.a.	227.7 to 449.2	n.a.	n.a.
Participant group mean						
Social/behavioral						
Absenteeism (days)	7.9	6.8	10.7	n.a.	14.8	n.a.
Cognitive						
Academic grade point average	203.5	244.3	78.4	n.a.	75.7	72.0
Reading test score[e]	n.a.	n.a.	0.0	n.a.	n.a.	n.a.
Attainment						
Probability of completing high school	n.a.	n.a.	n.a.	0.38 to 0.99	n.a.	n.a.
Years of schooling	n.a.	n.a.	n.a.	11.0 to 12.5	n.a.	n.a.
Probability of attending college for high school graduates	n.a.	n.a.	n.a.	0.10 to 0.31	n.a.	n.a.
Unconditional probability of attending college[f]	n.a.	n.a.	n.a.	0.10 to 0.17	n.a.	n.a.

Sources: Maynard, 1977, 373; Maynard and Murnane, 1979, 369; Mallar and Maynard, 1981, 131–133; Manheim a Minchella, 1978, 16–17.

Note: n.a. = Figures not available.

[a] Grades 2–8; total sample size for North Carolina and Iowa, grades 2–12 = 847 (Maynard, 1977, 373).

[b] Grades 7–10; sample size for abseenteeism = 829; academic GPA = 898; reading test score = 276 (Maynard a Murnane, 1979, 370).

[c] Sample of youths who were 16 or 17 when the NIT experiment began; sample size for probability of graduat high school and years of schooling = 138; the two variables concerning college attendance = 80. Results were compu separately for eight experimental groups for which the level of income guarantee and the tax rate varied (Mallar a Maynard, 1981, 131–33).

[d] Seattle sample size for absenteeism = 210; academic GPA = 453; Denver sample size for academic GPA = 7 (Manheim and Minchella, 1978, 16–17).

[e] Impact and mean reported in standardized raw scores from the Iowa Test of Basic Skills.

[f] Adjusted means obtained by multiplying those for high school completion with those for conditional college attendar

* Statistically significant at the 10 percent level.

** Statistically significant at the 5 percent level.

*** Statistically significant at the 1 percent level.

TABLE A.5.3. Estimated Program Impacts on Education-Related Outcomes of Adults

Population/ Program/Site	School Enrollment	Diploma/ GED	GED	Basic Skills
Estimated program impact (percentage of control/comparison group mean)				
Adult females				
California GAIN overall [a]	341.1	7.1*	n.a.	1.8
Alameda	607.6	7.7*	n.a.	2.3
Los Angeles	355.6	2.2*	n.a.	3.7
Riverside	180.0	2.6	n.a.	−19.0*
San Diego	256.8	4.2*	n.a.	33.8*
Tulare	393.2	19.0***	n.a.	−10.2
JTPA	n.a.	75.9***[a]	n.a.	n.a.
Minority Female Single Parent Program				
AUL	295.1	n.a.	492.3	n.a.
CET	300.9***	n.a.	180.6***	n.a.
OIC	332.4***	n.a.	200.0***	n.a.
WOW	250.0***	n.a.	223.5***	n.a.
Adult males				
JTPA	n.a.	89.6	n.a.	n.a.
Participant Group Mean				
Adult females				
California GAIN overall [a]	52.5%	2.1	n.a.	483
Alameda	65.1%	1.3	n.a.	491
Los Angeles	49.2%	0.5	n.a.	461
Riverside	40.6%	3.7	n.a.	411
San Diego	42.1%	1.9	n.a.	607
Tulare	65.6%	2.1	n.a.	429
JTPA	n.a.	19.1%[b]	n.a.	n.a.
Minority Female Single Parent Program				
AUL	64.8%	n.a.	15.4%	n.a.
CET	43.3%	n.a.	10.1%	n.a.
OIC	77.4%	n.a.	18.0%	n.a.
WOW	46.2%	n.a.	5.5%	n.a.
Adult males				
JTPA	n.a.	12.7%[b]	n.a.	n.a.

Sources: Sources of data presented in this table are detailed in table B.5.2.

Note: n.a. = Figures not available. Program descriptions are presented in table B.5.1. Data for GAIN pertain to three years after enrollment. Data for Minority Female Single Parent Demonstration pertain to the fourth quarter after baseline. Data for JTPA pertain to 18 months after enrollment.

[a] Determined to need basic education subgroup; no tests for statistical significance run on school enrollment.

[b] By month 18; attainment of diploma or GED and having attended school or training.

* Statistically significant at the 10 percent level.

** Statistically significant at the 5 percent level.

*** Statistically significant at the 1 percent level.

TABLE A.5.4. Estimated Education, Basic Skills, and Earnings Impacts of Participating in California's Work-to-Welfare Program on Adult Females (two to three years after enrollment)

	GED/HS Diploma (%)[a]		Test of Applied Literacy		Monthly Earnings ($)[b]	
	Participant Group Mean	Estimated Impact	Participant Group Mean	Estimated Impact[c]	Participant Group Mean	Estimated Impact
Alameda	1.3	7.7*	491	2.3	$110	$9
Los Angeles	0.5	2.2*	461	3.7	98	0
Riverside	3.7	2.6	411	−19.0*	186	73*
San Diego	1.9	4.2*	607	33.8*	173	14
Tulare	2.1	19.0*	429	−10.2	132	12
Total (N = 1,115)	2.1	7.1*	483	1.8	n.a.	n.a.

Sources: Martinson and Friedlander (1994, tables 1, 2); Friedlander et al. (1993, table 4).

Note: n.a. = Figures not available.

[a] Obtained after referral to California's welfare-to-work program, GAIN.

[b] Estimates pertain to the subgroup determined to need basic education, two years after enrollment.

[c] Calculated as 100*(Participant Group Mean − Control Group Mean)/Control Group Mean.

* Significantly different from zero at the .10 level.

TABLE A.5.5. Estimated Program Impacts on Education-Related Outcomes of Youth

Program/Population	School Enrollment	Diploma/ GED	GED	Basic Skills
Estimated program impact (percentage of control/comparison group mean)				
Teen parent welfare recipients				
Job Corps	−80.3**[a]	666.7***	n.a.	n.a.
Job Start	n.a.	57.3**	67.1**	n.a.
New Chance	84.9**	43.7**	74.9**	<0.1
Ohio Learnfare	15.5**	n.a.	62.5**	n.a.
Project Redirection	16.7	0.1	n.a.	n.a.
Teen Parent Welfare Demonstration	42.0**	4.0*	19.2	<0.1
Disadvantaged females				
JTPA	n.a.	7.9**[b]	n.a.	n.a.
Job Corps (nonmothers)	n.a.	1367.6***	n.a.	n.a.
Job Start (nonmothers)	n.a.	33.2**	n.a.	n.a.
Disadvantaged males				
JTPA	n.a.	7.7**[c]	n.a.	n.a.
Job Corps	n.a.	465.9***	n.a.	
Job Start	n.a.	48.4**	n.a.	n.a.
Participant group mean				
Teen parent welfare recipients				
Job Corps	5.3% of time	48.3%	n.a.	n.a.
Job Start	n.a.	42.0%	39.1%	n.a.
New Chance	33.0% of time	43.1%	36.8%	7.8 GE
Ohio Learnfare	67.4%	n.a.	3.9%	n.a.
Project Redirection	18.6%	48.3%	n.a.	n.a.
Teen Parent Welfare Demonstration	41.6%	48.4%	5.7%	8.1 GE
Disadvantaged females				
JTPA	n.a.	13.7%	n.a.	n.a.
Job Corps (nonmothers)	n.a.	54.3%	n.a.	n.a.
Job Start (nonmothers)	n.a.	41.6%	n.a.	n.a.
Disadvantaged males				
JTPA	n.a.	13.7%	n.a.	n.a.
Job Corps	n.a.	23.2%	n.a.	n.a.
Job Start	94.0%	42.0%	n.a.	n.a.

Sources: Sources of data presented in this table are detailed in table B.5.2.

Note: n.a. = Figures not available.

GE = grade equivalent score.

Program descriptions are presented in table B.5.1.

Data for Project Redirection pertain to five years after study enrollment. Data for Job Start and Job Corps pertain to four years after enrollment. Data for Ohio Learnfare pertain to three years after enrollment. Data for Teen Parent Welfare Demonstration pertain to two years after enrollment. Data for New Chance and JTPA pertain to 18 months after enrollment.

[a] Months 0–6 after enrollment.

[b] Attainment of diploma or GED and having attended school or training.

[c] Attended high school in first 12 months of program.

* Statistically significant at the 10 percent level.

** Statistically significant at the 5 percent level.

*** Statistically significant at the 1 percent level.

TABLE A.5.6.   Estimated Program Impacts on Employment-Related Outcomes of Youth

Program	Employment		Monthly Earnings[a]	
	Participant Group Mean	Estimated Impact[b]	Participant Group Mean	Estimated Impact[b]
Teen parent welfare recipients				
Job Corps	40.0% of weeks	−40.5**	$178	−44.4***
Job Start	49.1%	0.4	$187	$7.5
New Chance	42.6%	−4.9	$76	−33.4
Project Redirection	60.1%	15.1	$297	51.5*
Teen Parent Welfare Demonstration	48.2%	11.8**	$137	20.0**
Disadvantaged females				
JTPA	n.a.	2.8	$356	−2.9
Job Corps (nonmothers)	60.8% of weeks	31.9***	$293	19.7**
Job Start (nonmothers)	84.3%	−1.2	$290	4.6
Disadvantaged males				
JTPA	n.a.	1.5	$644	−7.9***
Job Corps	61.1% of weeks	11.1	$389	10.8
Job Start	94.1%	−0.4	$487	−1.2
Supported Work Demonstration	74.0%	12.3	$302	−10.2

Sources: Sources of data presented in this table are detailed in table B.5.2.

Note: n.a. = Figures not available.

Program descriptions are presented in table B.5.1.

Data for Project Redirection pertain to five years after study enrollment. Data for Job Start and Job Corps pertain to four years after enrollment. Data for Supported Work Demonstration pertain to 34 to 36 months. Data for Teen Parent Welfare Demonstration pertain to two years after enrollment. Data for New Chance and JTPA pertain to 18 months after enrollment.

[a] Earnings not corrected for changes in the buying power of the dollar.

[b] Calculated as 100*(Participant Group Mean − Control Group Mean)/Control Group Mean.

* Statistically significant at the 10 percent level.

** Statistically significant at the 5 percent level.

*** Statistically significant at the 1 percent level.

TABLE A.5.7. Estimated Program Impacts on Employment-Related Outcomes of Adult Females

Program	Employment		Monthly Earnings[a]	
	Participant Group Mean	Estimated Impact[b]	Participant Group Mean	Estimated Impact[b]
California GAIN (overall)	56.7%	11.8***	$216	22.3***
Alameda	48.8%	19.6***	$179	30.2**
Butte	63.4%	−0.3	$240	20.6
Los Angeles	39.4%	12.9***	$137	5.6
Riverside	67.1%	25.5***	$262	49.1***
San Diego	62.2%	10.1***	$272	22.1***
Tulare	59.5%	7.6**	$207	5.3
JTPA	80.0%	2.8**	$446	7.2***
Minority Female Single Parent Demonstration (overall)	47.7%	5.1	$321	8.7
CET	54.3%	30.5***	$420	49.6***
Supported Work Demonstration	42.0%	20.3*	$248	48.0**
WIN (Work Incentive Programs)				
Arkansas	50.4%	5.9	$124	16.0
Baltimore	77.9%	2.8	$276	13.5***
California	33.9%	16.7***	$268	14.8**
Virginia	75.7%	4.8**	$230	9.9*

Sources: Sources of data presented in this table are detailed in table B.5.2.

Note: n.a. = Figures not available.

Program descriptions are presented in table B.5.1.

Data for WIN pertain to five years after study enrollment. Data for GAIN pertain to three years after enrollment. Data for Supported Work Demonstration pertain to the twenty-fifth through the twenty-seventh months. Data for Minority Female Single Parent Demonstration pertain to the fourth quarter after baseline. Data for JTPA pertain to 18 months after enrollment.

[a] Earnings not corrected for changes in the buying power of the dollar.

[b] Calculated as 100*(Participant Group Mean − Control Group Mean)/Control Group Mean.

* Statistically significant at the 10 percent level.

** Statistically significant at the 5 percent level.

*** Statistically significant at the 1 percent level.

TABLE A.5.8. Estimated Program Impacts on Employment-Related Outcomes of Adult Males

Program	Employment		Monthly Earnings[a]	
	Participant Group Mean	Estimated Impact[b]	Participant Group Mean	Estimated Impact[b]
California GAIN (overall)	44.6%	11.2***	$282	12.3***
Alameda	n.a.	n.a.	n.a.	n.a.
Butte	48.1%	14.8*	$328	38.7***
Los Angeles	35.8%	37.7***	$139	21.6**
Riverside	44.8%	11.4**	$321	15.0**
San Diego	45.6%	3.9	$322	1.2
Tulare	48.9%	1.0	$301	−2.4
JTPA	86.4%	3.4**	$714	4.5
Supported Work Demonstration				
Former Drug Addicts[c]	48.8%	54.4**	$319	45.6**
Former Offenders[d]	50.9%	12.6	$361	22.3

Sources: Sources of data presented in this table are detailed in table B.5.2.

Note: n.a. = Figures not available.

Program descriptions are presented in table B.5.1.

Data for GAIN pertain to three years after enrollment. Data for Supported Work Demonstration pertain to the 34 to 36 months after enrollment. Data for JTPA pertain to 18 months after enrollment.

[a] Earnings not corrected for changes in the buying power of the dollar.

[b] Calculated as 100*(Participant Group Mean − Control Group Mean)/Control Group Mean.

[c] Sample was 83% male.

[d] Sample was 97% male.

* Statistically significant at the 10 percent level.

** Statistically significant at the 5 percent level.

*** Statistically significant at the 1 percent level.

TABLE A.5.9. Estimated Program Impacts for Teenage Parents on Repeat Pregnancies and Births

Program	Pregnancies	Abortions	Births
Estimated program impact (percentage of control/comparison group mean)			
Job Start	12.7**	n.a.	17.1**
New Chance	7.5*	34.2**	8.4
Ohio Learnfare	−25.9	n.a.	4.3
Project Redirection	6.9	−41.5*	20.0**
Teen Parent Welfare Demonstration	5.3	−16.9	6.6*
Participant group mean			
Job Start	76.1%	n.a.	67.8%
New Chance	57.0%	14.9%	28.4%
Ohio Learnfare	10.3%	n.a.	26.7%
Project Redirection	3.3 (#)	0.3 (#)	2.4 (#)
Teenage Parent Welfare Demonstration	52.5%	0.16 (#)	0.64 (#)

Sources: Sources of data presented in this table are detailed in table B.5.2.

Note: n.a. = Figures not available.

= number.

Program descriptions are presented in table B.5.1.

Data for Project Redirection pertain to five years after study enrollment. Data for Job Start pertain to four years after enrollment. Data for Ohio Learnfare pertains to three years after enrollment. Data for Teen Parent Welfare Demonstration pertain to two years after enrollment. Data for New Chance pertain to 18 months after enrollment.

 * Statistically significant at the 10 percent level.

 ** Statistically significant at the 5 percent level.

TABLE B.5.1. Key Employment and Training Program Evaluations

Program	Setting	Cost	Study Design	Sample Size
GAIN (California work-welfare)	CBOs and welfare offices in 6 counties in California	$3,422 net per experimental (1993 dollars)	Random assignment	33,000
Job Corps	78 Job Corps centers	$500 per month (1977 dollars)	Matched comparison	Youth parents: 1,008
Job Start	13 CBOs, vocational schools, and Job Corps programs	$771 per month (5.9 months)	Random assignment	Teen mothers: 508 Youth females: 533 Youth males: 900
JTPA (federal employment training)	16 local JTPA programs.	n.a.	Random assignment	AFDC: 4,376 Adult males: 4,419 Youth females: 2,300 Youth males: 1,748
Minority Female Single Parent Demonstration	CBOs in Atlanta, San Jose, Providence, and Washington, D.C.	n.a.	Random assignment	3,352
New Chance	16 CBOs, PICS, and schools	$1,525 per month (6 months)	Random assignment	2,088
Ohio Learnfare	County welfare program	$27.50 per eligibility month	Random assignment	4,225
Project Redirection	4 CBOs	$324 per month (1984 dollars)	Comparison sites	277
Supported Work Demonstration	CBOs in 10 cities, 1975–78	(1976 dollars)	Random assignment	AFDC: 587 Ex-drug addicts: n.a. Ex-offenders: 302 Youth: 153
SWIM (California WIN)	Welfare offices in San Diego County	$900 net per experimental (1986 dollars)	Random assignment	3,210
Teen Parent Welfare Demonstration	Welfare offices in 3 cities	$244 per month (9 months per year)	Random assignment	5,297
WIN (national work-welfare)	County welfare offices in Virginia, Arkansas and Baltimore	Virginia: $430 per experimental Arkansas: $140 Baltimore: $295	Random assignment	Virginia: 3,150 Arkansas: 1,127 Baltimore: 2,757

Sources: Sources of data presented in this table are detailed in table B.5.2.

Note: n.a. = not available; CBO = community based organization; PIC = private industry council; AFDC = Aid to Families with Dependent Children.

TABLE B.5.2.   Sources of Program Impact Estimates and Cost Data

Program	Sources
GAIN	Riccio, James, Daniel Friedlander, and Stephen Freedman. 1994. *Gain: Benefits, Costs, and Three-Year Impacts of a Welfare-to-Work Program. Executive Summary.* New York: Manpower Demonstration Research Corp.
Job Corps	Mallar, Charles, Stuart Kerachsky, Craig Thornton, and David Long. 1982. *Evaluation of the Economic Impact of the Job Corps Program: Third Follow-Up Report.* Princeton, NJ: Mathematica Policy Research, Inc.
Job Start	Cave, George, Hans Bos, Fred Doolittle, and Cyril Toussaint. 1993. *Job Start: Final Report on a Program for School Dropouts.* New York: Manpower Demonstration Research Corp.
JTPA	Bloom, Howard S., Larry L. Orr, George Cave, Stephen H. Bell, and Fred Doolittle. 1994. *The National JTPA Study:Title IIA Impacts on Earnings and Employment at 18 Months.* Bethesda, MD: Abt Associates.
Minority Female Single Parent Demonstration	Gordon, Anne, and John Burghardt. 1990. *The Minority Female Single Parent Demonstration: Short-Term Economic Impacts.* New York: The Rockefeller Foundation.
New Chance	Quint, Janet, Denise Polit, Hans Bos, and George Cave. 1994. *New Chance: Interim Findings on a Comprehensive Program for Disadvantaged Young Mothers and Their Children.* New York: Manpower Demonstration Research Corp.
Ohio Learnfare	Long, David, Judith M. Gueron, Robert G. Wood, Rebecca Fisher, and Veronica Fellerath. 1996. *LEAP: Three- Year Impacts of Ohio's Welfare Initiative to Improve School Attendance among Teenage Parents: Ohio's Learning, Earning, and Parenting Program.* New York: Manpower Demonstration Research Corp.
Project Redirection	Polit, Denise, and Cozette White. 1988. *The Lives of Young, Disadvantaged Mothers: The Five-Year Follow-up of the Project Redirection Sample.* Saratoga Springs, NY: Humanalysis, Inc.
Supported Work Demonstration	Hollister, Robinson G. Jr., Peter Kemper, and Rebecca A. Maynard, eds. 1984. *The National Supported Work Demonstration.* Madison, WI: The University of Wisconsin Press.
SWIM (California WIN)	Friedlander, Daniel, and Gayle Hamilton. 1993. *The Saturation Work Initiative Model in San Diego: A Five-Year Follow-up Study.* New York: Manpower Demonstration Research Corp.
Teen Parent Welfare Demonstration	Maynard, Rebecca, ed. 1993. *Building Self-Sufficiency among Welfare-Dependent Teenage Parents.* Princeton, NJ: Mathematica Policy Research, Inc. Maynard, Rebecca, Walter Nicholson, and Anu Rangarajan. 1993. *Breaking the Cycle of Poverty: The Effectiveness of Mandatory Services for Welfare-Dependent Teenage Parents.* Princeton, NJ: Mathematica Policy Research, Inc.
WIN	Friedlander, Daniel, and Gary Burtless. 1995. *Five Years After: The Long-Term Effects of Welfare-to-Work Programs.* New York: Russell Sage Foundation.

Note: Program descriptions are presented in table B.5.1.

REFERENCES

Advocates for Youth. 1994. *Teenage Pregnancy and Too-Early Childbearing: Public Costs, Personal Consequences,* 5th ed. Washington, DC: Advocates for Youth.

Ahn, G. 1994. Teenage Childbearing and High School Completion: Accounting for Individual Heterogeneity. *Family Planning Perspectives* 26:17–21.

Alan Guttmacher Institute. 1994. *Sex and America's Teenagers.* New York: Alan Guttmacher Institute.

Alwin, D., and A. Thornton. 1984. Family Origins and the Schooling Process: Early versus Late Influence of Parental Characteristics. *American Sociological Review* 49:784–802.

Anderson, E. 1994. *Sexuality, Poverty and the Inner City.* Menlo Park, CA: Henry J. Kaiser Family Foundation.

Annie E. Casey Foundation. 1993. *Kids Count Data Book: State Profiles of Child Well-Being.* Baltimore, MD: Annie E. Casey Foundation Center for the Study of Social Policy.

Averch, H. A., et al. 1972. *How Effective Is Schooling? A Critical Review and Synthesis of Research Findings.* Santa Monica: Rand Corp.

Barnett, W. S. 1985. *The Perry Preschool Program and Its Long-Term Effects: A Benefit Cost Analysis.* High/Scope Early Childhood Policy Paper, no. 2. Ypsilanti, MI: High/Scope Educational Research Foundation.

Barnett, W. S. 1991. Benefits of Compensatory Preschool Education. *Journal of Human Resources* 27:279–312.

Barnow, B. S. 1987. The Impact of CETA Programs on Earnings. *Journal of Human Resources* 22:157–91.

Behrman, J. R. 1996. Conceptual and Measurement Issues. Paper presented at the conference "Social Benefits of Education: Can They Be Measured?" sponsored by the Office of Research of the U.S. Department of Education, Washington, DC, 4–5 January (chap. 3 in this volume).

Behrman, J. R., M. R. Rosenzweig, and P. Taubman. 1994. Endowments and the Allocation of Schooling in the Family and in the Marriage Market: The Twins Experiment. *Journal of Political Economy* 102:1131–74.

Behrman, J. R., M. R. Rosenzweig, and P. Taubman. 1996. College Choice and Wages: Estimates using Data on Female Twins. *Review of Economics and Statistics.*

Berlin, G., and A. Sum. 1988. *Toward a More Perfect Union: Basic Skills, Poor Families, and Our Economic Future.* New York: Ford Foundation.

Berrueta-Clement, J. R., et al. 1984. *Changed Lives: The Effects of the Perry Preschool Program on Youths through Age 19.* Ypsilanti, MI: High/Scope Educational Research Foundation.

Berryman, S. 1988. *Literacy and the Marketplace: Improving the Literacy of Low Income Single Mothers.* New York: Rockefeller Foundation.

Blank, R. 1994. Outlook for the U.S. Labor Market and Prospects for Low-Wage Jobs. Paper presented at the conference on "Self-Sufficiency and the Low-Wage Labor Market: A Reality Check on the Welfare-to-Work Transition," sponsored by the Urban Institute, Washington, DC. Mimeo.

Blau, D., ed. 1991. Child Care Policy and Research: An Economist's Perspective. In *The Economics of Child Care*. New York: Russell Sage Foundation.

Bloom, D., et al. 1991. *LEAP: Implementing a Welfare Initiative to Improve School Attendance among Teenage Parents*. New York: Manpower Demonstration Research Corp.

Bloom, D., et al. 1993. *LEAP: Interim Findings on a Welfare Initiative to Improve School Attendance among Teenage Parents*. New York: Manpower Demonstration Research Corp.

Bloom, H., et al. 1993. *The National JTPA Study: Title II–A Impacts on Earnings and Employment at 18 Months*. Cambridge, MA: Abt Associates.

Bloom, H., et al. 1994. *The National JTPA Study: Overview of the Impacts, Benefits, and Costs of Title II–A*. Cambridge, MA: Abt Associates.

Bourdieu, P. 1984. *Distinction: A Social Critique of the Judgement of Taste,* trans. R. Nice. Cambridge: Harvard University Press.

Boyer, D., and D. Fine. 1992. Sexual Abuse as a Factor in Adolescent Pregnancy and Maltreatment. *Family Planning Perspectives* 24:4–19.

Braddock, J. H., II, et al. 1991. Bouncing Back: Sports and Academic Resilience among African-American Males. *Education and Urban Society* 24:112–31.

Burghardt, J., and A. Gordon. 1990. *More Jobs and Higher Pay: How an Integrated Program Compares with Traditional Programs*. New York: Rockefeller Foundation.

Burtless, G., ed. 1990. *A Future of Lousy Jobs? The Changing Structure of U.S. Wages*. Washington, DC: Brookings Institution.

Burtless, G. 1994. Who is Employable and What Can the Labor Market Absorb? Paper presented at the conference "Self-Sufficiency and the Low-Wage Labor Market: A Reality Check on the Welfare-to-Work Transition," sponsored by the Urban Institute, Washington, DC. Mimeo.

Cain, G., and D. Wissoker. 1990. A Reanalysis of Marital Stability in the Seattle-Denver Income-Maintenance Experiment, *American Journal of Sociology* 95:1235–69.

Cameron, S. V., and J. J. Heckman. 1993. The Nonequivalence of High School Equivalents. *Journal of Labor Economics* 11:1–47.

Campbell, F. A., et al. 1991. Parental Beliefs and Values Related to Family Risk, Educational Intervention, and Child Academic Competence. *Early Childhood Research Quarterly* 6:167–82.

Cattan, P. 1991. Child-Care Problems: An Obstacle to Work. *Monthly Labor Review* 114:3–9.

Cave, G., et al. 1993. *Job Start: Final Report on a Program for School Dropouts*. New York: Manpower Demonstration Research Corp.

Cherlin, A. J., and F. F. Furstenberg, Jr. 1994. Stepfamilies in the United States: A Reconsideration. *Annual Review of Sociology* 20:359–81.

Chubb, J. E., and T. M. Moe. 1990. *Politics, Markets, and America's Schools*. Washington, DC: Brookings Institution.

Cohen, E., et al. 1994. Welfare Reform and Literacy: Are We Making the Connection? Background briefing report for seminar/forum, Library of Congress, Washington, DC. Mimeo.

Cohen, M. 1991. Key Issues Confronting State Policy Makers. In *Restructuring Schools: The Next Generation of Educational Reform,* ed. R. F. Elmore. San Francisco: Jossey-Bass Publishers.

Coleman, J. S., and T. Hoffer. 1987. *Public and Private High Schools: The Impact of Communities.* New York: Basic Books.

Committee for Economic Development. 1994. *Putting Learning First: Governing and Managing the Schools for High Achievement.* New York: Committee for Economic Development.

Congressional Budget Office. 1990. *Sources of Support for Adolescent Mothers.* Washington, DC: Government Printing Office.

Corcoran, M., and L. Datcher. 1981. Intergenerational Status Transmission and the Process of Individual Attainment. In *Five Thousand American Families: Patterns of Economic Progress,* ed. M. Hill, D. H. Hill, and J. M. Morgan. Vol. 9. Ann Arbor: University of Michigan, Institute for Social Research.

Crane, J. 1991. The Epidemic Theory of Ghettos and Neighborhood Effects on Dropping Out and Teenage Childbearing. *American Journal of Sociology* 96:1226–59.

Currie, J. 1994. Welfare and the Well-Being of Children: The Relative Effectiveness of Cash and In-Kind Transfers. In *Tax Policy and the Economy,* ed. James M. Poterba. Cambridge: The National Bureau of Economic Research and MIT Press.

Datcher, L. 1982. Effects of Community and Family Background on Achievement. *Review of Economics and Statistics* 64:32–41.

Dryfoos, J. G. 1990. *Adolescents at Risk.* New York: Oxford University Press.

Dryfoos, J. G. 1994. *Full-Service Schools.* San Francisco: Jossey-Bass Publishers.

Ellwood, D. 1988. *Poor Support.* New York: Basic Books.

Erickson, F. 1987. Transformation and School Success: The Politics and Culture of Educational Achievement. *Anthropology and Education Quarterly* 18:335–56.

Ferguson, R. 1991. Paying for Public Education: New Evidence on How and Why Money Matters. *Harvard Journal on Legislation* 28:465–98.

Finkelhor, D. 1994. Current Information on the Scope and Nature of Child Abuse. *Future of Children* 4:31–53.

Friedlander, D., and G. Burtless. 1995. *Five Years After: The Long-Term Effects of Welfare-to-Work Programs.* New York: Russell Sage Foundation.

Friedlander, D., S. Freedman, and J. Riccio. 1993. *GAIN: Two-Year Impacts in Six Counties.* New York: Manpower Demonstration Research Corp.

Friedlander, D., and G. Hamilton. 1993. *The Saturation Work Initiative Model in San Diego: A Five-Year Follow-Up Study.* New York: Manpower Demonstration Research Corp.

Fuhrman, S., ed. 1993. *Designing Coherent Education Policy: Improving the System.* San Francisco: Jossey-Bass Publishers.

Fuhrman, S., R. Elmore, and D. Massell. 1993. School Reform in the United States: Putting It into Context. In *Reforming Education: The Emerging Systemic Approach,* ed. S. L. Jacobson and R. Berne. Thousand Oaks, CA: Corwin Press.

Furstenberg, F. F. Jr., and J. O. Teitler. 1994. Reconsidering the Effects of Marital Disruption: What Happens to Children of Divorce in Early Childhood? *Journal of Family Issues* 15:173–90.

Geronimus, A., and S. Korenman. 1993. The Socioeconomic Consequences of Teen Childbearing Reconsidered. *Quarterly Journal of Economics.* 107:281–90.

Goetz, K., ed., 1992. *Programs to Strengthen Families: A Resource Guide.* Washington, DC: Family Resource Coalition.

Goldberger, S., R. Kazis, and M. K. O'Flanagan. 1994. Learning through Work: Designing and Implementing Quality Worksite Learning for High School Students. New York: Manpower Demonstration Research Corp.

Gordon, A., and J. Burghardt. 1990. *The Minority Female Single Parent Demonstration: Short-Term Economic Impacts.* New York: Rockefeller Foundation.

Gramlich, E. 1986. Evaluation of Education Projects: The Case of the Perry Preschool Program. *Economics of Education Review* 5:17–24.

Hahn, A., with T. Leavitt, and P. Aaron. 1994. *Evaluation of the Quantum Opportunities Program (QOP): Did the Program Work? A Report on the Post Secondary Outcomes and Cost-Effectiveness of the QOP Program (1989–1993).* Waltham, MA: Brandeis University.

Hamburg, D. 1992. The Family Crucible and Healthy Child Development. In *Annual Report, 1990. Carnegie Corporation.* New York: Carnegie Corp.

Hannan M. T., N. B. Tuma, and L. P. Groeneveld. 1977. Income and Marital Events: Evidence from an Income Maintenance Experiment. *American Journal of Sociology* 82:1186–1211.

Hanushek, E. A. 1989. The Impact of Differential Expenditures on School Performance. *Educational Researcher* 18:45–50.

Hanushek, E. A. 1994. *Improving Performance and Controlling Costs in American Schools.* Washington, DC: Brookings Institution.

Haveman, R., and B. Wolfe. 1984. Schooling and Economic Well-Being: The Role of Nonmarket Effects. *Journal of Human Resources* 19:377–407.

Haveman, R., and B. Wolfe. 1994. *Succeeding Generations: On the Effects of Investments in Children.* New York: Russell Sage Foundation.

Haveman, R., B. Wolfe, and J. Spaulding. 1991. Childhood Events and Circumstances Influencing High School Completion. *Demography* 28:133–57.

Hayes, C., J. Palmer, and M. Zaslow. 1990. *Who Cares for America's Children? Child Care Policy for the 1990s.* Washington, DC: National Academy of Sciences.

Haynes, N. M., and J. P. Comer. 1993. The Yale School Development Program: Process, Outcomes, and Policy Implications. *Urban Education* 28:166–99.

Hedges, L. V., R. D., Laine, and R. Greenwald. 1994. Does Money Matter? A Meta-Analysis of Studies of the Effects of Differential School Inputs on Student Outcomes. *Educational Researcher* 23:5–14.

Hershey, A., N. Adelman, and S. Murray. 1995. Helping Kids Succeed: Implementation of the School Dropout Demonstration Assistance Program. Princeton, NJ: Mathematica Policy Research, Inc.

Hoffman, S., E. M. Foster, and F. Furstenberg Jr. 1993. Reevaluating the Costs of Teenage Childbearing. *Demography* 30:1–13.

Hollister, R., P. Kemper, and R. Maynard. 1984. *The Supported Work Demonstration.* Madison: University of Wisconsin Press.

Horwitz, S. M., et al. 1991. School-Age Mothers: Predictors of Long-Term Educational and Economic Outcomes. *Pediatrics* 87:862–68.

Hotz, V. J., S. McElroy, and S. Sanders. 1994. Assessing the Costs of Maternal Outcomes to Government of Teenage Childbearing in the U.S. University of Chicago. Manuscript.

Jencks, C., and S. Mayer. 1990. The Social Consequences of Growing Up in a Poor Neighborhood. In *Inner-City Poverty in the United States,* ed. L. Lynn and M. McGeary. Washington, DC: National Academy Press.

Johnson, T. R., and M. Troppe. 1992. Improving Literacy and Employability among Disadvantaged Youth: The Job Corps Model. *Youth and Society* 23:335–55.

Kantor, H., and B. Brenzel. 1993. Urban Education and the "Truly Disadvantaged": The Historical Roots of the Contemporary Crisis, 1945–1990. In *The "Underclass" Debate: Views from History,* ed. M. B. Katz. Princeton: Princeton University Press.

Kasarda, J. 1993. Inner City Concentrated Poverty and Neighborhood Distress: 1970–1990. *Housing Policy Debate* 3:253–302.

Katz, M. B. 1993. The Urban Underclass as a Metaphor of Social Transformation. In *The "Underclass" Debate: Views from History,* ed. M. B. Katz. Princeton: Princeton University Press.

Kemple, J. J., and J. Haimson. 1994. *Florida's Project Independence: Program Implementation, Participation Patterns, and First-Year Impacts, Executive Summary.* New York: Manpower Demonstration Research Corp.

Kerachsky, S. H., et al. 1985. *Impacts of Transitional Employment on Mentally Retarded Young Adults: Results of the STETS Demonstration.* Princeton: Mathematica Policy Research, Inc.

Kirby, D., et al. 1993. The Effects of School-Based Health Clinics in St. Paul on School-Wide Birthrates. *Family Planning Perspectives* 25:12–16.

Kirby, D., et al. 1994. School-Based Programs to Reduce Sexual Risk Behaviors: A Review of Effectiveness. *Public Health Reports* 109:339–60.

Kirsch, I., and A. Jungeblut. 1986. *Literacy Profiles of America's Young Adults.* Princeton: Educational Testing Service.

Kirsch, I., A. Jungeblut, L. Jenkins, and A. Kolstad. 1993. *Adult Literacy in America.* Washington, DC: Department of Labor.

Kirst, M. W. 1992. Supporting School-Linked Children's Services. In *Rethinking School Finance: An Agenda for the 1990s,* ed. A. R. Odden. San Francisco: Jossey-Bass Publishers.

Kisker, E., et al. 1989. *The Child Care Challenge: What Parents Need and What Is Available in Three Metropolitan Areas.* Princeton: Mathematica Policy Research, Inc.

Kozol, J. 1991. *Savage Inequalities: Children in America's Schools.* New York: Crown Publishing.

Krein, S. F., and A. H. Beller. 1988. Educational Attainment of Children from Single-Parent Families: Differences by Exposure, Gender, and Race. *Demography* 25:221–33.

Larner, M., R. Halpern, and O. Harkavy. 1992. *Fair Start for Children: Lessons Learned from Seven Demonstration Projects.* New Haven: Yale University Press.

Layzer, J., et al. 1982. Lasting Effects of Early Education: A Report from the Consortium for Longitudinal Studies. Monographs of the Society for Research in Child Development, vol. 47, no. 195. Chicago: University of Chicago Press for the Society for Research in Child Development.

Leibowitz, A. 1974. Home Investment in Children. *Journal of Political Economy* 82:111–31.

Lewitt, E. M. 1994. Child Indicators: Reported Child Abuse and Neglect. *Future of Children* 4:233–42.

Long, D., J. M. Gueron, R. G. Wood, R. Fisher, and V. Fellerath. 1996. *LEAP: Three-year Impacts of Ohio's Welfare Initiative to Improve School Attendance among Teenage Parents. Ohio's Learning, Earning, and Parenting Program.* New York: Manpower Demonstration Research Corp.

Long, D., R. G. Wood, and H. Kopp. 1994. *LEAP: The Educational Effects of LEAP and Enhanced Services in Cleveland: Ohio's Learning, Earning, and Parenting Program for Teenage Parents on Welfare.* New York: Manpower Demonstration Research Corp.

Lynn, L. E., and M. G. H. McGeary, eds. 1990. *Inner-City Poverty in the United States.* Washington, DC: National Academy Press.

Mallar, C., et al. 1982. *Evaluation of the Economic Impact of the Job Corps Program: Third Follow-Up Report.* Princeton: Mathematica Policy Research, Inc.

Mallar, C. D., and R. A. Maynard. 1981. The Effects of Income Maintenance on School Performance and Educational Attainment. *Research in Human Capital and Development* 2:121–41.

Manheim, L. M., and M. E. Minchella. 1978. The Effects of Income Maintenance on the School Performance of Children: Results from the Seattle and Denver Experiments. Mathematica Policy Research Discussion Paper DP–78C–01. Princeton: Mathematica Policy Research, Inc.

Martinson, K., and D. Friedlander. 1994. *GAIN: Basic Education in a Welfare-to-Work Program.* New York: Manpower Demonstration Research Corp.

Maynard, R. A. 1977. Some Aspects of Income Distribution: The Effects of the Rural Income Maintenance Experiment on the School Performance of Children. *American Economic Review* 67:370–74.

Maynard, R. A. 1980. *Supported Work: Impacts for Young School Dropouts.* New York: Manpower Demonstration Research Corp.

Maynard, R. A., ed. 1993. *Building Self-Sufficiency among Welfare-Dependent Teenage Parents.* Princeton: Mathematica Policy Research, Inc.

Maynard, R. A. 1994. The Effectiveness of Interventions Aimed at Reducing the Incidence of Teenage Pregnancy and Mitigating the Consequences of Early Childbearing. Paper presented at the annual meeting of the Association for Public Policy and Management. Mimeo.

Maynard, R. A., and R. J. Murnane. 1979. The Effects of a Negative Income Tax on School Performance: Results of an Experiment. *Journal of Human Resources* 14:463–76.

Maynard, R. A., W. Nicholson, and A. Rangarajan. 1993. *Breaking the Cycle of Poverty:*

The Effectiveness of Mandatory Services for Welfare-Dependent Teenage Parents. Princeton: Mathematica Policy Research, Inc.

McGroder, S. 1990. *Head Start: What Do We Know about What Works?* Washington, DC: Office of Assistant Secretary for Planning and Evaluation, Department of Health and Human Services.

McKey, R. H., et al. 1985. *The Impact of Head Start on Children, Families, and Communities.* Final report of the Head Start evaluation, synthesis, and utilization project. Washington, DC: Department of Health and Human Services.

McLanahan, S., and G. Sandefur. 1994. *Growing Up with a Single Parent: What Hurts, What Helps.* Cambridge: Harvard University Press.

Menacker, J. 1990. Equal Educational Opportunity: Is It an Issue of Race or Socioeconomic Status? *Urban Education* 25:317–25.

Moore, K. 1994. Trends in Teenage Childbearing. Paper presented at the seminar series on "Persistent Poverty Conference on the Causes and Costs of Teen Motherhood," sponsored by the American Enterprise Institute, Washington, DC.

Moore, K., et al. 1993. Age at First Childbirth and Later Poverty. *Journal of Research on Adolescence* 3:393–422.

Mott, F. L., and W. Marsiglio. 1985. Early Childbearing and Completion of High School. *Family Planning Perspectives* 17:234–37.

Moynihan, D. P. 1994. Presentation on Welfare Reform at the spring retreat of the Democratic National Policy Committee, Williamsburg, VA. Transcript.

Mulkey, L. M., R. L. Crain, and A. J. C. Harrington. 1992. One-Parent Households and Achievement: Economic and Behavioral Explanations of a Small Effect. *Sociology of Education* 65:48–65.

Munnell, A., ed. 1986. *Lessons from the Income Maintenance Experiments: Proceedings of a Conference Held at Melvin Village, New Hampshire, September 1986.* Sponsored by Federal Reserve Bank of Boston and the Brookings Institution. Boston: Federal Reserve Bank of Boston.

Murnane, R. 1993. *Microeconomics: A Policy Tool for Educators.* Cambridge: Harvard Graduate School of Education.

Murnane, R., and F. Levy. 1992. Education and Training. In *Setting Domestic Priorities: What Can Government Do?* ed. H. J. Aaron and C. L. Schultz. Washington, DC: Brookings Institution.

Murnane, R. J., R. A. Maynard, and J. C. Ohls. 1981. Home Resources and Children's Achievement. *Review of Economics and Statistics* 63:369–77.

Murnane, R., J. B. Willett, and K. P. Boudett. 1994. Do High School Dropouts Benefit from Obtaining a GED? Working paper, Harvard Labor Economics Seminar. Mimeo.

Natriello, G., ed. 1987. *School Dropouts, Patterns, and Policies.* New York: Teachers College Press.

NCES. 1993a. *Digest of Educational Statistics.* Washington, DC: National Center for Educational Statistics.

NCES. 1993b. *Youth Indicators 1993.* Washington, DC: National Center for Educational Statistics.

NCES. 1994. *The Condition of Education.* Washington, DC: National Center for Educational Statistics.

Nord, C., et al. 1992. Consequences of Teen-Age Parenting. *Journal of School Health* 62:310–18.

O'Conner, F., P. Madden, and A. Pringle. 1976. *Nutrition: Rural Income Maintenance Experiment, Final Report.* Madison, WI: Institute for Research on Poverty.

Odden, A. R., and L. Kim. 1992. Reducing Disparities across the States: A New Federal Role in School Finance. In *Rethinking School Finance: An Agenda for the 1990s,* ed. Allan Odden. San Francisco: Jossey-Bass Publishers.

Ogbu, J. U. 1987. Variability in Minority School Performance: A Problem in Search of an Explanation. *Anthropology and Education Quarterly* 18:312–34.

Olds, D., et al. 1988. Improving the Life-Course Development of Socially Disadvantaged Mothers: A Randomized Trial of Nurse Home Visitation. *American Journal of Public Health* 78:1436–45.

Orr, M. T. 1989. *Keeping Students in School.* San Francisco: Jossey-Bass Publishers.

O'Sullivan, A., and B. Jacobsen. 1992. A Randomized Trial of a Health Care Program for First-Time Adolescent Mothers and Their Infants. *Nursing Research* 41:210–15.

Pauly, E., H. Kopp, and J. Haimson. 1994. *Home Grown Lessons: Innovative Programs Linking Work and High School.* New York: Manpower Demonstration Research Corp.

Phillips, D., et al. 1993. Child Care for Children in Poverty: Opportunity or Inequity? Manuscript.

Polit, D., and C. White. 1988. *The Lives of Young, Disadvantaged Mothers: The Five Year Follow-Up of the Project Redirection Sample.* Saratoga Springs, NY: Humanalysis, Inc.

Quint, J., D. Polit, H. Bos, and G. Cave. 1994. New Chance: Interim Findings on a Comprehensive Program for Disadvantaged Young Mothers and Their Children. New York: Manpower Demonstration Research Corp.

Ramey, C T., and F. A. Campbell. 1990. Poverty, Early Childhood Education, and Academic Competence: The Abecedarian Experiment. In *Children in Poverty,* ed. Aletha Huston. New York: Cambridge University Press.

Ramey, C. T., and S. L. Ramey. 1992. At Risk Does Not Mean Doomed. National Health/Education Consortium Occasional Paper no. 4. National Health/Education Consortium. Mimeo.

Raywid, M. A., and T. A. Shaheen. 1994. In Search of Cost-Effective Schools. *Theory into Practice* 33:67–74.

Rhode, D. L. 1994. Adolescent Pregnancy and Public Policy. *Political Science Quarterly* 108:635–69.

Riccio, J., D., Friedlander, and S. Freedman. 1994. *GAIN: Benefits, Costs, and Three-Year Impacts of a Welfare-to-Work Program, Executive Summary.* New York: Manpower Demonstration Research Corp.

Robins, P. K. 1985. A Comparison of the Labor Supply Findings from the Four Negative Income Tax Experiments. *Journal of Human Resources* 20:567–82.

Roper, P., and G. Weeks. 1993. *Child Abuse, Teenage Pregnancy, and Welfare Dependency: Is There a Link?* Olympia: Washington State Institute for Public Policy, Evergreen State College.

Sawhill, I. 1989. The Underclass. *Public Interest* 96:3–15.

Schweinhart, L. J., H. V. Barnes, and D. P. Weikart. 1993. *Significant Benefits: The*

High/Scope Perry Preschool Study through Age 27. Ypsilanti, MI: High/Scope Press.

Smith, T. W. 1994. *The Demography of Sexual Behavior.* Menlo Park, CA: Henry J. Kaiser Family Foundation.

Stafford, F. P. 1986. Women's Work, Sibling Competition, and Children's School Performance. *American Economic Review* 77:972–80.

Stephens, S., S. Leiderman, W. Wolf, and P. McCarthy. 1994. *Building Capacity for System Reform.* Bala Cynwyd, PA: Center for Assessment and Policy Development.

Stern, D., M. Raby, and C. Dayton. 1992. *Career Academies: Partnerships for Reconstructing American High Schools.* San Francisco: Jossey-Bass Publishers.

Stern, M. J. 1993. Poverty and Family Composition since 1940. In *The "Underclass" Debate: Views from History,* ed. M.B. Katz. Princeton: Princeton University Press.

St. Pierre, R., B. Goodson, J. Layzer, and L. Bernstein. 1994. *National Impact Evaluation of the Comprehensive Child Development Program.* Cambridge, MA: Abt Associates.

Summers, A., and A. Johnson. 1994. A Review of the Evidence on the Effects of School-Based Management Plans. Paper presented at the conference "Improving the Performance of America's Schools: Economic Choices," National Academy of Sciences.

Summers, A., and B. Wolfe. 1977. Do Schools Make a Difference? *American Economic Review* 67:639–52.

Swanson, D. P., and M. B. Spencer. 1991. Youth Policy, Poverty, and African-Americans: Implications for Resilience. *Education and Urban Society* 24:148–61.

Tanner, D. 1993. A Nation "Truly" at Risk. *Phi Delta Kappan* 75:288–97.

University of Pennsylvania. 1994. *Universities and Community Schools.* Philadelphia: University of Pennsylvania.

Urbanski, A. 1993. Real Change is Hard: Lessons Learned in Rochester. Paper presented at the 1993 National Center for Research on Evaluation, Standards, and Student Testing conference "Assessment Questions: Equity Answers."

U.S. Bureau of the Census. 1991. *Fertility of American Women, June 1990: Current Population Reports, Series P20–454.* Washington, DC: Government Printing Office.

U.S. Bureau of the Census. 1993a. *Fertility of American Women, June 1992: Current Population Reports, Series P20–470.* Washington, DC: Government Printing Office.

U.S. Bureau of the Census. 1993b. *Household and Family Characteristics, March 1992: Current Population Reports, Series P20–467.* Washington, DC: Government Printing Office.

U.S. Bureau of the Census. 1993c. *Poverty in the United States, 1992: Current Population Reports, Series P20–478.* Washington, DC: Government Printing Office.

U.S. Bureau of the Census. 1994a. *The Diverse Living Arrangements of Children, Summer 1991: Current Population Reports, Series P70–38.* Washington, DC: Government Printing Office.

U.S. Bureau of the Census. 1994b. *Household Wealth and Asset Ownership, 1994:*

Current Population Reports, P70–34. Washington, DC: Government Printing Office.

U.S. Bureau of the Census. 1994c. *Marital Status and Living Arrangements, March 1993: Current Population Reports, Series P20–478.* Washington, DC: Government Printing Office.

U.S. Department of Commerce. 1987. *Who's Minding the Kids?* Washington, DC: Department of Commerce.

U.S. Departments of Education and Labor. 1995. *The Bottom Line: Basic Skills in the Workplace.* Washington, DC: Department of Labor.

U.S. Department of Labor. 1995. *What's Working (and What's Not): A Summary of Research on the Economic Impacts of Employment and Training Programs.* Washington, DC: Department of Labor.

U.S. General Accounting Office. 1987. *School Dropouts: Survey of Local Programs.* Washington, DC: Government Printing Office.

U.S. General Accounting Office. 1992. *School-Linked Human Services: A Comprehensive Strategy for Aiding Students at Risk of School Failure.* Washington, DC: Government Printing Office.

U.S. General Accounting Office. 1993. *Demographics of School-Age Children.* Publication no. HRD–93–105BR. Washington, DC: Government Printing Office.

U.S. House of Representatives. 1993. *The Green Book.* Washington, DC: House Ways and Means Committee.

Walker, E. M., and M. E. Sutherland. 1993. Urban Black Youths' Educational and Occupational Goals: The Impact of America's Opportunity Structure. *Urban Education* 28:200–220.

Walberg, H. H., and W. J. Fowler Jr. 1987. Expenditure and Size Efficiencies of Public School Districts. *Educational Researcher* 16:5–13.

Weiss, H., and F. Jacobs. 1988. *Evaluating Family Programs.* New York: Aldine de Gruyter.

Werner, E. E., and R. S. Smith. 1992. *Overcoming the Odds: High Risk Children from Birth to Adulthood.* Ithaca: Cornell University Press.

Whelage, G. G., et al. 1989. *Reducing the Risk: Schools as Communities of Support.* New York: Falmer Press.

Willer, B., et al. 1991. *The Demand and Supply of Child Care in 1990.* Washington, DC: National Association for the Education of Young Children.

Wilson, W. J. 1987. *The Truly Disadvantaged: The Inner City, the Underclass, and Public Policy.* Chicago and London: University of Chicago Press.

Wolfe, B. 1994. Externalities of Education. In *The International Encyclopedia of Education.* Oxford: Pergamon Press.

Wolfe, J. 1982. The Impact of Family Resources on Childhood IQ. *Journal of Human Resources* 17:213–235.

Wolfner, G. D., and R. J. Gelles. 1993. A Profile of Violence toward Children: A National Study. *Child Abuse and Neglect* 17:197–212.

Young, T. W. 1990. *Public Alternative Education.* New York: Teachers College Press.

Zill, N. 1994. Characteristics of Teenage Mothers. Talking points for the AEI conference "The Costs of Teenage Child Bearing." Mimeo.

Zill, N., and C. Nord. 1994. *Running in Place: How American Families are Faring in a Changing Economy and an Individualistic Society.* Washington, DC: Child Trends, Inc.

Zill, N., and C. Rogers. 1988. Trends in Indicators of Academic Achievement. In *The Changing American Family and Public Policy,* ed. A. Cherlin. Washington, DC: Urban Institute Press.

CHAPTER 6

Feedback Effects and Environmental Resources

V. Kerry Smith

Richer countries are safer, healthier places to live.[1] They pollute less and enjoy a higher standard of material well-being.[2] Several recent statistical studies have used aggregate cross-country data to suggest a causal link between level of economic activity, safety (Lutter and Morrall 1994), and the environment (Grossman and Krueger 1991). Is education the *real* source of these positive results? The answer to this question will not be found in aggregate statistical models. Evaluating the indirect, nonmarket effects of education requires detailed, microeconomic analyses of education's causal role in people's behavior. While there is extensive evidence that education and training enhance people's productivity and earnings, what we know about education's effects outside markets is much more limited.

The purpose of this chapter is to consider how education might influence the environmental quality people experience. Education could promote private behavior that enhances environmental quality for everyone or increase people's effectiveness in protecting themselves from negative environmental effects. These negative influences result from conventional externalities or unrecognized impacts of the environment on people (e.g., radon and lung cancer).

Thanks are due to Ray Kopp for collaborating in the development of the general conceptual issues associated with valuing nonmarket resources; to Jere Behrman, Winston Harrington, Nevzer Stacey, Albert Tuijnam, and Dennis Yang for constructive comments on earlier drafts; and to Paula Rubio, Terrie Rouse, and Tricia Shore for assuring that a continuously changing manuscript was completed. Partial support for this research was provided by the U.S. Department of Education and the University of North Carolina Sea Grant Program under grant R/MRD25.

1. This observation was first made by Wildavsky (1988) in considering the apparent contradiction between concerns about risk among people in developed economies and the actual risks they experience.

2. Given the concern over environmental quality in the United States and most developed economies, this comparison may seem surprising, but it is readily confirmed for air and water quality where there are reasonable monitoring data and may well be an adequate summary for hazardous substances as well. See the World Bank's 1992 report *Development and the Environment* or the United Nations Environment Programme's *Urban Air Pollution in the Megacities of the World* (1992).

In order to attribute an indirect social benefit to one of these behavioral responses, we must establish that it resulted from a causal rather than a taste-related association with education. There is *no* direct evidence of these types of connections in the environmental economics literature. Economists who evaluate people's behavior in avoiding environmental externalities or enhancing environmental quality have not tested these hypotheses.

Because there is no literature on education's role in improving environmental quality, this chapter considers three questions: (1) How should we define the social or nonmarket benefits of education? (2) Do existing studies of people's mitigating behavior, avoiding environmental hazards, offer any indirect evidence of a causal link between education and increased activities to improve the environment people experience? (3) Assuming that there might be a causal relationship between education and people's nonmarket behavior, would that connection have implications for the design and evaluation of environmental policy?

6.1. Defining Terms and Examining Trends

6.1.1. What Is Education?

Education is both a process and a set of outcomes. For the issues discussed in what follows, I am interested in what the educational process conveys to the individual. Today's students at all levels are involved in activities that enhance environmental quality, in many cases as part of their science courses. While these programs may be important as vehicles for teaching environmental stewardship, there is insufficient information about them to permit any evaluation. As a result, specific environmental education is not a focus of my analysis. Rather, the primary concern is whether the outcomes resulting from education as a whole alter people's behavior toward the environment when they leave school.

Because the outcomes resulting from education are diverse and often difficult to measure in quantitative terms, most studies of the effects of education have focused on duration and degree-based measures—years of schooling and completion of specific stages of the process (i.e., high school diploma, college degree, graduate degree, and so on). Refined outcomes such as cognitive reasoning skills, mathematical ability, or understanding of science are more difficult to measure and are usually not available. This is potentially important. If we hypothesize that education affects people's ability to protect themselves from environmental hazards or increases their understanding of the environmental system and, as a result, their concern for protecting it, then we should expect to see specific causal links to what takes place in school. That is, it seems reasonable to expect that these changes could be related to specific aspects of the educational process such as a set of environmental science modules in the primary, secondary, and college curricula. Indeed, it is a belief that these activities promote such responses that has increased their presence in instructional programs.[3]

Unfortunately, the measures available do not offer this level of resolution. This limitation has at least two implications. Finding a correlation between a general measure of education such as years of schooling and an individual's actions to improve environmental quality is more difficult to accept as a causal relationship. Equally important, the prospect of detecting these correlations is small. Years of schooling can involve many different mixes of activities and patterns of learning. There is no reason to believe all aspects of an educational program will be equally relevant to behavior that either contributes to enhancing environmental quality or promotes people's understanding of how to protect themselves from environmental hazards.

6.1.2. Social versus Public Benefits

Conventional economic discussions of the motives for public intervention arise from some type of "market failure." Externalities and public goods are the most prominent examples of these failures. To the extent that a private activity has an impact on the production process or well-being of others that is *outside* any market-determined transaction, we consider it to be an externality. When an individual acquires the skills and understanding provided through education, these may enhance the others' well-being in some way (e.g., each citizen makes "better" decisions in a democratic society). This is an external effect.

To the extent that residents of a community demand and experience welfare gains when their school systems (whether primary, secondary, or tertiary) are enhanced, then these gains may reflect some public good aspects of these educational programs. This effect is, in principle, different from what happens to each individual through education. Of course, it may well be that the reason for these "public" values arises as an ex ante expectation that the citizens emerging from enhanced educational programs will create externalities for the community in the future at the time they finish.

Nonetheless, these explanations are "stories" an analyst offers to explain a set of choices. As I argue subsequently, they do not necessarily mean that people have these values unless their choices were, in fact, motivated by them.

---

3. Indeed, the National Environmental Education Act of 1990 sought to develop educational programs and curricula that respond to the complex nature of environmental problems. The legislation notes that "effective response to complex environmental problems requires understanding of the natural and built environment, awareness of environmental problems and their origins, and the skills to solve these problems." More recently, the National and Community Service Trust Act of 1993 sought to expand community service and student service activities as part of social learning that it argued provided visible benefits to the participants in such programs and to their communities.

Why do we make a distinction between private and public benefits from education and how does the issue of social benefits enter an economic evaluation? The answers to these questions relate to two concerns. Do the conventional private returns from education, measured using education's effects on productivity and earnings, reflect the total value of education to each individual? Here the answers relate to the role of the social effects. To the extent that education enhances a person's abilities in nonmarket activities, the private-earnings-related measures would be only a partial gauge of the economic value of education *to that individual*. Omitting these effects could lead the analyst to incorrectly interpret comparisons of education's costs with its benefits measured solely from earnings effects as indicating irrational behavior. This follows because the benefit side of the comparison omits the nonmarket or social influences. Nonetheless, this type of comparison does not in itself motivate public intervention because the gains are "captured" by the individual. The only issue is one of measurement and, perhaps, testing the hypotheses implied by revealed preference.

Externalities and public goods do motivate intervention because private action alone would not necessarily assure an efficient level of the activity that contributes to these effects. Both the nonmarket private and the public good effects of education must rely on methods of nonmarket valuation to evaluate their impact. Thus, a substantial component of the discussion in this chapter will consider whether existing analyses of the demand for and value of education have adequately accounted for these potential impacts.

6.1.3.   Trends in Support for the Environment

Over the past decade, environmental quality in the United States has generally improved. It would be difficult to establish whether these types of changes were in any way linked to changes in education. There are no systematic records of household activities related to promoting environmental quality or sustaining private averting behavior over time. The only consistent long-term information about attitudes toward the environment can be found in the National Opinion Research Center (NORC) General Social Surveys. From 1972 to 1993, 19 national samples were asked the same questions about support for environmental and other programs. These consist of independent samples of English-speaking persons, 18 years of age or over, living in noninstitutional arrangements in the United States.

Figure 6.1a plots the results for four of a total of six questions derived in each of these 19 surveys. The first curve includes the average years of schooling (relative to 13 to represent high school equivalent), RAVED. The remaining curves plot the fractions indicating that we are spending too little money on improving and protecting the environment (mean env. high) and too

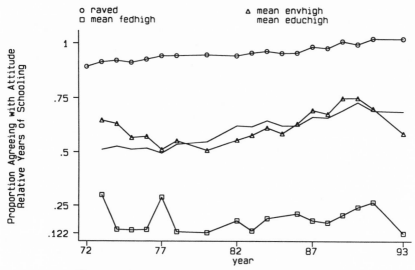

Fig. 6.1a.   Trends in attitudes and education, 1972–93

little money on improving the nation's education system (mean educ. high), as well as the fraction indicating that they had "a great deal" of confidence in those people running the executive branch of the federal government (mean fed. high). As the graph indicates, there is a slight upward trend in the years of schooling completed over the 21 years covered by these samples. Support for education is also consistent with a somewhat more pronounced upward trend. The most surprising outcome of the comparison is the decline, beginning about 1991, in those indicating that we are spending "too little" on the environment. This change is not sufficient to change a positive and significant trend in the fraction agreeing that too little is being spent over the full time period, but it is a departure in a trend that appears to have begun about 1977. This result does not seem to be related to any change in the educational levels of those surveyed and does not in itself indicate that people would be less willing to take private actions to enhance the environment. It may be the result of a decline in confidence in the executive branch of government as well as other public functions, as illustrated by the lowest line in figure 6.1a, displaying those respondents expressing "a great deal" of confidence in those running the executive branch of government. Indeed, a similar pattern arises when this type of question was asked about those running education in this country (mean educ. high) and about scientists (mean sci. high), plotted in figure 6.1b in comparison with education and the confidence in those running the executive branch (plotted again for comparison).

Thus, the overall conclusion to be drawn from these trends parallels the judgment from cross country studies. Aggregate trends in one country are

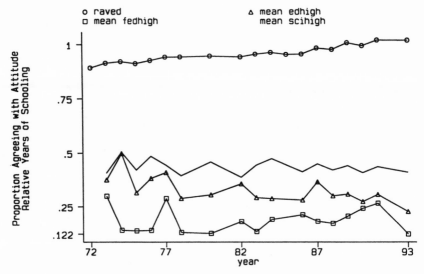

Fig. 6.1b.   Trends in attitudes and education, 1972–93

the result of complex processes. Even at the level of suggestive evidence, there is little in the trends in support for environmental programs and in the average levels of schooling over time that would imply a close link. Evaluating the prospects for these connections will require more detailed microanalyses that incorporate the reasons for connections between education and individual behavior that improves environmental quality. These conceptual and empirical issues will be the primary focus of this chapter.

6.2. Willingness to Pay for Education: The Role of Preference and Household Production Functions

6.2.1. Background

Measures of economic value are commonly understood to be constructed from people's choices. A choice defines a lower bound for an individual's willingness to pay (WTP) for any commodity—marketed or not. For example, when a person gives up one or more years of work to pursue an advanced degree, the economic value must be at least as great as what was foregone. Under ideal conditions, we expect people to adjust until the value of the last unit selected exactly equals its incremental cost. By reconstructing the implicit net "price" in this tradeoff and expressing it as a rate of return on an investment, Becker (1964) and Mincer (1974) developed a model that has been one of the key organizing frameworks for evaluating education over the past 30 years.

Education was an investment providing each individual who decided to pursue more schooling a private rate of return. This return could be estimated directly from the time profile of costs, together with foregone and final earnings (Becker), or from earnings functions (Mincer). Each approach was derived by assuming that the market experience of people "revealed" their economic values. While this model had most of its early applications in evaluating the returns to college and on the job training, it has also been extended to consider a number of policy issues, including, more recently, the effects of educational quality on the rates of return for primary and secondary education (see Behrman and Birdsall 1983; Card and Krueger 1992; and Betts 1995).

Models based on an alternative framework, consistent with revealing individual WTP for primary and secondary education, have also been developed from a completely different perspective—that of local public finance. Two approaches for estimating the demand for local education can be distinguished. The first of these, sometimes described as the "standard model," postulates a functional form for the median voter's demand for a local public good (in this case education) based on what is assumed to be the individual's (or the household's) tax rate and a measure of income.[4] With a variety of assumptions (see Oates 1994), it is possible to recover estimates of the price and income elasticities of demand by relating the per capita expenditures for the local "public good" to constructed measures for the median voter's tax rate and income. A variation on the framework relies on household surveys. This approach is sometimes referred to as the "micro" method. It can use either households' actual choices (Gertler and Glewwe 1990) or stated choices (Bergstrom, Rubinfeld, and Shapiro 1982) to estimate a representative household's preferences for different types of educational alternatives.

In comparing these three sources of information about people's willingness to pay for education, it seems natural to ask whether each approach is capturing the same type of economic tradeoff and, therefore, would imply comparable estimates for the typical individual's WTP for education. I believe the answer is *no*. These models actually measure the demands for *different* commodities.

To understand why, we need to consider the assumptions implicit in each framework, including the economic agent hypothesized to make educational decisions and the specification of education as the object of choice. With that background, it is possible to relate what can be learned from the models about the economic value of education.

---

4. These models were proposed by Borcherding and Deacon (1972) and Bergstrom and Goodman (1973) as theoretically consistent alternatives to an earlier literature that used regression models that sought to describe public expenditures per capita in a variety of different categories as a function of state and local area characteristics. The standard models usually maintain a constant elasticity demand function.

6.2.2. Interpreting Past Modeling Strategies

Two features distinguish the economic decision underlying the Becker-Mincer framework from the models used in local public finance. First, the human capital model assumes each individual decides about education, evaluating his (or her) market alternatives with added schooling in comparison with what they would be without it. In the terminology used in the nonmarket valuation literature, the model assumes that education is a *weak complement* in production to labor market time.[5] That is, if we use a Becker-Mincer estimate of the rate of return on education as the basis for computing education's social value, then from society's perspective the enhanced value of labor time (due to education) is being assumed to capture all of the relevant economic value of education.[6] Second, the basic unit of measurement for the amount of education selected is usually expressed in years of schooling or variables that identify a set of discrete intervals corresponding to the degrees received with different levels of schooling (i.e., high school, college, and so on).

In contrast to this approach, models of the demand for local education based on household surveys (and the median voter framework) shift the decision context from the individual deciding about her education to an adult deciding about the *education provided to children*. Usually this choice involves public education (certainly this is the case for median voter models). Both the object of choice and the individual making the choice are different. It is an educational system for most local public-finance applications. Demands are acknowledged to be different for people with children in comparison with those who do not have children (Wyckoff 1984) and sometimes between property owners versus renters (Oates 1994).

These differences are most often explained as the result of price effects rather than of the nature of the object of choice and what motivates each type of agent's decision. For example, in comparing the responses of households with and without children, differences in the demands for public schools are assumed to arise because the former consumes the education services, pays the tax price, and experiences the resulting net appreciation (or depreciation) arising from the mix of tax rate/educational services provided (i.e., the so-called Tiebout effects [1956]). By contrast, the household without children (or with children beyond school age) faces the tax price and experiences only the property value appreciation effects of education.

---

5. See Huang and Smith (1995) for further discussion of the production interpretation of weak complementarity as a basis for measuring the economic value of nonmarketed resources that affect production activities.

6. Becker's (1964) discussion of differences between the private and social rates of return on education focuses primarily on the subsidies and indirect costs not reflected in his estimates. No consideration was given to nonmarket effects.

To consider how an economic model conceptualizes the economic value of education to the individual hypothesized to be making educational choices, we need to consider what each model implies about the object of choice and how it is assumed to affect each individual. This shifts the focus of the analysis away from imputed net prices, the issue emphasized in the comparisons between these approaches, to all aspects of these decisions.

Consider first the Becker-Mincer labor market model. Education is represented by the years of schooling selected by each individual. This formulation implies that all sources of education are perfect substitutes (from the perspective of any market evaluation of the added value of labor time due to education) and ignores any role of education in contributing to other aspects of an individual's activities. Incorporation of quality into the Mincer earnings model (as in Behrman and Birdsall 1983), relaxes the first of these assumptions, and the use of the household production framework (HPF) broadens the second, allowing for a wider set of potential motives for the private demands for education. Within it, education can be interpreted as a "public input" to several household production activities. Indeed, this is exactly the argument made by Haveman and Wolfe (1984) in their proposed method for calculating the WTP values for nonmarket impacts.

Nonetheless, this formulation does not necessarily alter any efficiency judgment about the private decisions for education implied by the Mincer model.[7] Instead, it suggests that the labor market tradeoff may not accurately capture the complete marginal value an individual places on education. Indeed, based on Haveman and Wolfe's arguments, one might suggest that labor market estimates provide a poor lower bound for an individual's full marginal WTP. Because these values accrue to private individuals, this expansion in the sources of value for education would help to explain why individuals would select educational investments when they yield lower rates of return relative to comparable investment alternatives. However, it would not provide a basis for measuring whether education had additional social effects that might be considered "public goods."

This conclusion may be seen more directly by applying the revealed preference logic used in the nonmarket valuation of environmental resources to this model. The key elements in the economic tradeoff used to reconstruct values are given in the model's specification of the marginal rate of substitution (MRS) between education, as an argument in individual preferences, and a numeraire. To gauge the tradeoff between added education and some reference good, or numeraire, the analyst must consider all of the effects on these within

---

7. The HPF framework allows the analyst to introduce structure into the way goods, services, and time combine to yield increases in well-being. See Smith (1991a) for a discussion of other restrictions commonly used to estimate nonmarket values within this framework.

home activities. The simple "individual preferences" model has education as a private good entering in preferences with all gain from an additional "unit" captured by the individual. The HPF generalization has education exerting effects on the production of multiple final services, but they are all captured by the individual (or her household) who has invested in education. This makes the resulting expression for the MRS more complex (because it now combines the contributions of final service flows linked together through the effects of education on each) but does not necessarily imply effects outside the household (see Haveman and Wolfe's [1984] equation 3 as an example). To gauge the tradeoff between added education and a numeraire, the analyst must consider all of the effects on these within home activities.

With aggregate versions of the median voter model, the object of choice, or specification for the commodity used to represent education is *never* developed. Indeed, in most cases the price of a unit of education is also left undefined. The empirical models are based on demand specifications that allow estimates of the price and income elasticities to be recovered from per capita expenditure models.[8] The object of choice in the survey-based models is also described by responses to questions about increasing "expenditures on local public schools" together with an analyst's construction of what prices people perceive they are paying for these increases. Private benefits from enhanced education in this model are derived by families with children in the schools and by homeowners through any positive net capitalization of the local public education in their property values.

Wyckoff (1984) has argued that, after taking account of property value effects, households with no children (or with children beyond school age) have demands for local public education that are motivated exclusively by its public good characteristics.[9] Those with children in school have demands due to both the private and public components. Thus, in his framework, by sorting the sample into these two groups and assuming common underlying preferences, these different sources of demand for local public education (as a mixed good) can be distinguished. His estimates imply that the total demand (considering both the private and public components) is more inelastic than the public component. With further assumptions, they would imply that the share of WTP for local education due to the public component is about 90 percent.[10]

8. These models sometimes include constructed price measures (see Gramlich and Rubinfeld 1982 for an example).

9. Martinez-Vazquez (1981) considered local bond referenda to evaluate whether public goods effects (beyond direct private use benefits) appear to influence voting behavior. He concluded that private net benefits was a weak explanatory factor because high-income groups voted in favor of proposals that would have benefited lower-income groups.

10. This estimate assumes a locally constant elasticity demand function and computes the consumer surplus per unit of education based on the elasticity from total demand (including private

The strategy used to develop Wyckoff's estimates is comparable to the distinction drawn in the valuation of environmental resources between use and nonuse values for these resources. The former correspond to economic values attributed to in situ uses, while the latter do not require any form of observable consumption. Nonuse values correspond to the values for any pure public good service a resource provides (see Plourde 1975; and McConnell 1983). One early approach for measuring these components of total value distinguished users from nonusers.[11] The latter's economic values for improvements in a resource were assumed (by definition) to reflect nonuse values.

The only relevant definition of economic value derives from a choice. It is the *object of choice* that provides the basis for how we interpret that value. When analysts adopt a revealed preference approach to estimate people's economic values, they must focus on situations where there is some reason to observe people's decisions. The linkage between the observed decision and the underlying object of choice is then used to construct the necessary tradeoff information for estimating economic values.

To illustrate how this works, consider two of the Haveman-Wolfe (1984) estimates of the incremental WTP for education arising from its effects on nonmarket activities. The first of these is their calculation of the value of education through its impact on the attainment of "desired family size and child spacing." Their calculations estimate the marginal effect of schooling on family size and child spacing. The net changes in household time related to their activities are then interpreted in terms of the nonmarket time effects of these decisions and valued at the husband's market wage rate to estimate the marginal value. The second considers the effects of education on criminal activity. Here, these authors evaluate the years of schooling that would be *equivalent* to an additional unit of police time in a local jurisdiction in terms of its contribution to the probability of criminal apprehension and punishment. Using the dollar cost of police time, an individual's incremental WTP is imputed from these two sources. The community effect (or public good) value of the increment is derived by multiplying the estimated individual value by the number of people in the community. This approach relies on an analogy to the traditional public good logic (i.e., $n \times$ MRS, with $n =$ number of people).[12]

Neither of these estimates is an economic value for the public good effects of education. Each is a clever economic reconstruction of the values of time (household and police) in specific activities that are *attributed to* education.

---

and public components in Wyckoff's framework) and public component elasticity. See Smith and Desvousges (1986b) for the derivation.

11. See Freeman (1993) for an overview of the issues associated with defining and measuring existence (or nonuse) uses.

12. See Wolfe with Zuvek (n.d.) for an update of the Haveman-Wolfe analysis.

This attribution arises because there were models "describing" how levels of schooling influence these outcome variables. Even if the models correctly reflect an effect due to education, people did *not* make the *choice* to undertake the education in order to accomplish these goals. They are constructed values akin to what would be expected if all these activities took place in ideal markets, so that any discrepancies in implied values would create incentives for arbitrage.

Decompositions of value into use (or private good) related measures of WTP reflect only the fact that a private decision can be recorded, and it is assumed that a reason for the decision is found in the object being valued. In the Becker-Mincer human capital model this amounts to *requiring* that the exclusive basis for an individual valuing education is due to the enhanced labor market returns. By contrast, for local public finance, any recovery of components of the total value relies on observable characteristics of a household (i.e., on school-age children). These are used to identify those households with both private and public demands along with their associated "contributions" to each one's total value. Experience with these types of approaches in estimating values for nonmarketed environmental resources suggests that a more fruitful strategy may be found in specifying more completely the economic commodity of interest and how it affects people.

6.2.3. Describing Education's Role in Individual Behavior

One lesson that emerges from these past efforts is the central role of the linkages between education and other types of decisions that are used to reconstruct people's values. In this section we consider three preference specifications and describe how each might be used to evaluate connections between education and other public goods. While the primary focus of the discussion will be on how they could be used to consider the relationship between education and environmental quality (as a public good), the arguments are general. My objective is to evaluate two aspects of modeling decisions that attempt to explain the sources of "public good" values for education. First, I consider whether indirect links between education and other public goods are capable of providing one explanation for what are sometimes postulated as the "public good" services or social components of education (see, e.g., Wyckoff 1984). Second, to the extent that there is empirical evidence to support such links, I discuss whether observed behavior (or the responses captured in traditional models) could be used to estimate these public benefits.

The first model is the simplest, with a private good, X, a public good, Q, and education, E. It is given in equation 1. The additional term, θ, is a parameter included to reflect the heterogeneity in individual preferences.

Model 1

$$U = U(X, Q, E; \theta). \tag{1}$$

As noted earlier, restrictions on preferences (or physical connections due to location) link X to Q and generally provide the basis for revealed preference measures of the implicit tradeoff perceived to be involved in increasing Q. For example, weak complementarity (see Mäler 1974; and Bradford and Hilderbrandt 1977) restricts the marginal rate of substitution between Q and X to be zero when the demand for X is zero (i.e., $(U_Q/U_X)_{X=0} = 0$). A connection between Q and E would be difficult to interpret from an empirical model based on this framework. Is E serving as an indicator of differences in individual preferences (i.e., as a proxy for the unobserved sources of heterogeneity assumed to be present in θ or a component of a composite good with Q that is linked to X? Pursuing the second part of this question is easier with a more structured model, building on the household production framework and will be discussed subsequently as part of the development of model 2.

We could also simply postulate a public good element to education (though the measure used to represent E would likely be different from what has been used in most empirical studies) and argue that it was linked with Q in any relationship hypothesized to govern X. For example, Bockstael and Kling (1988) have discussed situations in which sets of public goods can be treated as weak complements with specific private goods. This would imply that the values for Q could not be recovered from individual decisions about X, without also considering E. Here, too, the distinction between a public good rationale for E and a difference in the taste for Q *due to varying levels of education* is largely an assumption. We can reinforce the assumption in empirical modeling through the ways our models measure E. The public good effects would most likely be based on community-level measures for E, while the private good is more likely to be captured with individual measures of education such as years of schooling.

The logic underlying such a restriction is that people's enjoyment of the set of Qs can only be realized if they undertake some private activity. For example, the preservation of unique artistic, scientific, or historical material can only be appreciated as "enhancing culture" if the citizens involved in such activities simultaneously attain the levels of education necessary to understand their significance. Then we take the next step (required to use a revealed preference method) and assume that for these composite gains to be realized people must be able to devote time to visiting museums and unique scientific, historical, or cultural sites.

These analytical arguments raise more general questions about how we describe commodities that have public good attributes. Are they part of more general composites that involve an array of services? And do these broader relationships condition how the group of public goods influences preferences? This point was raised, implicitly, in the discussion of the embedding question as part of a set of issues recently raised about the use of survey methods to value environmental resources.[13] Because all of these types of assumptions must be maintained hypotheses, they cannot be tested. Informal, qualitative evaluations, relying on cognitive interviews and focus groups, may provide insights into how people evaluate groups of public goods and whether they evaluate them as composites. Nonetheless, for the short term, specifying groups of public goods, including education in that group, as weak complements to a private commodity, is unlikely to offer practical empirical insights.

The second type of modeling structure, the one with the most direct empirical relevance to environmental resources, is the "household production story," and it follows the Haveman-Wolfe (1984) framework. As in the examples they identified, education is assumed to enhance production of those activities involving environmental resources. However, this effect is unlikely to be comparable with a pure public good. For this second model, we would rewrite equation 1 with more specific implicit structure on how goods, services, environmental resources, and education combine to enhance well-being as in equation 2:

Model 2

$$U = U(f_1(X_1, Q_1, E), f_2(X_2, Q_2), f_3(X_3, Q_1, E), f_4(X_4, E), \ldots; \theta). \quad (2)$$

Each $f_i(\cdot)$ corresponds to a household production activity with private goods (X_i), environmental public goods (Q_i) and education (E). The form given in equation 2 illustrates the variety of specifications that would be possible. For example, in the first household production function (HPF) a vector of private goods (X_1), a unique environmental resource (Q_1), and education contribute to production, E. That same Q_1 is seen to enhance $f_3(\cdot)$, as does education. Education could enter production relationships without Q_1, as was the case in several of the Haveman-Wolfe studies and is illustrated in my expression for the first activity. The situation described by $f_1(\cdot)$ is also analogous to their example of education's contribution to reducing crime.

Lest we get carried away with the possibilities of "storytelling," it is important to acknowledge the limitations in what can be learned from observations

13. The embedding issue was first identified by Kahneman and Knetsch (1992) as a fundamental problem in the use of survey techniques in nonmarket valuation. Support for this view was offered in some of the studies reported in Hausman (1993), notably the Kemp and Maxwell (1993) and Diamond, Hausman, Leonard, and Denning (1993) papers. By contrast, an explanation that recognizes embedding as an aggregation issue can be found in Smith (1992) and Carson and Mitchell (1995).

of people's behavior. More than 20 years ago, Mäler (1974) demonstrated that the marginal willingness to pay for *any* nonmarketed good could be expressed in terms of the price of any private good and the marginal rate of substitution between that private good and the nonmarketed good as in equation 3.

$$\text{MWTP}_Q = -\frac{\partial e(\cdot)}{\partial Q} = P_{X_i} \cdot \text{MRS}_{Q,X_i}, \tag{3}$$

where MWTP equals marginal willingness to pay for Q and $e(\cdot)$ equals the Hicksian expenditure function P_{X_i} = price of X_i.

Unfortunately, when Q is not a choice argument, there is no real basis for observing the MRS. This is where the maintained hypotheses restricting preferences and the HPF "stories" enter. They describe cases in which the decisions observed provide the analyst with sufficient information to reconstruct measures of economic value. One of the most widely used such assumptions is perfect substitution. That is, we can estimate an individual's MWTP for Q if there is a perfect substitute using the change in expenditures for the private good that accompanies any change in Q (see Smith 1991a for the details). As a rule, this restriction has been used for empirical models of averting behavior. Consider, for example, the case of a deterioration in air quality. If a household cleaning activity is a perfect substitute for air quality in completely mitigating the full effects of that pollution on people (e.g., air pollution causes increased soiling of houses, automobiles, clothing, and so on), then the MWTP would be measured by the increased cleaning expenditures required by increased pollution.[14] To the extent that education contributes to the effectiveness of such a production process, we could argue that incremental cost savings (reduced expenditures required for cleaning), because of the learning accompanying education, offer a measure of this component of education's economic value.

This connection does not imply that education is a public good. Any public action such as an information or risk communication program that is described within the averting behavior framework relies on one of the following conditions:

1. Consumers' incomplete knowledge about an environmental problem or method to reduce its effects
2. Consumers' "inappropriate" risk perceptions in comparison with experts' judgments about environmental risk
3. Cost advantages to the collective provision of information
4. Cost advantages to decentralized responses for mitigating the effects of an environmental externality

---

14. See Ridker (1967) for the first example using this basic idea for measuring the value of reducing air pollution.

In each case, education can be argued to have a complementary effect by enhancing the effectiveness of a household's private responses. To understand how the logic works, consider an example. Suppose the action to be evaluated concerns contamination of groundwater that is used as a drinking water source through private wells (see Poe and Bishop 1993). Private household action with testing and filters may be the most cost effective response, but this would require household recognition of the problem and a corresponding set of actions. The externality motivates the public intervention and education enhances the effectiveness of that intervention. The opportunity for a household to mitigate individually creates a private commodity—"clean" water from that household's perspective. If this is the least-cost response and education enhances its success, then education reduces the cost of responding to a local public "bad"—the contaminated groundwater.

A second line of reasoning, popular among environmental policymakers, is that people's risk perceptions for environmental sources of risk are incompatible with the experts' judgments.[15] In this case, too much private (and public) action is taken for some environmental problems and too little for others (because of these misperceptions). This can also be described as a type of HPF model (see Erlich and Becker 1972). Treating self-protection as an influence on subjective probabilities, with education as a factor in "improving" perceptions, allows a comparable explanation to be presented. It can either be in reducing the "incorrect perceptions" or enhancing the effectiveness of risk communication.

In all of these cases, education is not a public good. It has social consequences because it affects the performance of other private or public actions. These examples avoid the criticism that might be made of many of the Haveman-Wolfe nonmarket effects. In several of their cases, the consequences of which were also specific to the household, education enhanced effectiveness. Why, then, would this not be acknowledged by the household and reflected in its educational choices? The policy implications of the existence of these types of effects would not be to call for increased public intervention but rather a realization that more detailed models are needed to explain behavior. That is, when analysts reconstruct what those choices mean, account must be taken of these effects.

Here the externality-mitigating or cost-reducing properties of an information program create the "publicness." Education of the targeted population simply reduces the "costs" of actions taken to respond to these problems.

---

15. See Slovic et al. (1985) and the National Research Council (1989) for discussions of these discrepancies and their policy implications. Viscusi's (1993) prospective reference theory offers a different interpretation for this research, suggesting it is a reflection of the informal Bayesian formulation of subjective risk perceptions.

The last category of model for individual (or household) behavior does provide a link between education and a public good that could be interpreted as expanding its public dimension. It is given in equation 4 and requires some explanation.

Model 3

$$U_1 = U_1(X_1, q_1, h(q_1, q_2, \ldots, q_N), E_1; \theta).$$ (4)

This preference specification is intended to describe an individual identified by the subscript "1" for convenience. It includes a vector of private goods, education (treated here as a private good), and the middle terms with q_1 and the function $h(\cdot)$. The intention is to reflect a set of models describing how people's actions contribute to the availability of public goods.

The most common application in these models has been for describing charitable contributions (see, e.g., Andreoni 1989), but the implications of the models are much more general. Each person can engage in activities (or contribute) to their production. This type of action is represented here for individual 1 as q_1. The collection of all individuals' actions leads to a public good, represented here with the function $h(\cdot)$. The other arguments in $h(\cdot)$ are the activities of others. In the simplest models

$$h(\cdot) = \sum_i q_i.$$

This specification has been used for the charitable contributions literature where the total "output" of the charity is the sum of all contributors. It is also one that is frequently adopted for describing public goods that result from individual action (see Cornes and Sandler 1986, 1994; and Sandler 1992).

It is written generally in equation 4, with the function $h(\cdot)$, used to acknowledge that people's responses to the anticipated actions of others depend on how each person perceives the public good is linked to individual behavior. Vivid examples of this relationship were provided in Hirshleifer's (1983) description of the role of the function, labeled by him as a *social composition function*. More recently, both experimental (Harrison and Hirshleifer 1989) and conceptual (Cornes 1993) analysis have confirmed and extended his arguments.

How do these analytical details relate to the treatment of education as having an "indirect" public good effect through its impact on environmental quality? The answer lies in the chain of effects of education on each q_i, such as the one identified for individual 1, and then each q_i on the resulting public good represented through $h(\cdot)$. In the environmental context, does education promote environmentally "responsible" behavior? This could be the specific context for interpreting a measure of $P_X \cdot \text{MRS}_{Eq_i}(\partial h/\partial q_i)\text{MRS}_{QX}$ as an estimate of the incremental WTP of education because of its public goods effects. They arise from education's induced effects on private behavior that in turn contributes to providing a larger amount of public good.

Of course, this type of logic is not limited to private behavior that might be described environmentally responsible. Often in describing the potential for education's public good effects analysts have suggested that an informed population is likely to act more responsibly in other ways that have been associated with externalities, including actions that might take place in a public choice context (see Jimenez 1995). Nonetheless, to move from concept to practice, three connections must be measured:

A relationship describing the effect of education on the specific type of private behavior that contributes to a public good (i.e., MRS_{Eq_i})

A relationship specifying how an increment in private behavior changes the level of the public good (Hirshleifer's [1983] arguments clearly document that this relationship is important and it need not be a one-for-one relationship, $\partial h/\partial q_i$).

A function describing how the measure of the economic value varies with the amount of the public good (i.e., $P_x \cdot \text{MRS}_{QX}$).

As the next section discusses, we usually do not have the ability to completely construct this sequence for a typical household. Instead, empirical studies will reflect one or more parts of the sequence (often from different studies). Usually these types of studies report the results as suggestive of education's public good (or social values) or develop illustrative calculations by supplementing what is available with maintained assumptions in order to estimate the desired economic value (this was the strategy adopted in Haveman and Wolfe 1984).

6.3.   Implications of the Models for Measurement

Table 6.1 summarizes the issues identified in this overview of three alternative conceptual structures for describing the role of education for people's behavior. My discussion has considered the types of assumptions required to evaluate whether private decisions about education, interpreted as a private good, can have nonmarket, and especially public good, consequences. The primary focus of the applications considered (in a few simple examples) has been with respect to environmental resources because they are the source of the empirical results discussed in the next section.

TABLE 6.1. Overview of Modeling Implications

Framework	Potential Theoretical Restrictions	Education Causal or Source of Unobserved Heterogeneity	Measurement Issues	Types of Environmental Application
Model 1 (simple)	Weak complementarity; potential for cascading chain of linkages; group linkage across public goods	Difficult to establish causality with theoretical restrictions in this format and only revealed preference data (RPD)	Measuring amount of education-years of schooling versus average level of overall education; allocation of "joint" benefits	Unique or rare environmental resources in groups with education; examples include biodiversity and historic and cultural resources
Model 2 Household production functions (HPF)	Group private commodities based on a priori restrictions due to defined activities; assumes knowledge of a process; links education to activities based on assumed a priori knowledge	Likely to define rationale for causality with prior HPF restrictions and RPD	Estimating HPF functions; time allocation measures of pollution; jointness in education's role across HPF as a type of public input; and maybe jointness in other inputs confounding role of education	Mitigating exposure to pollution; recreation; self-protection and risk perception
Model 3 Public good production by individuals	Structure of Hirshleifer's Social composition function (SCF)	Comparable to simple model	Substantial data issues; measuring behavioral activities; estimating SCF	Green labeling; environmental altruism

Two of the elements in the table have not been explicitly discussed. Both of the new items relate to informal judgments about the prospects for success in addressing specific empirical questions. Thus, there seems to be little basis for an extensive discussion. The first of these involves whether the models used to describe behavior are likely to permit distinguishing education's role as a proxy for taste (i.e., an unobserved source of heterogeneity) rather than as a causal factor. My evaluation is that only in the case of household production models does this type of distinction seem likely to have reasonable chance of success.

The second measurement issue concerns questions that would need to be addressed in order to implement the models. Here my judgments are more diverse, depending on the particular framework and application to be considered. Nonetheless, there are a few common themes. The measure intended to represent education as an object of choice—whether it is specific to the individual, such as years of schooling (as in models 2 and 3), or more general, as a measure of the educational output in a community will be important to the ability to distinguish heterogeneity from causal relationships. It is also important to consider the specific measures used to describe the outcomes influenced by education and how these will be used in nonmarket benefit measurement. Without restrictive assumptions such as perfect substitution in HPF relations, estimates like those proposed by Haveman and Wolfe (1984) will not accurately reflect Hicksian WTP.

Finally, when models acknowledge a jointness, we face a problem in isolating the value attributed to education. The source of that jointness, whether with other public goods, across HPF descriptions of private activities, or due to the effect education has on people and their joint actions for a common good (i.e., Hirshleifer's [1983] social composition function [SCF]) does not necessarily affect the relevance of the issue. All sources lead to questions comparable with those found in cost allocation problems. That is, to attempt to distinguish the social benefits of education how do we allocate what might be argued to be the joint benefits due to either a composite of public goods or arising from people's actions?

The last column in table 6.1 identifies some conceptual issues that may offer opportunities for further research with greater interaction between economists who attempt to use people's behavior to value environmental resources and those interested in comparable issues for public education. The first of these is an analogy to the Baumol, Panzar, and Willig (1982) concept of a distinction in the properties of costs when they are involved in producing individual outputs separately versus producing them together. Economies of scope refer to the reduced total cost argued (in some cases) to be associated with producing outputs together. Bockstael and Kling's (1988) suggestion of weak complementarity between groups of public goods and a private commodity may well reflect a preference equivalent of this type of relationship. That is, when combined, the public goods are more valuable. Exceptional visibility and a view from the South Rim of the Grand Canyon are a pair that might be cited in discussions of environmental resources. However, one can also identify education with cultural, historic, or scientific resources. Would biodiversity be a different public good to a community with a higher overall level of education that appreciates the interconnections linking ecological resources?

Finally, there is an important omission in the analyses reviewed here, which have provided the primary basis for describing people's behavior and its implications for the value of education. They all have focused on interior solutions, considering the effects of education on MRSs. By conducting the analysis at the intensive margin of choice, these models overlook a view of education that describes economic behavior as a composite of decisions made at the extensive and intensive margins of choice. That is, there will be people who do not participate or who change their decisions to participate based on the action under study (see Bergstrom, Blume, and Varian 1986 for a discussion of this issue in the context of charitable contributions). The conditions defining decisions at the extensive margin are often referred to as individual rationality or participation constraints, and they require evaluation of total gains and losses arising from choices. For marketed commodities, these conditions define *the extent of the market.*

Together with the MRS, these two types of conditions combine to lead to measures of the benefits of a public good. As the next section discusses, in several cases empirical evaluations of information or risk communication policies have encountered both types of responses without having a unified conceptual framework. The point to be made here is that education can in principle also influence *both*—the choice over amounts of an environmental resource and whether or not to participate or be concerned about it.

6.4. Education and Environmental Resources

6.4.1. Background

To my knowledge, there have been no attempts, comparable in objectives to Haveman and Wolfe (1984) and the recent update by Wolfe and Zuvekas (n.d.), to estimate education's effects on improving environmental resources. Because education is frequently argued to be a "control" variable reflecting the influence of taste- and knowledge-related effects, the empirical studies do not claim a causal relationship.[16] Instead, they acknowledge that people with

---

16. Behrman's (1996) discussion of this issue in a general context, reflects the long-standing examples. One that is relevant to some of my discussion, by Fuchs (1982), argues that unobservables, such as differential rates of time preferences, could have been responsible for more-educated

certain amounts of education can be different in their propensities to undertake averting behavior, respond to information programs, and form risk perceptions for different types of environmental hazards.

To evaluate whether a causal argument could be made requires another look at these empirical findings. In the first subsection, I provide that overview. However, it is not a comprehensive review. Instead, I focus on four sets of research: (1) my own work on averting behavior with hazardous waste risks and the implications of information programs for averting behavior intended to reduce risks of exposure to an indoor pollutant, radon; (2) Viscusi's findings concerning the impacts of labels on people's precautionary intentions along with some of my own work on a radon risk communication program; (3) a recent contingent valuation study describing the effects of the framing of risk information about the risks of groundwater contamination; and (4) the work of Ippolito and Mathios and Kenkel concerning health information, nutrition, and behavior because the issues involved are closely aligned with some new research reported later in the section.

6.4.2. Averting Behavior and Information Policies

The logic underlying these types of models can be described within an HPF framework. Indeed, the conceptual arguments suggesting that these actions offer opportunities to observe people's values for environmental resources are widespread in the literature. Unfortunately, empirical tests using people's decisions and linking them to environmental resources have been limited. Two types of studies have been used—reports of actual averting or mitigating behaviors and stated choices in response to predefined situations. Each has advantages and disadvantages for estimating people's marginal valuations or testing the role of education in enhancing the effectiveness of public information or risk communication programs.

Studies relying on actual reports necessarily use indirect measures of the policy and/or behavior of interest. Nonetheless, the responses studied are reports of actual choices. By contrast, the stated choice studies often have greater control over the way the policy is presented and the object of choice framed to people, but this comes at the cost of the use of statements about choices that *would* be made.

The first study (Smith and Desvousges 1986a) involved both types of responses. It was based on a survey of households in suburban Boston. Conducted during the spring and summer of 1984 using a stratified sample selected from two strata, the town of Acton and the rest of suburban Boston, the survey was

---

individuals making greater health investments rather than a causal link between education and health.

designed to estimate people's willingness to pay for reductions in the risk of being exposed to hazardous waste (see Smith and Desvousges 1987). A number of different types of actual and stated response measures were collected from respondents during in-person interviews lasting nearly an hour each. Acton was oversampled because its residents had experienced several incidents in which hazardous wastes contaminated their drinking water supply.

One aspect of the information collected in the survey involved a household's decisions to undertake one of three "averting" activities during the five years preceding the survey for the sole purpose of reducing the risk of exposure to hazardous waste. These activities were: installation of water filters, purchase of bottled water, and attendance at public meetings concerning hazardous waste. Nearly 30 percent of the respondents indicated that they purchased bottled water regularly to avoid hazardous waste, 7 percent had installed water filters, and 8 percent had attended public meetings.

Probit estimates for each activity individually and for a composite (designed to measure whether a person had undertaken any one of the three types of averting behavior) indicated that attitudes concerning the degree to which hazardous waste was harmful, experience, and recent knowledge of the problem in the respondent's town as well as proxy variables for overall attitudes toward risk and the effectiveness of public mitigation were significant, and consistent with a priori sign expectations, as determinants of several of these reported actions, whether measured individually or as a composite variable. Education (measured as years of schooling) *was not.*

By contrast, when the home owners in the sample (approximately 44 percent of the sample) were asked about their willingness to move to avoid proximity to a landfill with hazardous waste, the respondents' years of schooling were a significant, positive determinant of their demand for distance. These demand-intention models included income, age, family size, and years at the address, as well as experience and attitude measures. The question providing the basis for the demand model was framed following the logic of a hedonic model (see Freeman 1993) in which home owners were told houses like their current home would vary in price depending on their distance from landfills with hazardous waste (see Smith and Desvousges 1986b).[17] This difference in findings illustrates the complexity in linking specific reported behaviors to goals that might be associated with environmental resources and then distinguishing an additional contributing factor, such as education's role, in these decisions.

There are any number of explanations for the limited nature of the factors identified in the actual behavior models. The actions are likely to be multiple purpose, and we do not know how people interpreted the original question's

---

17. Separate examples for this type of relationship using information from actual housing sales can be found in Michaels and Smith (1990) and Kolhase (1991).

request that they report only activities whose "sole purpose" was related to reducing exposure of hazardous waste. Recall of behavior, especially actions that are not important or regular, can have substantial error, and finally the categorical nature of our outcome measure limits the ability of statistical models to capture potentially important, but subtle effects.[18] With these caveats, it is not clear that the interpretation of education as enhancing people's understanding of the issues would have implied a clear-cut sign for its implied effects—either positive or negative.

To evaluate the benefits of education's role in inducing people to take action, we must first judge whether the action would be warranted by some "objective" standard. If the exclusive pathway of exposure to hazardous waste is through drinking water and the household is served from a community source, proximity between one's house and a landfill will *not* influence the pathway. Similarly, if experts judge a particular risk to be small and education has a positive, significant effect on subjective risk perceptions for that source, we must ask whether the educational effect is meaningful.[19] It may be that education heightens awareness of the source (a "good" outcome) and does not influence perceived risk greatly across individuals (a "neutral" outcome) but is found to be a significant positive influence in empirical models (a seemingly "bad" outcome) because of the type of measures of risk perception available.

Where does this leave my discussion of the conflicting results from the role of education in the first area? I believe it implies that, if we are seeking a clear interpretation that education has a social benefit due to its effects in enhancing the performance of environmental policies directed at private responses to externalities or inducing people to undertake behavior that makes "more" environmental quality available, then the cases must involve actions with unambiguous interpretation and substantial control over how the policy or activity influences the "claimed" environmental benefits.

Use of behavioral intentions for products labeled as having specific hazards defines both the context and the judgment about what is a "correct" outcome for each person. To do so requires that the analysis be based on respondents'

---

18. There was subsequent evidence of systematic recall errors as the time horizon for the summary judgment of activity is increased (see Westat, Inc. 1989).

19. Machina (1990) has argued that in evaluating the economic efficiency of allocation decisions, analysts should be prepared to intervene and "correct" risk misperceptions people form in valuing policy intervention if they are based on incorrect interpretations or incorrect use of logical methods (i.e., probability theory) with the available information on the risk. His arguments raise important questions about how consumer sovereignty affects the analyst's interpretation of "mistakes." Education presumably enters this brew by influencing the rate of mistakes. This would seem to be especially relevant to decisions involving risk, where people seem to have a very difficult time understanding probability concepts. I return to this point as a more general issue in the section 6.4.

statements about their intentions for using this hypothetical commodity. While this research may seem far afield from applications to environmental resources, Viscusi's research (see Viscusi and Magat 1987; and Magat and Viscusi 1992) was designed as part of a larger effort to evaluate information programs in implementing environmental policies (e.g., regulating the use of pesticides).

A variety of products and outcome measures were considered using both computer-assisted, mall intercept, and telephone surveys. Two outcome measures are potentially important in evaluating the role of education: (1) recognizing the warning message and (2) being able to use the information to undertake (or intend to undertake) the recommended mitigating behavior.

Under a variety of controlled conditions, Magat and Viscusi (1992) report that education enhances recognition and ability to recall warning messages (see their appendix H for specific multivariate results). Open-ended questions seeking information about the warnings yielded responses that identified the precautionary words and the prospects respondents would remember those warnings as positively related to education. While these results are related to specific types of consumer products with hypothetical labels, my risk communication experiments evaluating brochures explaining radon's risk confirm their findings (see Smith et al. 1988).

That is, by exploiting the panel design of a study intended to evaluate the effectiveness of a risk communication program, this analysis was able to consider whether different types of information materials influenced people's knowledge about radon, its risk, and how to mitigate its effects. Years of schooling was a positive and highly significant determinant of participants' scores on a quiz given after they had received the risk information treatments; it positively contributed to their learning (as measured by correctly answering questions previously answered incorrectly) and to their "correct" interpretations of the risks associated with radon and the mitigation recommendations they would make. While this study used a specific set of questions (and not the often preferred open-ended approach used in Magat and Viscusi), it involves real risks and controls over the circumstances in which learning is measured.

Thus, both of these studies would support the type of link hypothesized in the conceptual discussion between education and household production functions. However, this evidence alone does not indicate whether years of schooling increases the rate of mitigation or reduces its costs (by improving household production activities). It simply suggests that people recognize the message.

If we consider that next step, mitigation, the record is mixed with some encouraging evidence on an indirect effect. To some degree, the conclusions here overlap with activities in the health area noted in the Ippolito-Mathios and Kenkel research soon to be discussed. For these applications, there are fewer assumptions required to connect behavior (stated or actual) with education.

Viscusi's research with product warnings does *not* find a significant role for education in enhancing the effects of a warning on promoting the recommended behavior (as a stated intention). The variable, years of schooling, is a positive contributor to the behavioral intention, but it is not significant. (Viscusi, Magat, and Huber 1986). In a continuing evaluation of the panel of households' decisions, some years after the learning questions were posed, we (Smith, Desvousges, and Payne) investigated their reported mitigation and found no direct effect. That is, with a sample of 853 households that had participated in the original analysis, received radon readings, and been given differing information materials, we found there was no significant separate effect of education on mitigation. However, there *was* a significant positive effect of respondents' knowledge (measured by the score of the same individual on the quiz taken two years prior to the mitigation survey). Because education was a key determinant of the effectiveness of information programs in conveying the correct messages, these results would suggest the types of impacts outlined in the HPF model.

Nonetheless, it is important to acknowledge that these effects need not be uniform for all people. That is, if people already know about radon, its risks, and the mitigation options, then the information programs do not change their knowledge base. They may well choose not to do anything about it. Hence, for these people, education, by enhancing their effectiveness in test scores but not their choices (stated or actual), would not yield indirect benefits. This conclusion reinforces the distinction between the effects of education on participation and marginal conditions in describing its indirect benefits. Unfortunately, the data available do not permit measuring the cost of the activities to the people involved. Thus, an incremental tradeoff, similar to that suggested by Haveman and Wolfe (1984), is not possible. The next two sets of research would allow some version of this type of tradeoff, but neither is ideal.

The first is a contingent valuation study focused on how risk information was presented to respondents. The design relies on the Smith and Desvousges (1987) study of people's willingness to pay for reducing the risk of exposure to hazardous wastes. Using a split-sample design, Loomis and DuVair (1993) evaluate whether the method used to explain a proposed risk reduction (i.e., a risk ladder versus pie charts) influences respondents' willingness to purchase plans (identified with different costs) to reduce risk. The most interesting aspect of the findings for judging the effects of education is the *differential* impact of education on a stated behavior (i.e., purchasing a program to reduce exposure to risk) using the two different information approaches. Education is a highly significant, positive influence on the likelihood of supporting the plan when a more complex, compound lottery format (involving pie charts) was used. It was a positive, but insignificant influence when a single risk measure, with a risk ladder, was used. If we interpret education's role as permitting increased understanding of the object of choice in the complex case and not necessarily important to the questions posed in the other subsample, then the behavioral link suggested by the mitigation results described previously would appear to be present for decisions in which both prices and information matter.

The last set of research returns to actual behavior in a health-related context and considers the effects of information on continuous measures of activity. The reason for considering it here is to evaluate whether education would influence both the decision to undertake activities and the amount of those activities.[20] The results from Ippolito and Mathios (1990, 1989) suggest that education may be enhancing the effect of fiber information available through cereal ads on the amount of fiber consumed as a result of a person's cereal choice. Their analysis uses the difference in these fiber consumption patterns before and during a period when cereal manufacturers were permitted to use fiber-related health claims in their advertisements. Education is a significant determinant of the selected fiber content in cereal in each of the two periods studied. Its estimated effect increased on fiber consumption for the period with the fiber-health claims, but these differences would not be judged as significantly greater than those for the period before the advertisements. Moreover, the results relate to two *different* samples of women with somewhat different educational levels (12.72 years of schooling for the sample before the advertising and 12.84 after). Supporting evidence is also available in their summary of the fiber consumption of women based on the *USDA Continuing Survey of Food Intakes by Individuals* in the same years when it is decomposed by education (Ippolito and Mathios 1989). This comparison indicates significant differences in fiber consumption between 1985 and 1986 for those with some college (i.e., 13–15 years of reported schooling) but no significant differences at other educational levels.

Perhaps the strongest evidence of an interaction effect is found in Kenkel's (1991) study of the interaction effects of knowledge of the "harms" posed by smoking and drinking and the benefits of exercise with the level of education as a differential factor influencing reported behavior. As in the work associated with radon, Kenkel uses respondents' answers to questions about each source

---

20. Separate analysis of these mitigation decisions of households in the New York panel study, considering their dollar expenditures, have a number of problems. Because the activities do not have well-defined prices (i.e., the radon mitigation must be adjusted to the characteristics of each house) it was not possible to obtain meaningful price measures. Equally important, the actions involved a mix of private home owners' activities and monetary expenditures. The latter can include equipment that serves multiple objectives (e.g., a new furnace ventilation system). Finally, the mitigation reports included a limited number of observations reporting expenditures exclusively for radon reduction. Thus, there are reasons to question what can be learned from the monetary expenditures data. A tobit analysis was consistent with these reservations. The overall signs of effects identified with the discrete classification of activities were consistent, but few of the variables would have been judged statistically significant by conventional criteria.

of health effect to measure knowledge and then investigates, using interaction terms, education's additional influence for each type of behavior (i.e., cigarettes per day, alcoholic drinks in the past two weeks, and minutes of exercise in the past two weeks). He interprets a significant interaction effect between a knowledge measure and education as supporting a differential effect of education. For example, education enhances the impact of knowledge about the ill effects of smoking, and that increase in impact is unlikely to be taste related.

There are two problems with these results. The first arises with the interpretation of a knowledge variable as a measure for what an information program would accomplish. The second is recognized by Kenkel but not fully developed in his results. That is, it concerns the separate effect of education on knowledge. Education influences both knowledge and behavior, so the interaction effect may simply reflect simultaneity in Kenkel's knowledge and behavior variables. Because both variables are based on reports elicited *after* the learning and the activity studied have taken place, they may well be jointly determined.

Equally important, Kenkel's argument that an interaction effect of knowledge can distinguish causality from taste assumes a fairly simple relationship. As the earlier work suggests, there is clear evidence of a link between knowledge and policies in more controlled settings, but it is difficult to establish the "knowledge equivalent" of a policy. Simple interaction effects do not in themselves distinguish taste from the role of education in enhancing the effectiveness of an information program. They could reflect the need for a more detailed specification. Indeed, these interaction effects were significant and *incorrectly* signed (if the argument is intended to suggest that they provide evidence of the complementary effects) with two of the three other activities using his male subsample. Simultaneity between knowledge levels and the activities studied also poses a potential problem in interpreting these interaction effects. Unfortunately, Kenkel does not report enough information to resolve matters. Models based on estimates adjusting for simultaneity are reported, but they do not include the interaction terms.

The lessons from my selective review of links between education and people's behavior in learning about sources of environmental externalities, and what the people can do to protect themselves from these hazards, confirms education's role in enhancing learning. Both specific information (Smith et al. 1988) and general reports (Viscusi, et al. 1986) suggest that the number of years of schooling improves the transmission of information from brochures and labels.

Education also seems to increase the likelihood of undertaking behavior because of this *enhancement in knowledge.* Thus, the effect is unlikely to be taste related, but it may also be possible to accomplish this increase in the effectiveness of information programs in other ways (i.e., with different information messages, as in Loomis and DuVair 1993). Moreover, education's impact on the amount of effort devoted to mitigation has not been unambiguously established with models based on actual behavior. At this point, the empirical findings are suggestive "hints" about an association. To extend the link beyond this point would seem to require more control than is usually available. To illustrate whether such a strategy can be successful, the next section summarizes the findings from an earlier evaluation of a public information program about radon (Desvousges, Smith, and Rink 1992) and a reanalysis of those results to determine whether the complementary effects of education could be detected using actual behavior and the experimental controls that were present as part of an evaluation of that program.

6.4.3. Some New Evidence on Education and Averting Behavior

This section describes the results of an extension to Desvousges, Smith, and Rink (1992) investigating education's interactive role with information programs and controlling for knowledge as well as other economic and demographic effects. The context of this evaluation is a panel study designed to evaluate two different risk communication programs intended to increase the likelihood that home owners would test their residences for radon. Three communities in Maryland were selected for that evaluation. All had high reported levels of radon and similar socioeconomic characteristics. Table 6.2 identifies the treatment and control communities and describes the characteristics of the two programs—an extensive program in Frederick and a more modest campaign in Hagerstown. Unfortunately, the control that can be exercised in "real world" experiments is limited. Moreover, confounding effects can arise independent of experimental controls. Independent of our study, a Washington, D.C., television station (WJLA) launched an information campaign during the same time period consisting of public service announcements about radon and a prime-time special. Because this activity had its primary effects on Hagerstown and Frederick, *not* our study's control community, this independent effort confounded our ability to unambiguously evaluate the impact of our controlled program, but it does not affect the objective of gauging education's causal role with information programs. As table 6.2 indicates, the WJLA program appears to have had its greatest effect on the community that also received the most extensive risk communication campaign.

Baseline surveys were conducted in each city prior to each program (December 1987), to obtain information about attitudes, knowledge, prior radon testing, and demographic information for each subsample. A random-digit-dialed survey screened the initial sampled telephone numbers to be sure they were associated with owner-occupied dwellings and obtained a listing of adult decision makers. We randomly selected one of these identified decision makers and conducted a baseline and follow-up (after the program) interview with that

TABLE 6.2. Design Features of the Maryland Public Information Program

Community	Role in EPA Test	Elements of Treatment[a]			Impact of Independent WJLA Program[b]	Sample Size	
		Media	Mailings	Outreach		Baseline	Follow-up[c]
Randallstown	Control	None[d]	None[d]	None[d]	10 kits	495 (48)	307 (78)
Hagerstown	Modest media campaign	Five different public service announcements (PSAs) on three radio stations every two weeks; project-designed posters ran in newspaper one week in February; four additional articles in paper	Pamphlet inserted in utility bills during February-March billing cycle	None	93 kits	529 (64)	432 (82)
Frederick	Extensive media campaign	Five different PSAs on two radio stations every two weeks; five of eight articles in local newspaper were project related	Pamphlet inserted in utility bills during February-March billing cycle	Four posters in locations around town; nine presentations to community groups between January and March 1988; organized Radon Awareness Week; arranged for mayor and alderman to monitor their homes	669 kits	523 (56)	432 (83)

[a]The primary messages emphasized in the public service announcements (PSAs), posters, public meetings, etc. were: (1) Radon is a serious health risk. *You* may be at risk. The only way to find out is to test. (2) Testing is easy and inexpensive. (3) Radon problems can be fixed.

[b]Independent of the EPA Project, a Washington, D.C., television station, WJLA, conducted a month-long campaign to encourage people to test their homes for radon during January and February of our study period. The campaign had multiple components, with coordination by television and newspapers, and availability of radon test kits at a reduced price at Safeway Supermarkets. The campaign began on 12 January 1988, included a three-part news series during the week of 18 January, and ended with another three-part series during the week of 15–19 February. Advertisements for the effort appeared in the *Washington Post* and on television. One hundred thousand radon tests kits were purchased, with 70,000 returned for analysis. Television ratings indicated an audience of 76,000 viewers. The television programs targeted the Washington, D.C., viewing area. Residents of Frederick were most likely to watch the station airing the programs. Hagerstown residents could view WJLA, but reception is poor without cable. Randallstown is outside the viewing area, but reception is good. Numbers refer to the radon test kits returned from each community.

[c]The numbers in parentheses beside the sample sizes are the response rates in percentage terms. For the details of how they were computed, see Desvouges, Smith, and Rink 1989.

[d]*None* refers to the fact that there were no project-initiated information materials presented in public media mailings or meetings. Some independent articles did appear in a local newspaper.

person. This follow-up interview took place in April 1988.[21] Table 6.3 includes the response rates for the two surveys and the sample sizes for each community and interview.

The panel design of the study, together with the experimental variation in the risk communication programs, allows the separate effects of education on

TABLE 6.3. Testing Education's Role with the Maryland Risk
Communication Experiment: Probit Analysis

Independent Variables	Full Sample	Greater Than High School	High School or Less
Intercept	−3.072*	−4.113*	−3.422*
	(−7.50)	(−4.99)	(−2.80)
Years of schooling	.007	.066	.063
	(0.25)	(1.32)	(0.60)
Family Income	.050	.065	.028
(in thousands)	(1.45)	(1.50)	(0.46)
Health Attitude[a]	.195†	.078	.361†
	(1.62)	(0.51)	(1.80)
Identified TV[b]	.156	.127	.167
	(1.28)	(0.79)	(0.85)
Know[c]	.239*	.229*	.244*
	(6.17)	(4.48)	(3.86)
Improve[d]	.230*	.183†	.253*
	(3.61)	(1.81)	(2.97)
Frederick (=1)	.418*	.659*	−.025
	(2.61)	(3.28)	(-0.09)
Hagerstown (=1)	.082	.163	−.175
	(0.46)	(0.71)	(-0.61)
Pseudo R^2	.148	.160	.152
n	1,132	633	499

Note: The numbers in parentheses below the estimated coefficients are Z-statistics based on the estimated asymptotic standard errors for the null hypothesis of no association.

[a] This is a qualitative variable (0,1) for a health attitude question asked during the baseline overview. It asks respondents to describe themselves in terms of the statement: "I ask my physician a lot of questions about my health." The question asks the respondent whether the following things are true always, often, sometimes, or never. Those answering always or often were coded as health concerned (1) and otherwise as less concerned (0).

[b] This variable attempts to take account of the effects of the WJLA radon information program. Because these efforts were largely related to public service announcements on TV, a qualitative variable coded as one for those individuals identifying TV as the source of their information and zero otherwise.

[c] "Know" is a count of the correct answers for the seven questions asked during the baseline interview.

[d] "Improve" is the proportionate change in the number of correct answers between the baseline and follow-up interviews. This is interpreted as the effect of the program on learning.

* Significantly different from zero at least at the 5 percent level.
† Significantly different from zero at least at the 10 percent level.

---

21. There was also an independent sample collected after the public information programs were conducted in each town to evaluate the potential for sensitization of respondents in the panel sample due to the baseline survey. These results did not appear to be important (see Desvousges, Smith, and Rink 1989).

learning and then mitigation to be evaluated. The outcome variables used in this analysis are learning measures and mitigation in the form of conducting a home radon test. The latter was a key objective of the communication program—to promote testing and self-protection where it was needed.

The original analysis of this experiment focused on attitude change, learning, and testing as measures of the results of each program. There was no attempt to evaluate whether education enhanced either program's effectiveness. Our earlier conclusions on the mitigation decisions were that the concentrated media campaign (in Frederick) did significantly increase testing but the modest media campaign did not lead to any difference from the control community in radon testing. Moreover, the sensitization associated with the survey activity itself did not alter these general conclusions.

My reanalysis of these data focused on distinguishing the effects of education through learning versus its direct impact on program effectiveness using the new testing decision as the outcome measure. Tables 6.3 and 6.4 report these results based on probit and ordinary least squares models with the panel sample pooled across the three communities. There is clear evidence

TABLE 6.4.   Education's Impact on Learning: The Maryland Risk
Communication Experiment

Independent Variables	Full Sample	Greater Than High School	High School or Less
Intercept	.448*	1.192*	−.939†
	(2.09)	(−3.67)	(−1.91)
Years of schooling	.008	−.034	.107*
	(0.74)	(−1.46)	(3.00)
Health attitude	.061	.024	.112
	(1.07)	(0.33)	(1.27)
Age (in years)	−.004*	−.004	−.001
	(2.14)	(−1.59)	(−0.44)
Male (=1)	−.153*	−.142†	−.138
	(2.62)	(−1.89)	(−1.51)
Identified TV	.090	.016	.159†
	(1.55)	(0.22)	(1.76)
Frederick	.118†	−.004	.317*
	(1.64)	(−0.05)	(2.59)
Hagerstown	.122†	.163†	.141
	(1.67)	(1.72)	(1.21)
Pseudo R^2	.015	.018	.046
n	1,315	721	594

Note: These estimates are based on ordinary least squares with the dependent variable defined as the proportionate increase in the count of correct answers to a seven-question multiple-choice quiz, asking the same respondent about radon's effects, home testing, and mitigation. The numbers in parentheses below the coefficients are t-ratios for the null hypothesis of no association. The variables are defined in table 6.3.

  * Significantly different from zero at least at the 5 percent level.
  † Significantly different from zero at least at the 1 percent level.

of education's complementary effect with risk communication programs on people's home testing decisions. Indeed, the initial analysis overlooked an important component of this effect by failing to allow for this complementarity.

Table 6.3 considers the effects of selected attitude and demographic variables on each respondent's decision to test his (or her) home for radon *after* the risk communication program is completed.[22] The first column reports a somewhat different specification than that originally reported in Desvousges, Smith, and Rink (1992), changing the treatment of information available through television (the WJLA effect) and introducing a specific learning variable measured by the percentage of improvement on a seven-question quiz given during the baseline interview and then again in the follow-up interview. Concerns about health, initial knowledge, learning, and the qualitative variable identifying the more extensive program were all significant positive influences on these people's decisions to test. While the learning effect was not recognized before, measures for the remaining variables were reported in that earlier analysis. Education has no apparent separate effect with this model. However, we never considered the possibility of a complementary effect with the program.

The next two columns divide the sample into those respondents with more schooling than high school and those with a high school education or less. Here we begin to see the potential for interaction effects. The intensive information program has a differential impact for *only* those respondents with more than a high school level of schooling. This would suggest that the complementary effects are selective, depending on the level of education and potentially the type of activity involved.

However, this is not the end of the story. Based on the earlier conceptual argument, as well as the Viscusi et al. (1986) and Smith et al. (1988) results, we would also expect to see an impact of the risk communication programs on learning. Under this hypothesis, some of the effect captured in the learning measure would be due to any indirect effect of the communication programs. Table 6.4 tests this hypothesis using a regression analysis of the learning measure, "improve," as a function of demographic and program-related variables. The first column reports the full sample. The second and third columns provide the same two subsamples (i.e., greater than high school education and high school or less) as considered in describing radon testing decisions.

These findings are important to the earlier conclusions (i.e., Desvousges, Smith, and Rink 1992). By failing to take explicit account of learning, our

---

22. This outcome measure is a *new* decision to test for radon. The panel survey was evaluated three ways—without the home owners' reporting that they had undertaken tests in the baseline survey, adjusting for prior tests as a selection effect, and the current method that treats them as unaffected by the program. All three approaches yield comparable conclusions about the complementary role of education. The current method was selected because it makes the impact "most difficult" to isolate and offers the largest sample for disaggregated analysis.

evaluation of each program overlooked the potential for differences in the direct and indirect impacts with education. These new findings indicate a small effect of the media-only program (Hagerstown) on testing through enhancements in people's learning.

More specifically, it appears that the more extensive program has its greatest effect on learning for those respondents with a high school education or less. The WJLA television-based program also enhanced learning for this group. Within this group, there is also a separate effect of years of schooling. By contrast, in those households with greater than high school education, there appears to have been a learning effect due to the media-only format. The primary effect of the extensive program (Frederick) takes place directly in inducing them to undertake home testing once they already know about radon.

6.4.4. Implications

Three cases were distinguished in developing a model that would permit estimation of education's social value: (1) education as a public good complementary with other public goods (i.e., the preference equivalent of economies of scope); (2) education as a private good that improves the effectiveness or reduces the cost of programs intended to promote private actions mitigating public bads; and (3) education as a private good that induces people to pursue activities that contribute to public goods.

This section concerned the empirical evidence on these types of relationships linking education to environmental resources. To my knowledge, there has been no research on the first type of relationship.[23] The last requires an external, generally agreed-upon set of private activities that actually contribute to an environmental public good. Private efforts at recycling or in the definition of eco-labels illustrate the difficulties in making judgments about what is in fact "environmentally good," private behavior (see Menell 1993). To pursue this line of research further would also require that there be general recognition and acceptance that these activities were consistent with producing improved environmental quality. There did not appear to be examples that would meet these criteria.

As a result of these constraints, the bulk of this section was devoted to a selective review of the literature on averting and mitigating behavior models to gauge whether a complementary role for education (separate from taste effects)

---

23. Three studies, Cummings, et al. (1994), Hoehn (1991), and Hoehn and Loomis (1993) have considered how people's responses to valuation questions are influenced by the sequencing of changes in closely related environmental public goods. This research seeks to evaluate the effects of contemporaneously provided public goods due to substitution and complementarity relationships that may exist between the goods. See Madden (1991) and Carson, Hanemann, and Flores (1994) for discussions of the conceptual rationale for these types of tests. Because education's public good effects are presumably long-term impacts, this type of contemporaneous effect seems unlikely.

could be established. The available results seem to suggest a complementary role in learning tasks. The level of education enhances the effectiveness of information and risk communication programs in increasing people's ability to learn. No separate complementary effect of education has been detected for precautionary activities with either the environmental or health issues. Part of the reason for this conclusion (in the environmental research) was that few of the studies were looking for these types of effects. Education was largely a control variable. Distinguishing the effects of education as a proxy for taste rather than a causal factor was not important to the objectives of that research. Moreover, the level of control necessary to do so seems beyond most of this past research.

The last part of this section then asked whether it would be possible to evaluate the potential for a complementary role when there was sufficient control available in the research design. Here the discussion offers one example— a reexamination of an early risk communication program for home owners' decisions to test for radon. The results were surprising. In contrast with earlier conclusions, not only were the effects of the risk communication programs more detailed and complex than originally concluded, but the complementary role of education seems to help in explaining them. For this one example, then, there appears to be an effect of education in enhancing learning *and* a separate effect in promoting action.

6.5.   Environmental Policy Design and Evaluation

6.5.1.   Speculations on Education's Impact on Environmental Policy

To the extent that education plays a role in influencing people's performance in market and nonmarket tasks, recognition of these impacts should alter policy. This implication is simply an extension of Blinder and Rosen's (1985) recognition of the importance of heterogeneity for the design of tax policies (i.e., creating "notches" or budget discontinuities to target the distortionary effect of these policies).

Targeting policies, based on other criteria, are not new. Differential policies for large and small firms, minority groups, gender groups, age groups, and so on have been developed to achieve policy objectives related to these groups. Targeting based on educational levels has generally been regarded as more difficult because of the transaction costs of identifying and separating the groups.

A better understanding of how education serves as a complementary resource, enhancing the effectiveness of environmental and other policies, may change this preconception. Moreover, to the extent that differentiated programs already exist (or would need to be developed to meet declining educational levels among large segments of the population), then direct efforts to promote enhanced education offer a substitute for these program adjustments.

There is another way in which policy design is affected by education. In a democratic society, to the extent that the public has unwarranted fears of any phenomenon—such as the risks arising from exposure to hazardous wastes— and policymakers direct resources to mitigate these problems (and away from more serious hazards according to "the experts"), then one might argue that education could improve the allocation of public resources by changing the perceived fears driving the policy agenda.

This suggestion is not a random speculation. The disparities between expert and public evaluations of environmental risks has been argued to provide the reason why the EPA's policy initiatives appear inconsistent with technical risk estimates. Indeed, the EPA's Science Advisory Board identified this disparity in beliefs between experts and laypersons as a central problem facing the agency in its policy making.[24] Education is related to subjective risk perceptions, and there is now wide appreciation in economics of the importance of the cognitive problems that can arise when people consider environmental risks. However, to evaluate the full consequences of this misperception requires the definition of a standard. Someone must specify the "right risk perception" for each person.

Subjective risk perceptions are the result of both an understanding of the process giving rise to risk and individuals' preferences (e.g., judgments of the importance to that individual of what is at risk). Thus, we cannot be sure that stated risk perceptions are "mistakes" due to cognitive errors in interpreting risk information or simply reflections of preferences. To alter the latter as a correction would abandon consumer sovereignty. Nonetheless, because there are very large discrepancies between public and expert perceptions for important sources of risk, there is certainly scope for improved efficiency without necessarily defining a "best" subjective risk perception for each person. Education's role in reducing simple cognitive errors and information limitations would no doubt lead to substantial gains before entering into discussions that could be argued as questioning consumer sovereignty. Unfortunately, beyond identifying the issues and empirical research on risk perception processes (e.g., Viscusi 1993; and Smith et al. 1990), there has been no research on how enhanced education might influence the policy agenda.

6.5.2. Education and Policy Evaluation

Information is essential in evaluating any policy activity. There has been increasing recognition of how education is impacting the collection of information

---

24. The EPA Science Advisory Board report that started these activities—*Unfinished Business: A Comparative Assessment of Environmental Problems* (1987) contributed to changing the agency's approach to evaluating its policy goals.

from surveys. At the simplest level, average reading skill among the U.S. population (currently at about the seventh-grade level) limits the methods used to both convey information and collect it.[25] Thus, to the extent that mailed surveys are used to collect information for policy evaluation, education has a long-term effect on the types of information that can be collected using this format.

To my knowledge, there is little direct evidence on the effects of education on response rates and survey administration. There is a developing set of literature indicating that the cognitive effort devoted to answering attitude and related questions is influenced by educational attainment. Krosnick (1991), for example, suggests that the likelihood that respondents will adopt "satisfying" approaches to answering questions (i.e., offering answers that appear acceptable but do not result from a thoughtful evaluation of the issues posed) will be inversely related to the respondents' cognitive sophistication. This sophistication is described in Krosnick's and others' work as an ensemble of abilities associated with retrieving information from memory and integrating it into verbally expressed summary judgments. These skills are related to *both* innate factors and learning experiences.

Thus, education can, in principle, affect who participates in surveys designed to collect information used in policy evaluation as well as the quality of the responses they provide. In short, it contributes to the measurement error in the economic models we use to evaluate programs and policy outcomes. In the long term, these errors are influenced by the educational level (and associated cognitive skills) of the population providing that information. Thus, we have short-term effects on the design of mechanisms to collect information comparable in its role to the design of policies as responses to existing educational levels.

There is also a longer-term return to education for both policy and evaluation. These influences may be especially relevant to environmental policies in which the issues involved are complex and require detailed understanding of the interactions within ecosystems and between people and their environment. Educational constraints may well limit the ability to convey information about such complex policy issues. A few examples illustrate the dilemma. Decisions about biodiversity and species loss, climate change, and the long-term hazards posed by alternative management policies for high-level nuclear waste require extensive technical information to appreciate their short- and long-term implications. Informed choices cannot be made without an understanding of the technical issues involved. In these areas, one might ask whether education

---

25. A recent study of adult literacy in the United States sketches an even more discouraging picture, suggesting that language barriers and insufficient education are important barriers to such common tasks as "writing a letter about a billing error or calculating the length of a bus trip from a schedule" (see Kirsch et al. 1993).

imposes a constraint on the ability to rely on consumer sovereignty in such large-scale choices (see Ecosystem Valuation Forum 1992; and Weitzman 1992, 1993; for more technical arguments).

6.6.   The Environment's Role in Education's Social Benefits: Next Steps

More than 30 years of empirical research on the impact of education has focused the greatest attention on its private returns. While social returns to education have been informally acknowledged for most of this time, systematic efforts to estimate these benefits have been limited. This overview of the relationship between education and efforts to enhance environmental quality has identified a more general set of questions associated with developing measures of education's social benefits. Past efforts to explain the demand for education have used two quite different specifications for education as an object of choice or an economic commodity. One focuses on years of school and each individual's choice to pursue increased education. Within this framework, social benefits have been defined as a composite of the effects of education on that individual's nonmarket activities and any private decisions that relate to social objectives. These linkages are best described in a household production framework in which education *must be* considered an input that has a causal role in improving the effectiveness of these activities. The classification of activities based on their relationships with private services or public goals determines whether this causal link would imply a public benefit.

The second approach measured the object of choice attributed to education as some type of average level of activity for students within an educational system. Usually these evaluations focused on primary and secondary education, but the same logic could be applied to public higher education. The only attempt to distinguish social from private benefits in this context was based on the attributes of households (e.g., presence of children and capitalization effects) in comparison with those without the possibility of these sources of private gains.

Using either approach to construct separate measures for the social benefits of education requires the analyst to compose what is taken to be the object of choice motivating people's decisions. This strategy is *the* accepted paradigm for revealed preference approaches to economic analysis. Results are evaluated, in part, by how much can be inferred from extremely limited information.[26] An alternative strategy would suggest that the analyst should begin by determining

---

26. A vivid example of this tendency can be found in Fuchs's foreword to Mincer's classic study (1974) of experience and earnings. Fuchs observes: "In the pages that follow Mincer demonstrates his skill as a wielder of Occam's razor. His objective is to explain a great deal with a little" (xiii). What he does not say is whether the explanations are consistent with what people believed they were doing when they made those decisions.

how people conceive of education as an object of choice. While there are limits to what can be learned from this approach, the literature seems to be in little danger of reaching the point of diminishing returns. No economic research has considered this option.

Why might it be important, given the prospect of success with the alternatives? The reasons arise in the role attributed to education and measures of economic value. The conventional strategy relying on cost savings due to education's role in improving households' abilities to accomplish tasks that are related to private or public goals imputes values to each of these savings by considering a substitute for what was accomplished with education. Education is a means to some other objective. It enhances private activities or improves public mechanisms (i.e., public information or risk communication policies), but *no independent role can ever be detected.* This follows because maintained assumptions are required to link education to the activities in the first place. Even if people appreciate these connections, they may have other objectives (unrelated to private returns) for supporting public education.

These more general efforts should be regarded as requiring longer-term research programs. In the short term, there does appear to be a significant role for education as a complementary factor in improving the performance of public information and risk communication related to environmental resources. With the increasing complexity of environmental resource problems, programs to communicate information about environmental resources seem likely to play a growing role in future environmental policy design and evaluation. Because of these trends, it would be desirable to consider opportunities for short-term research insights from investigating links between education and these past policy initiatives.

Over the past decade, the Environmental Protection Agency sponsored a substantial program of research on public information and risk communication. These efforts involved job-related risk, product labeling, indoor radon, food safety (i.e., pesticide residues), siting decisions involving undesirable land uses, recycling, and others. In some cases, the studies had a specific component designed to evaluate the effectiveness of the policy interventions being considered. To my knowledge, none of these efforts attempted to evaluate how education might have enhanced programmatic objectives or if the policies could be designed to reflect the effects of education on people's responses. My reanalysis of one of these earlier research efforts indicates evidence of a complementary role for education "waiting in the responses" that was never observed because the researchers did not look. Equally important, there are new initiatives, such as the EPA's Toxic Release Inventory, that make emission information generally available to the public. These programs could be leading to changes in community response activities that differ by education levels. Such differences in education may offer a natural experiment to further investigate these complementarities, provided causal and taste-related effects can be separated.

In all of these efforts, it is important to distinguish social from public values, where the latter are assumed to arise from public goods. There is also a need to distinguish value from monetary benefit. Reconstructions of imputed cost savings due to measures of education's effects on household or policy performance do not mean that people would, in fact, pay these amounts for the education. They are an analyst's imputation. Measuring willingness to pay from these implicit decisions requires that people recognize the objects of choice in ways that are consistent with what analysts assume.

REFERENCES

Andreoni, J. 1989. Giving with Impure Altruism: Applications to Charity and Ricardian Equivalence. *Journal of Political Economy* 97:1447–58.

Baumol, W. J., J. C. Panzar, and R. D. Willig. 1982. *Contestable Markets and the Theory of Industry Structure*. New York: Harcourt Brace Jovanovich.

Becker, G. S. 1964. *Human Capital*. New York: Columbia University Press.

Behrman, J. R. 1996. Conceptual and Measurement Issues. Chapter 3 of this volume.

Behrman, J. R., and N. Birdsall. 1983. The Quality of Schooling: Quantity Alone is Misleading. *American Economic Review* 73:928–46.

Bergstrom, T. C., L. Blume, and H. Varian. 1986. On the Private Provision of Public Goods. *Journal of Public Economics* 29:25–49.

Bergstrom, T. C., and R. Goodman. 1973. Private Demand for Public Goods. *American Economic Review* 63:286–96.

Bergstrom, T. C., D. L. Rubinfeld, and P. Shapiro. 1982. Micro-Based Estimates of Demand Functions for Local School Expenditures. *Econometrica* 50:1183–1206.

Betts, J. R. 1995. Does School Quality Matter? Evidence from the National Longitudinal Survey of Youth. *Review of Economics and Statistics* 77:231–50.

Blinder, A. S., and H. S. Rosen. 1985. Notches. *American Economic Review* 75:736–47.

Bockstael, N. E., and C. L. Kling. 1988. Valuing Environmental Quality: Weak Complementarity with Sets of Goods. *American Journal of Agricultural Economics*, 70:654–62.

Borcherding, T. E., and R. T. Deacon. 1972. The Demand for the Services of Non-federal Governments. *American Economic Review* 62:891–901.

Bradford, D., and G. Hilderbrandt. 1977. Observable Preferences for Public Goods. *Journal of Public Economics* 8:111–31.

Card, D. E., and A. B. Krueger. 1992. Does Schooling Quality Matter? Returns to Education and the Characteristics of Public Schools in the United States. *Journal of Political Economy* 100:1–40.

Carson, R. T., W. M. Hanemann, and N. E. Flores. 1994. On the Creation and Destruction of Public Goods: The Matter of Sequencing. University of California, San Diego. March. Mimeo.

Carson, R. T., and R. C. Mitchell. 1995. Sequencing and Nesting in Contingent Valuation Surveys. *Journal of Environmental Economics and Management* 28:155–73.

Cornes, R. 1993. Dike Maintenance and Other Stories: Some Neglected Types of Public Goods. *Quarterly Journal of Economics* 108:259–72.

Cornes, R., and T. Sandler. 1986. *The Theory of Externalities, Public Goods, and Club Goods.* Cambridge: Cambridge University Press.

Cornes, R., and T. Sandler. 1994. The Comparative Static Properties of the Impure Public Good Model. *Journal of Public Economics* 54:403–22.

Cropper, M. L. 1994. Comments on Estimating the Demand for Public Goods: The Collective Choice and Contingent Valuation Approaches. World Bank, Washington, DC. Mimeo.

Cummings, R. G., P. T. Ganderton, and T. McGuckin. 1994. Substitution Effects in Contingent Valuation Estimates. *American Journal of Agricultural Economics* 76:205–15.

Desvousges, W. H., V. K. Smith, and H. H. Rink III. 1989. Communicating Radon Risk Effectively: Radon Testing in Maryland. Final report to the U.S. Environmental Protection Agency, EPA–230–03–89–048. March. Mimeo.

Desvousges, W. H., V. K. Smith, and H. H. Rink III. 1992. Communicating Radon Risks Effectively: The Maryland Experience. *Journal of Public Policy and Marketing* 11:68–78.

Diamond, P. A., J. A. Hausman, G. K. Leonard, and M. A. Denning. 1993. Does Contingent Valuation Measure Preferences? Experimental Evidence. In *Contingent Valuation: A Critical Assessment*, ed. J. A. Hausman. Amsterdam: North-Holland Publishing Co.

Ecosystem Valuation Forum. 1992. Report to the U.S. Environmental Protection Agency. Conservation Foundation, Washington, DC. Mimeo.

Erlich, I., and G. Becker. 1972. Market Insurance, Self-Insurance and Self-Protection. *Journal of Political Economy* 80:623–48.

Freeman, A. M. III. 1993. Nonuse Values in Natural Resource Damage Assessment. In *Valuing Natural Assets: The Economics of Natural Resource Damage Assessment*, ed. R. J. Kopp and V. K. Smith. Washington, DC: Resources for the Future.

Fuchs, V. R. 1982. Time Preference and Health: An Exploratory Study. In *Economic Aspects of Health,* ed. V. R. Fuchs. Chicago: University of Chicago Press.

Gertler, P., and P. Glewwe. 1990. The Willingness to Pay for Education in Developing Countries. *Journal of Public Economics* 42:251–75.

Gramlich, E. M., and D. L. Rubinfeld. 1982. Micro Estimates of Public Spending Demand Functions and Tests of the Tiebout and Median Voter Hypotheses. *Journal of Political Economy* 90:536–61.

Grossman, G. M., and A. B. Krueger. 1991. Environmental Impacts of a North American Free Trade Agreement. NBER Working Paper no. 3914, National Bureau of Economic Research. November. Mimeo.

Harrison, G. W., and J. Hirshleifer. 1989. An Experimental Evaluation of Weakest Link/Best Shot Models of Public Goods. *Journal of Political Economy* 97:201–26.

Hausman, J. A., ed. 1993. *Contingent Valuation: A Critical Assessment.* Amsterdam: North-Holland Publishing Co.

Haveman, R. H., and B. L. Wolfe, 1984. Schooling and Economic Well-Being: The Role of Non-market Effects. *Journal of Human Resources* 19:408–29.

Hirshleifer, J. 1983. From Weakest-Link to Best Shot: The Voluntary Provision of Public Goods. *Public Choice* 41:371–86 and correction in *Public Choice* (1985).

Hoehn, J. 1991. Valuing the Multidimensional Impacts of Environmental Policy: Theory and Methods. *American Journal of Agricultural Economics* 73:289–99.

Hoehn, J. P., and J. B. Loomis. 1993. Substitution Effects in the Valuation of Multiple Environmental Programs. *Journal of Environmental Economics and Management* 25:56–75.

Huang, J. C., and V. K. Smith. 1995. Weak Complementarity and Quasi-Rents. Center for Environmental and Resource Economics, Duke University. October. Mimeo.

Ippolito, P. M., and A. D. Mathios. 1989. *Health Claims in Advertising and Labeling: A Study of the Cereal Market.* Washington, DC: Federal Trade Commission.

Ippolito, P. M., and A. D. Mathios. 1990. Information, Advertising, and Health Choices: A Study of the Cereal Market. *Rand Journal of Economics* 21:459–80.

Jimenez, E. 1995. Human and Physical Infrastructure: Public Investment and Pricing Policies in Developing Countries. In *Handbook of Development Economics,* ed. J. R. Behrman and T. N. Srinivasan, vol. 3B. Amsterdam: North-Holland Publishing Co.

Kahneman, D., and J. Knetsch. 1992. Valuing Public Goods: The Purchase of Moral Satisfaction. *Journal of Environmental Economics and Management* 22:55–70.

Kemp, M. A., and C. Maxwell. 1993. Exploring a Budget Constraint for Contingent Valuation Estimates. In *Contingent Valuation: A Critical Assessment,* ed. J. A. Hausman. Amsterdam: North-Holland Publishing Co.

Kenkel, D. S. 1991. Health Behavior, Health Knowledge, and Schooling. *Journal of Political Economy* 99:287–305.

Kirsch, I., A. Jungeblut, L. Jenkins, and A. Kolstad. 1993. *Adult Literacy in America.* Washington, DC: Office of Educational Research and Improvement, Department of Education.

Kolhase, J. 1991. The Impact of Toxic Waste Sites on Housing Values. *Journal of Urban Economics* 30:1–26.

Krosnick, J. A. 1991. Response Strategies for Coping with the Cognitive Demands of Attitude Measures in Surveys. *Applied Cognitive Psychology* 3:213–36.

Loomis, J. B., and P. J. DuVair. 1993. Evaluating the Effect of Alternative Risk Communication in Devices of Willingness to Pay: Results from a Dichotomous Choice Contingent Valuation Experiment. *Land Economics* 89:289–98.

Lutter, R., and J. F. Morrall III. 1994. Health–Health Analysis: A New Way to Evaluate Health and Safety Regulation. *Journal of Risk and Uncertainty* 8:43–66.

Machina, M. 1990. Choice under Uncertainty: Problems Solved and Unsolved. In *Valuing Health Risks: Costs and Benefits for Environmental Decision Making,* ed. R. B. Hammond and R. Coppock. Washington, DC: National Academy Press.

Madden, P. 1991. A Generalization of Hicksian Substitutes and Complements with Application to Demand Rationing. *Econometrica* 59:1497–1508.

Magat, W. A., and W. K. Viscusi. 1992. *Informational Approaches to Regulation.* Cambridge: MIT Press.

Mäler, K. G. 1974. *Environmental Economics: A Theoretical Inquiry.* Baltimore: Johns Hopkins University Press.

Martinez-Vazquez, J. 1981. Selfishness versus Public "Regardiness" in Voting Behavior. *Journal of Public Economics* 15:349–62.

McConnell, K. E. 1983. Existence and Bequest Value. In *Managing Air Quality and Scenic Resources at National Parks and Wilderness Areas,* ed. R. D. Rowe and L. G. Chestnut. Boulder: Westview Press.

Menell, P. S. 1993. Eco-Information Policy: A Comparative Institutional Perspective. Working Paper no. 104, Stanford Law School, John M. Olin Program in Law and Economics. April. Mimeo.

Michaels, R. G., and V. K. Smith. 1990. Market Segmentation and Valuing Amenities with Hedonic Models: The Case of Hazardous Waste Sites. *Journal of Urban Economics,* 28:223–42.

Mincer, J. 1974. *Schooling, Experience, and Earnings.* New York: Columbia University Press.

Mitchell, R. C., and R. T. Carson. 1989. *Using Surveys to Value Public Goods: The Contingent Valuation Method.* Washington, DC: Resources for the Future.

National Research Council. 1989. *Improving Risk Communication.* Washington, DC: National Academy Press.

Oates, W. E. 1994. Estimating the Demand for Public Goods: The Collective Choice and Contingent Valuation Approaches. Department of Economics, University of Maryland. January. Mimeo.

Plourde, C. 1975. Conservation of Extinguishable Species. *Natural Resources Journal* 15:791–97.

Poe, G. L., and R. C. Bishop. 1993. Prior Information, General Information, and Specific Information in the Contingent Valuation of Environmental Risks: The Case of Nitrates in Groundwater. Working Paper no. SP93–11, Department of Agricultural Economics, Cornell University. July. Mimeo.

Ridker, R. G. 1967. *Economic Costs of Air Pollution.* New York: Praeger Publishers.

Sandler, T. 1992. *Collective Action: Theory and Application.* Ann Arbor: University of Michigan Press.

Slovic, P., B. Fischoff, and S. Lichtenstein. 1985. Regulation of Risk: A Psychological Perspective. In *Regulatory Policy and the Social Sciences,* ed. R. G. Noel. Berkeley: University of California Press.

Smith, V. K. 1991a. Household Production Functions and Environmental Benefit Estimation. In *Measuring the Demand for Environmental Quality,* ed. J. B. Braden and C. D. Kolstad. Amsterdam: North-Holland Publishing Co.

Smith, V. K. 1991b. Environmental Risk Perception and Valuation: Conventional Versus Prospective Reference Theory. In *The Social Response to Environmental Risk,* ed. D. W. Bromley and K. Segerson. Boston: Kluwer Academic Publishers.

Smith, V. K. 1992. Arbitrary Values, Good Causes, and Premature Verdicts. *Journal of Environmental Economics and Management* 22:71–89.

Smith, V. K. 1993. Nonmarket Valuation of Environmental Resources: An Interpretive Appraisal. *Land Economics* 69:1–26.

Smith, V. K., and W. H. Desvousges. 1986a. Averting Behavior: Does It Exist? *Economic Letters* 20:291–96.

Smith, V. K., and W. H. Desvousges. 1986b. The Value of Avoiding a LULU: Hazardous Waste Disposal Sites. *Review of Economics and Statistics* 68:293–99.

Smith, V. K., and W. H. Desvousges. 1987. An Empirical Analysis of the Economic Value of Risk Changes. *Journal of Political Economy* 95:89–114.

Smith, V. K., W. H. Desvousges, A. Fisher, and F. R. Johnson. 1988. Learning about Radon's Risk. *Journal of Risk and Uncertainty* 1:233–58.

Smith, V. K., W. H. Desvousges, F. R. Johnson, and A. Fisher. 1990. Can Public Information Programs Affect Risk Perception? *Journal of Policy Analysis and Management* 9:41–59.

Smith, V. K., W. H. Desvousges, and J. W. Payne. 1995. Do Risk Information Programs Promote Mitigating Behavior? *Journal of Risk and Uncertainty* 10:203–21.

Smith, V. K., D. J. Epp, and K. A. Schwabe. 1994. Cross Country Analyses Don't Estimate Health-Health Responses. *Journal of Risk and Uncertainty* 8:67–84.

Smith, V. K., and J. C. Huang. 1995. Can Markets Value Air Quality? A Meta Analysis of Hedonic Property Value Models. *Journal of Political Economy* 103:209–27.

Tiebout, C. 1956. A Pure Theory of Local Expenditures. *Journal of Political Economy* 64:416–24.

United Nations Environment Programme. 1992. *Urban Air Pollution in the Megacities of the World.* Oxford: Blackwell Publishers.

Viscusi, W. K. 1993. *Fatal Tradeoffs: Public and Private Responsibilities for Risk.* New York: Oxford University Press.

Viscusi, W. K., and W. A. Magat. 1987. *Learning about Risk: Consumer and Worker Responses to Hazard Warnings.* Cambridge: Harvard University Press.

Viscusi, W. K., W. A. Magat, and J. Huber. 1986. Informational Regulation of Consumer Health Risks: An Empirical Evaluation of Hazard Warnings. *Rand Journal of Economics* 17:351–65.

Weitzman, M. L. 1992. On Diversity. *Quarterly Journal of Economics* 107:363–406.

Weitzman, M. L. 1993. What to Preserve? An Application of Diversity Theory to Crane Conservation. *Quarterly Journal of Economics* 108:157–84.

Westat, Inc. 1989. Investigation of Possible Recall Reference Period Bias in National Surveys of Fishing, Hunting and Wildlife Associated Recreation. Final Report to the U.S. Department of the Interior. Rockville, MD: Westat, Inc.

Wildavsky, A. 1988. *Searching for Safety.* New Brunswick, NJ: Transaction Books.

Wolfe, B. L., with S. Zuvek. N.d. Nonmarket Outcomes of Schooling. University of Wisconsin, Madison. Mimeo.

World Bank. 1992. *World Development Report 1992: Development and the Environment.* New York: Oxford University Press.

Wyckoff, J. H. 1984. The Nonexcludable Publicness of Primary and Secondary Public Education. *Journal of Public Economics* 24:331–52.

CHAPTER 7

Crime

Ann Dryden Witte

Most crime, particularly street crime,[1] is committed by young men. The more serious the offense, the higher is male relative to female participation. For example, in any given year approximately 25 percent more males than females are involved in delinquent acts. Female participation in the most serious crimes (FBI Index offenses) is generally only one-third that of males.

Most young men and the majority of young women participate in some delinquent acts during their teen years. As one careful researcher has observed: "Actual rates of illegal behavior soar so high during adolescence that participation in delinquency appears to be a normal part of teen life" (Moffitt 1993, 675). By the age of 18 possibly over 90 percent of young males have participated in delinquent acts and approximately half have been *arrested* for nontraffic offenses by the time they are 30. Only 50 to 60 percent of young females have been involved in delinquent acts by the time they are 18 and less than 10 percent have been arrested by the age of 30.

Participation in criminal activity is restricted to the juvenile years for most individuals. By their midtwenties perhaps as many as three-quarters of individuals who began offending as juveniles have ceased offending according to official records.

To set the scene, I will briefly review trends in crime during the last 20 years. The public, even the informed public, as was demonstrated at the conference, believes that the level of crime is unprecedentedly high and increasing at an alarming rate. Actually, the most reliable evidence available, information from the National Crime Survey, indicates that the level of crime today is

---

This chapter was commissioned by the Office of Research of the U.S. Department of Education. While it has benefited from the comments of the conference organizers and other participants, I alone am responsible for all material in it.

1. I concentrate on street, or "blue collar," crime in this chapter because the public fear of crime results mainly from these types of offenses. This is not meant to downplay the importance or seriousness of "white collar" crime. Rather, it reflects my judgment that the likely effects of education on the two types of crime are quite different and a single essay cannot do justice to both "white collar" and "blue collar" crime.

lower than in the late 1970s and early 1980s. This is true for the most feared crimes such as rape, aggravated assault, burglary, and larceny, as well as for less-serious offenses. See Donohue and Siegelman (1994) for a compilation of crime statistics and a well-informed discussion of various types of data on crime.

The composition of crime has changed, however. For example, while the overall murder rate in the United States has declined since the late 1970s, the murder rate for young males, particularly young black males, has increased. Beginning in 1985, the murder victimization rate for blacks aged 15 to 24 began to increase dramatically. The victimization rate for young blacks exceeded the previous record levels of the early 1970s in the late 1980s and has continued to grow during the 1990s. Murder victimization rates for whites between the ages of 15 and 24 only began increasing in the late 1980s and reached the rate of the late 1970s only in the early 1990s. It appears that while we are not experiencing more violent crime we are experiencing unusually high levels of violent crime for young males.

Crime and education are approximately equally prevalent activities for young males. Are they related? There is, unfortunately, little evidence on this point. However, there are a number of potential linkages between crime and education. Further, if there are types of educational experiences that can lower the level of juvenile offending or lead to desistance once offending has begun, crime reduction can be a substantial benefit of education.

The organization of the chapter is as follows. In section 7.1, I survey models that suggest possible crime-reducing effects of education, and in section 7.2, I survey the empirical literature. In section 7.3, I use insights from the theoretical and empirical literature to suggest possible models for the effect of education on crime. Section 7.3 also contains a discussion of methods of measuring crime and reflecting deterrent effects. Section 7.4 contains a discussion of potential economic justifications for education programs designed to reduce crime, and section 7.5 considers alternative institutional structures designed to reduce crime. The final section suggests directions for future research.

7.1. The Effect of Education in Models of Criminal Behavior

Models of criminal behavior have not directly addressed the role of education in offending. Economic models have focused on the deterrence issue and the relationship between work and crime and sociological models on community and other macrosocial effects. Psychological models are primarily concerned with mental states and mental processes. I will briefly survey existing models with an emphasis on economic models.

7.1.1. Economic Models of Criminal Behavior

Economic modeling of criminal behavior began with Becker's pioneering work (Becker 1968). Becker developed a comparative-static model that considered primarily the deterrent effect of the criminal justice system. He used the expected utility model as a basis for his work. As developed subsequently by his students (e.g., Ehrlich), Becker's model was extended to encompass the relationship between crime and work.

Economic models, including Ehrlich's, developed during the 1970s and 1980s generally see crime as similar to work in that it takes time and produces income or other utility-enhancing effects (e.g., the joy of eliminating an enemy). Education played no role in these models. See Schmidt and Witte (1984) for a survey of these first-generation economic models of crime. As pointed out by Felson (1993), these models have limited relevance for juvenile offending, a substantial and increasing part of the crime problem.

Time-allocation models of crime imply that crime and work are substitute activities. If an individual allocates more time to work, he will commit less crime because he will have less time to do so. Since education also takes time, it would be easy to incorporate education in time-allocation models. Such models would imply that crime and education, like crime and work, are substitute activities.

As economists began to work with individual data for young adults and began to consider addiction and other types of persistent behaviors, different types of models were developed. While these models do not explicitly incorporate education, they do suggest possible ways of incorporating education in economic models of crime. These models are generally based on psychological processes (e.g., Dickens, 1986; and Lattimore and Witte 1986) or are dynamic (e.g., Becker and Murphy 1988; Davis 1988; Flinn 1986; and Tauchen and Witte, 1995).

Flinn's model, which incorporates human capital formation, suggests but does not detail a possible direct role for education. Like most economic models, Flinn's model deals with adult rather than juvenile offending. In his model, human capital is accumulated at work, not at school. Like earlier models, Flinn's model is a time-allocation model. He sees crime as taking time away from work and hence diminishing the amount of human capital accumulated. The diminished human capital leads to lower future wages and hence less time spent working. Since crime and work are substitutes in his model, the decline in time allocated to work leads to increased participation in criminal activities.

A major role of education is human capital formation. Flinn's model suggests that human capital formation decreases crime directly because it raises wages. Under Flinn's model, participation in criminal activity also has an effect on human capital formation because it decreases the amount of time that the individual can spend accumulating human capital.

More recently, economists, including Becker, have become interested in habit formation, addiction, and peer group effects. Labor economists have long been interested in state dependence, the fact that activities chosen in the current period may be strongly affected by the individual's activities in the previous period (e.g., Heckman 1981). In terms of the effect of education on crime, models incorporating state dependence suggest that those who stay in school are less likely to become delinquent than are those who drop out. Such models would have to rely on heterogeneity to explain why some individuals drop out (e.g., individuals with attention deficits or low IQs).

Economists interested in consumer demand (e.g., Pollak 1978; Theil 1980; and Phlips 1983) have long considered the ways in which information, an individual's time uses, and an individual's associates affect demand. These types of consumer demand models see external information, time uses, and an individual's associates as affecting the parameters of the utility function. Crime models might be developed using this literature as a basis. This type of crime model might incorporate education by having education impart information about the "rules of the game' " (i.e., what is legal and/or moral) or the benefits of legal activities and the costs of illegal ones. More time spent in school might affect tastes both directly (e.g., making individuals more future oriented) and indirectly (e.g., providing associates who are less crime prone).

Becker and Murphy (1988) build on consumer demand theory and develop a model of rational addiction. Their model relies on "adjacent complementarities" in consumption to produce habit formation. Under their model, the marginal utility of consuming a good that is an adjacent complement is higher if the good has been consumed in the previous period. They also incorporate myopia to explain why people become addicted to harmful goods. Under a model of the type developed by Becker and Murphy, education might affect the level of criminal activity by encouraging good habits (e.g., industriousness), discouraging bad habits (e.g., drug use, and violent methods of coping with difficult situations), and increasing future orientedness. See Grossman and Kaestner (in this volume) for a fuller exposition of this model and for a discussion of empirical work using it.

Economists at least since the time of Veblen have been interested in the interdependence of preferences. Economists have used interdependent preferences to explain conspicuous consumption and fads. Ehrlich (1975) developed a comparative-static model with interdependent preferences to explain murder. More recently, economists have suggested that consumption decisions (e.g., Karni and Schmeidler 1990) and peer groups may be determined simultaneously (e.g., Evans et al. 1992). Such models have been used to explain teenage pregnancy and school dropout behavior and might be adapted to explain juvenile offending. Under such models, a major role of education would be to provide peer groups that discourage criminal behavior.

7.1.2. Other Models of Criminal Behavior

Like economic models, other models of criminal behavior have not emphasized the role of education. In this subsection, I will briefly describe one sociological and one psychological model that could have important implications for the effect of education on crime.

7.1.2.1. A Sociological Model

In an important early work, Shaw and McKay (1969) suggest that disorganization in urban communities leads to increased levels of crime and delinquency. Community disorganization, they believed, was associated with low economic status, ethnic heterogeneity, residential mobility, and family disruption. Until quite recently, researchers using Shaw and McKay's model have considered mainly the causes of community disorganization (e.g., ethnic heterogeneity) and have neither measured nor modeled community disorganization.

In an interesting paper, Sampson and Groves (1989) estimate a structural model that considers the effect of sociodemographic factors on measures of community disorganization and the effect of measured community disorganization on crime. An important innovation in their work is the use of social-network theory to measure social organization. They see disorganized communities as characterized by sparse friendship networks, unsupervised teenagers, and low organizational participation. A finding of potential importance for understanding the impact of education on crime is that low socioeconomic status, ethnic heterogeneity, family disruption, and urbanization are all significantly associated with higher levels of unsupervised teenagers. They also find that communities with higher levels of unsupervised teenagers have significantly higher crime victimization rates. Indeed, the number of unsupervised teenagers has both the largest and the most significant effect on community victimization rates. An additional important finding is that communities with higher levels of participation in community organizations have significantly lower crime rates.

The work just described provides interesting potential paths for exploring the effect of education on crime. Schools can be a source for organizing the community and can have as a subsidiary role the supervision of teenagers.

7.1.2.2. A Psychological Model

Based on an extensive survey of work on crime and delinquency, Moffitt (1993) has developed an interesting dual typology of offenders. Research has shown that crime is a pervasive activity for teenagers. Longitudinal studies indicate that a few offenders are responsible for a disproportionate amount of offending. Building on these and other findings, Moffitt suggests that there are two types of offenders. One group exhibits long-term and persistent criminal behavior while the other group's criminal behavior is limited to the teenage years.

Moffitt sees persistent, long-term offenders exhibiting a wide range of antisocial behaviors during their lifetimes. As she describes the behavior of this type of offender, he may begin by biting and hitting other children at the age of four; he may skip school and shoplift at age 10; by 16 he may be selling drugs and stealing cars; at 22, rape and robbery may be among his activities; and at 30 he may be defrauding his employer and abusing his children. This heterogeneity in behavior is consistent with the persistent finding of little specialization among criminals. The causes of the behavior of this type of individual must, according to Moffitt, be sought in prenatal, perinatal, and early childhood experiences (e.g., exposure to lead, parental abuse and neglect).

Moffitt sees adolescent-limited criminal behavior as pervasive and exacerbated by "a maturity gap" that has widened during the post–World War II period. Teenagers now mature earlier, but their transition to adulthood is more delayed than ever before. This maturity gap causes frustration and may make deviant companions and a deviant lifestyle attractive.

As far as I am aware, there has only been one attempt to discern the degree to which Moffitt's typology is supported empirically (Nagin et al. 1995). This work is only partially supportive of Moffitt's typology. The work is able to identify a group of chronic offenders of the type described by Moffitt. However, it finds that what appears to be a group of adolescent-limited offenders on the basis of official records is actually a group of offenders who have changed their modus operandi. This group appears to have adopted traditional lifestyles. For example, they work, by and large have families, and have few arrests. Self-reports indicate that this group continues to offend. The offenses, however, are those with low probabilities of detection such as employee theft and drug use.

This work suggests a number of possible anticrime roles for education. For the persistent offender, intervention must come early and must involve the family as well as the child. It is more difficult to discern the educational implications of the high rate of adolescent offending. If adolescent offending is, indeed, not adolescent limited but continues well into adulthood (Nagin et al. follow their subjects to the age of 32), it is very important to channel adolescent energies into legal activities (e.g., sports or work) and to strongly and consistently punish adolescent offending when it occurs. For the adolescent offender, schools may need to have more adultlike environment. Such environment might combine work and school and should facilitate the integration of adult and teen cultures. It should also provide rules that are strongly inculcated and consistently enforced.

7.2. Empirical Evidence

The empirical evidence regarding the effect of education on crime is limited. Evaluations of educational programs have generally not considered crime. Correlational studies of crime often include various measures of education as "control" variables, but educational variables have not received a great deal of attention in this multivariate statistical work. I will survey briefly the experimental, quasiexperimental, and correlational literatures that provide insights regarding the effect of education on crime.

7.2.1. Experiments

Experimental evidence suggests that programs that provide intensive education for preschool children and their parents result in the most persistent crime-reduction effects. Programs for high-risk youth have generally not been effective. Education programs for prison inmates have yet to show significant effects on future criminal activity.

A number of small-scale studies have shown that *intensive* early childhood interventions that combine early childhood education with family support and education in parenting can reduce juvenile delinquency. Successful programs work with high-risk parents and children for a least two years before children enter school, provide high-quality infant day care or preschool programs for the children, provide informational and emotional support on child-development and child-rearing issues for parents, provide prenatal/postnatal health care, and either provide or make sure that vocational counseling or training are available for parents. Such programs are expensive, but cost-effectiveness studies indicate that they are less costly than the criminal justice system costs of dealing with crime after it has occurred. The lesson here, as in other areas of policy, is that prevention works and is generally cheaper than dealing with problems after inception. See Zigler et al. (1992) for a discussion of the effect of early childhood interventions and Yoshikawa (1994) for a thorough review.

We do not know whether the results of these early childhood programs would be forthcoming if they were to be adopted for broad population groups. However, we do know that broad-based, low-intensity programs such as Head Start have not been shown to have significant effects on juvenile delinquency (see Yoshikawa 1994).

During the 1970s, experiments were carried out to determine the effect of an intensive education and job placement program called the National

Supported Work Demonstration. The demonstration was carried out in a number of cities around the country. It provided training and work experience in supportive environments for four high-risk groups—ex-addicts, school dropouts, prison releasees, and women on welfare. Only women on welfare and ex-addicts appear to have benefited significantly from the program. While the level of criminal activity of these two groups declined, the level was not very high initially (Manpower Development Research Corporation 1980). A recent analysis of eight years of follow-up data for the participants in the Supported Work experiment found no discernible long-term impact (Couch 1992).

Published results for a carefully designed but poorly implemented vocational training and job placement program for youthful offenders show significant crime reduction effects (see Lattimore et al. 1990). However, the unpublished longer-term follow-up results show no significant differences in criminal activities between the experimental and the control groups.

The recently completed nationwide evaluation of employment and training programs under the Job Training Partnership Act (JTPA) found that youths in the experimental group had *higher* reported arrest rates than did youths in the control group. The JTPA program had no standard content. Rather, intake staff placed individuals in the treatment group in one of three programs depending on need. One program stressed classroom training in occupational skills. Another emphasized on the job training. The final, catchall program provided a diverse set of services that included job search assistance and basic education (see Orr et al. 1994).

Preliminary results for the Children at Risk Program (CAR) are promising although they are open to alternative interpretation. CAR is a carefully designed, theoretically based, multifaceted program for at-risk youth between the ages of 11 and 13. The program consists of eight components considered key to comprehensive delinquency prevention: case management, family services, educational services, after-school and summer activities, mentoring, incentives, community policing and enhanced enforcement, and criminal-juvenile justice intervention. Five cities (Austin, Bridgeport, Memphis, Savannah, and Seattle) where CAR has been implemented are participating in an experimental evaluation of program effects. Preliminary results indicate that program participants had significantly fewer contacts with the criminal justice system during the first year of program participation compared with youths in a randomly assigned control group. As the report of preliminary results is careful to point out, this outcome may indicate that CAR is succeeding in reducing delinquency or it may indicate that it is simply changing the way the target communities handle delinquent acts (see Harrell 1995).

Results for the Alternative Schools Initiative of the U.S. Departments of Labor and Education are not yet in. A personal communication from Mark Dynarski of Mathematica Policy Research indicates that preliminary results find no significant differences in arrest rates.

7.2.2. Quasi Experiments

There have been literally hundreds of quasi experiments designed to assess the effect of various educational interventions on crime. All such experiments are open to numerous methodological challenges. However, in this arena, these challenges may be superfluous since there is no consistent evidence from these quasi experiments that educational programs significantly reduce crime. For good surveys of this literature, see Wilson and Herrnstein (1985) and Gendreau and Ross (1987).

Preliminary results for an *intensive* residential program of work and education for high-risk urban youth called the Job Corps are more promising. Participation in the program significantly reduced the level of criminal activity while individuals were in the program (an incapacitation or supervision effect?). Postprogram follow-up results show no significant effect on arrest rate, but corps members are found to be involved in significantly less serious offenses (see Mallar et al. 1982). The Job Corps currently enrolls around 40,000 disadvantaged youth, and an experimental evaluation of its effects is under way (Dynarski, personal communication).

7.2.3. Correlational Studies

The role of education has not, as far as I am aware, been analyzed in great detail in correlational studies of crime. However, various measures of education are included in many studies. Education is generally measured by school grade completed, the receipt of various credentials (e.g., a high school diploma), or by scores on tests designed to measure educational attainment. Studies that include such variables generally find that they are insignificantly related to crime (e.g., Witte and Tauchen 1994).

A few correlational studies (e.g., Gottfredson 1985; Farrington et al. 1986; Viscusi 1986; and Witte and Tauchen 1994) incorporate the time spent in educational activities as an explanatory variable. They find that both time spent at school and time spent working are associated with a significantly lower level of criminal activity. Further, time spent in educational activities appears to have, if anything, a larger crime reduction effect than does time spent at work. These results have been interpreted as indicating that it is important to keep young people occupied in some legal endeavor and off the streets. The finding of a high correlation between unsupervised teenagers and crime would be consistent with such an interpretation.

These results must, however, be viewed with caution. Correlational studies of crime are difficult for a number of reasons. First, most measures of criminal activity are either qualitative (e.g., a binary variable equal to one if the individual offends and zero otherwise) or limited (e.g., an index of the seriousness of offenses committed, which is equal to zero if the individual is not an offender).

As is well known, such dependent variables require specialized econometric techniques. Most researchers now use specialized techniques when estimating crime models. However, the use of such techniques makes adjustment for other statistical problems more difficult.

Correlational studies of crime have generally used either aggregate, time-series data or individual, cross-sectional data. The specification of crime models requires the combination of these two types of data since both theory and empirical work indicate that understanding criminal activity requires detailed information about the individual, his associates, and the community in which he lives and offends. Researchers are beginning to use data that combine individual with community-level variables (e.g., Tauchen et al. 1994) and there is a large-scale effort under way in Chicago to collect prospective longitudinal data on individuals and the communities in which they live (see Earls and Mcguire 1993).

The use of aggregate data to test individual models of behavior is subject to aggregation bias and possibly insurmountable identification difficulties. Careful reviews of this research have concluded that little would come of further use of aggregate official records to test individual models of criminal behavior (e.g., Blumstein et al. 1978).

This suggests that research on the benefits of education would be wise to avoid the kind of aggregate data research that was common in crime causation studies until around the mid-1980s. Models of the type estimated by Sampson and Groves (1989), which seek to explain victimization rates, may be more promising, although they do not explain why individuals offend. Such models might be used to discern the effect of different types of schools and community outreach programs on crime.

Studies using individual, cross-sectional data suffer from a number of weaknesses. First, these studies generally use data for individuals already involved in criminal activity (see, e.g., Witte 1980). Such studies can uncover the effect of education on return to criminal activity (i.e., recidivism), but they cannot reveal the effect of education on initiation of criminal activity. They are also subject to potential simultaneity biases.

To evaluate this work, consider a carefully specified model of individual criminal activity that incorporates a range of the factors believed to affect criminal activity. To be well specified, such a model would need to incorporate variables that reflect both general deterrence (the effect of apprehension and punishment on individuals contemplating but not actually committing crimes) and specific deterrence (the effect of apprehension and punishment on those actually committing crimes), measures of participation and performance in legal endeavors (e.g., education and work), measures related to peer groups (e.g., gang or church affiliation), measures of community structure (e.g., the quality of local school and outreach programs), a vector of variables reflecting past criminal activities (e.g., criminal record), and a vector of sociodemographic variables.

The empirical model estimated in most work falls far short of this ideal. The work tends to concentrate on either deterrence or the relationship between work and crime. For example, studies concentrating on the relationship between work and crime either include no variables related to deterrence (e.g., Thornberry and Christenson 1984) or include only variables that reflect specific deterrent effects (e.g., Viscusi 1986; and Grogger 1994). Work concentrating on deterrence (e.g., Montmarquette and Nerlove 1985) has not considered the ways in which community actions (e.g., criminal justice system actions and community disapproval) produce deterrence.

Work using individual data generally fails to deal with the possible endogeneity of measures of work, schooling, and deterrence. This is quite understandable because dealing with these issues in the context of qualitative or limited dependent variables is not easy. Sickles and Schmidt (1978) have developed a method of estimating a simultaneous equation model with a limited dependent variable, and there have been a number of methods developed for estimating simultaneous probit models (e.g., Rivers and Vuong 1988). These techniques have been used occasionally to estimate simultaneous equation models of crime and work (e.g., Schmidt and Witte 1984) and to test for the endogeneity of general deterrence variables (Tauchen et al. 1994). As far as I am aware, no study has carefully considered the possible endogeneity of school attendance and achievement in crime models. Such endogeneity seems particularly likely for juveniles.

Beginning in the second half of the 1980s, researchers have used longitudinal data to estimate crime models (see, e.g., Farrington et al. 1986; Good et al. 1986; and Tauchen et al. 1994). Work with longitudinal data appears to offer the greatest promise for understanding the effect of education on crime.

A number of data bases currently available that contain longitudinal data on crime have yet to be used to estimate multivariate models of crime of the type considered in this section. These data have been collected in Philadelphia (see Wolfgang et al. 1987), Denver, Rochester, and Pittsburgh. Issue 1 of the 1991 volume of the *Journal of Criminal Law and Criminology* contains descriptions of the Denver, Rochester, and Pittsburgh data. There are also a number of international longitudinal data bases available. Both U.S. and European data bases are discussed in Weitkamp and Kerner (1994).

To illustrate the type of work that has been done using longitudinal data and to suggest ways in which recently available data sets might be used to understand the effect of education on crime, I will examine the recent work of Tauchen et al. (1994). For convenience, I will refer to this as the Philadelphia study. In this work, Tauchen and her colleagues use data for a seven-year period. These data reflect the activities of a random sample of all males born in 1945 and residing in Philadelphia between their tenth and eighteenth birthdays. The seven-year panel covers the activities of the young men from ages 18 through 25.

Both self-reports and official records are available in the Philadelphia study. Tauchen and her colleagues use official records to construct their measures of criminal activity. They use official records rather than self-reports for two reasons. First, the official records contain the date of each arrest, while the self-reports only indicate whether an offense occurred before or after the individual was 18. Construction of a multiyear panel requires information on the year in which offenses occur. Second, the official record data available in the Philadelphia study contain detailed descriptions of the offense, while the self-reports contain little information on the nature of the offense committed. I will discuss and compare the merits of official records and self-reports in more detail in the next section.

The Philadelphia study uses two measures of criminal activity, a binary measure indicating whether or not an individual committed an offense during the year and an index measure that reflects both the number and the seriousness of offenses committed during the year.[2] The binary measure of criminal activity treats all offenses as identical and treats a high-rate offender precisely like a low-rate offender.

To date, the literature has used primarily binary measures of criminal activity. Index measures of criminal activity either develop weights for different offenses based on such things as citizens' evaluation of the relative seriousness of various offenses or, as in the case of the Sellin and Wolfgang (1964) index used in the Philadelphia study, score each offense based on its characteristics (e.g., the amount of money stolen or the amount of harm inflicted) and sum the resulting scores over all offenses committed. Index measures of criminal activity seem better to me, but Tauchen and her colleagues obtained similar results for the binary and index measure of criminal activity.

Since the literature consistently reports that a small number of high-rate offenders are responsible for a disproportionate amount of crime, it would seem important to be able to identify these offenders. An index measure of criminal activity is far better able to do this than is a binary measure.

In contrast with other work I am aware of, Tauchen and her colleagues use a data base that contains both detailed individual information and data describing the community. Both the individual and aggregate data in the Philadelphia study contain educational variables. Tauchen and her colleagues enter three individual measures of education (i.e., a binary equal to one if the individual had a high school diploma, the fraction of the year the individual was in school, and a binary variable equal to one if the individual attended a parochial high school)

---

2. The index measure is constructed using a measure of crime seriousness developed by Sellin and Wolfgang (1964).

in the crime equation. They enter no aggregate variables describing schools in Philadelphia in their crime model but use two community-level education variables (i.e., public school enrollment and public school enrollment per capita) to test for the endogeneity of their general deterrence variables.

To evaluate the community-wide effect of education, it would be necessary to enter either citywide or neighborhood measures of educational activities in the crime equation. The literature suggests that such community-wide effects might emerge from better supervision of teenagers or from community outreach activities that help to organize the community and make it more cohesive.

Future efforts to evaluate the effect of community-level indicators of education (e.g., the level of discipline and types of educational or community outreach programs available) on individual criminal activity will benefit from recent econometric work on methods of combining aggregate and individual data when estimating multivariate models. In an important article, Moulton (1990) points out that the standard errors obtained when incorporating aggregate variables in models of individual behavior are generally underestimated. The reason is that individual behavior is generally correlated within an aggregate unit (e.g., a state or city) during a given time period. Models incorporating aggregate and individual data need to adjust standard error (generally upward) to account for this correlation.

Tauchen et al. (1994) approach the problem directly by adding a component to their error term. This portion of the error term allows for correlation in the random portion of criminal behaviors during any given year. There are a number of reasons why individuals' behaviors might be correlated in any given year such as changes in youth culture and the effect of unmeasured citywide social, political, or economic changes. While the Philadelphia study finds no significant correlation, other work finds that this type of correlation leads to substantial understatements of standard errors. See Moulton (1990) or Borjas and Sueyoshi (1993).

As is well known, the use of longitudinal data requires that the persistent nature of individual behavior be recognized. This is generally accomplished by adopting either a random-effects or fixed-effects model. A fixed-effects model assumes that individual effects can be incorporated by allowing the intercept of the crime function to be different for different individuals. This is equivalent to assuming that there is a level of criminal activity inherent in each person and that observed characteristics and activities simply lead to deviation from this innate level. One might conceive of the fixed effect as measuring the innate law abidingness of the individual. A fixed-effects model assumes that the unique attribute of the individual does not change over time. Fixed-effects models do not allow one to estimate the effect of time-invariant (e.g., race, sex, or ethnic group) or predetermined (e.g., juvenile record, or previous educational attainment) variables on the level of criminal activity.

By way of contrast, a random-effects model sees different individuals as characterized by a different random element. The random-effects model contains an error composed of two parts. One part is the standard identically and independently distributed random error found in most statistical models. The other is unique to the individual. This component is correlated across time for any individual and might reflect such unmeasured factors as habituation. To obtain consistent and asymptotically efficient estimates, the error in the random-effects model must be uncorrelated with the explanatory variables.

There are many potentially endogenous variables in a fully specified crime model (e.g., deterrence variables, educational variables, and work variables). Researchers have carefully considered the endogeneity of deterrence and work variables, but they have not considered in detail the possible endogeneity of educational variables. Recent research suggests that police resources, often used as general deterrence variables, are not endogenous (e.g., Trumbull 1989; and Tauchen et al. 1994). However, it appears that an individual's wage rate is endogenous in models of individual offending (e.g., Schmidt and Witte 1984).

When estimating the effect of education on criminal activity, it will be important to make extensive tests for endogeneity. When endogeneity is found, researchers must use estimation techniques that incorporate the endogeneity to obtain reliable estimates of the effects of education.

As noted earlier, estimates of the full effect of education on crime will require that both measures of individual educational activities and community-wide measures of education be included in the crime equation. At first blush, it would seem that only the individual variables would be endogenous. However, as Cushing and McGarvey (1985) show, this is not the case. Aggregate variables included in models of individual behavior may be endogenous. Estimating the full effect of education on crime will require careful consideration of potential endogeneity of both individual and community educational variables.

Exploration of potential endogeneities can begin with tests for the robustness of results and with specification tests. The presence of endogenous explanatory variables will generally cause parameter estimates to be unstable as one moves from models with unquestionable exogenous variables (e.g., family socioeconomic status at birth or sex) to models with variables where endogeneity is more likely. Viscusi (1986), Tauchen et al. (1994), and Grogger (1994) estimate a number of models and find the coefficients on major variables of interest, including educational variables, to be robust across specifications.

Formal specification tests are also available for some qualitative and limited dependent variable models (see, e.g., Rivers and Vuong 1988). These tests could be used to test explicitly for the endogeneity of education variables. Thus far, these tests have only been used to test for the endogeneity of general deterrence variables (Tauchen et al. 1994).

If education variables are found to be endogenous, researchers must use statistical models that allow for the endogeneity (see Sickles and Schmidt 1978; and Rivers and Vuong 1988). If only deterrence and work variables are found to be endogenous, it would be possible to estimate the effect of education on crime by estimating a reduced-form model for crime that contained educational variables.

7.3. Major Problems in the Literature

As is clear from this review of the theoretical and empirical literature on the effect of education on crime, the crime literature is now quite sophisticated. However, the literature has not carefully considered the role of education in preventing or controlling crime. To measure the effect of education on crime, we require theoretical models that explicitly incorporate the role of education, careful measurement of crime and deterrence variables, and the use of carefully chosen statistical techniques. Having discussed statistical techniques in the previous section, I will consider theory and measurement in this one.

7.3.1. Models of the Role of Education in Controlling Crime

The review of the literature provides a number of stylized facts and insights upon which an explicit model for the impact of education on crime might be constructed. The first insight is that most crime is committed by young men during their adolescent years. Crime is an integral part of the lives of male adolescents. The second insight is that a disproportionate amount of the most violent crime is committed by a relatively small group of persistent offenders who begin their antisocial behavior at a very young age. A third finding is that neither years of schooling completed nor receipt of a high school degree has a significant affect on an individual's level of criminal activity. However, greater amounts of time in school are associated with lower levels of criminal activity. Attendance at parochial school and church attendance have been shown to be consistently associated with lower levels of criminal activity. Communities with larger numbers of unsupervised teenagers and little community involvement among residents have higher crime rates.

These facts, when coupled with the theories surveyed in section 7.2, suggest a number of possible avenues for the crime-reducing effect of education. An adequate model of criminality needs to account for underlying criminal proclivity that may be chemically induced or genetically determined. Any innate proclivity that exists may be altered by prenatal, perinatal, and early childhood experiences. Mother's use of drugs, head injuries, exposure to lead, and poor parenting are factors that can either cause or exacerbate criminal tendencies.

Persistent, high-rate offenders have been consistently shown to have low IQs, low verbal abilities, and early antisocial behavior. Psychologists have found that good parenting, community support, and early childhood education can overcome the effect of many factors that predispose some individuals to crime (for a survey, see Rutter 1985). This research suggests that a model for the effect of education on crime would contain a measure of criminal proclivity. This individual effect would need to be mutable, with early childhood education and training in parenting being sources for restraining the individual's underlying level of criminality.

As children age, the community at large, peer groups, and schools play a larger role in the child's world and, hence, have larger potential effects on crime. There are many possible roles for education. Education affects children directly through the milieu it provides. There is increasing evidence that schools with clear goals, clear rules, and consistently firm discipline, and schools that actively involve parents, have students that commit fewer crimes and have fewer crimes committed by outsiders. Such schools keep teenagers busy and under supervision. They can instill values and become a force for community organization. See Bryk, Lee, and Holland (1993) for a discussion of the effect of school atmosphere on children and Rutter (1983) for a comprehensive review of school effects.

A useful theoretical model of the effect of education must incorporate the effect of schools carefully. Recall that there is no empirical evidence that traditional measures of human capital accumulation such as school grade or receipt of a high school diploma have a significant effect on crime. The crime-reducing effect of well-organized, well-disciplined, and community-oriented schools might come through the supervision of teenagers, imparting information about or strictures against certain types of destructive behaviors (e.g., early sex, drug use, or violence), raising self-esteem, improving community organization, or involving parents more actively in the lives of their children. At this juncture, models that allow school curricula to affect rates of time preference and see school management styles and school outreach programs as increasing the potential costs of offenses by more closely supervising teens and decreasing the opportunity for crime seem promising. See Grossman and Kaestner (chap. 4, this volume) for a discussion of the potential effects of schooling on time preference.

7.3.2. Measurement Issues

To estimate the effect of education on crime, one requires measures of both crime and education. In chapter 3 of this volume, Behrman provides an excellent discussion of the general issues involved in measuring education. In the preceding material, I have suggested that traditional measures of education such as school grade will not adequately capture the effects of education on crime.

Thus far, I have only briefly discussed how one might measure crime. It is to this issue that I now turn.

In large individual data bases, there are generally only self-reports of criminal activity or official records. Many recently collected, longitudinal data bases (see the preceding discussion) contain both self-reports and criminal records. At the community level, victimization surveys that obtain information on criminal victimizations from nationally representative samples are available in Britain, the United States and a number of other countries. Smaller-scale studies sometimes rely on direct observation and reports of third parties such as parents, teachers, and peers. Since both large-scale experiments and correlational studies rely on self-reports or official records, I will discuss only the relative merits of these two types of data.

Researchers who have carefully compared self-report data and official records conclude that most correlational relationships for broad population groups are largely unaffected by whether one uses self-reports or official records (see, e.g., Farrington and Wikstroem 1994, Thornberry and Farnworth 1982; and Weiss 1986). However, recent research suggests that some offenders shift to crimes with low probabilities of detection (such as employee theft) as they age (e.g., Nagin et al 1995). Thus, longitudinal studies of crime may need to use self-reports as well as official records.

Official records reflect the behavior of the criminal, the victim (if any), and the police. To fully understand the correlational results that one obtains using official records, one needs to understand how explanatory variables in crime models affect citizens' reporting of crime and the reporting behavior of the police. There is some progress in this area, but much remains to be done (see Reiss and Roth 1993, app. B; and Carr-Hill and Carr-Hill 1972).

To illustrate the possible effects of reporting behavior on the coefficients obtained when estimating crime models, I will consider the coefficient on race. Research using victimization surveys shows that blacks are more likely to report violent crimes than are whites (Reiss and Roth 1993). In addition, research suggests that, at least during the 1960s in Philadelphia, blacks were more likely to be arrested for an offense than were whites (Collins 1985).

These reporting behaviors will affect the coefficient one obtains on race in crime models. Specifically, these reporting behaviors would seem likely to inflate the coefficients one obtains on a black binary in models of criminal behavior. Such results could lead to overestimates of the criminal proclivities of blacks.

While it is generally agreed that most cross-sectional correlations between crime and explanatory variables will be approximately the same whether one uses self-reports or official records, the magnitude of coefficients will vary substantially. In general, self-reports reflect higher levels of offending than do official records.

Self-reports, like criminal records, are subject to reporting bias. In the case of self-reports, one needs to carefully consider both response and nonresponse bias. Such biases can be substantial and can vary across studies since there are no generally accepted methods for collecting self-report data.

Methods of obtaining self-reports have improved markedly in recent years (see, e.g., Elliott et al. 1988). However, most careful researchers are skeptical about relying entirely on either self-reports or official records. For example, it is believed that self-reports substantially undercount offenses by high-rate offenders, while official records substantially underreport less-serious offenses. See Tarling (1993) for a balanced discussion of these issues. The conclusion of most researchers is that the two approaches to measuring offending are complementary.

Many of the evaluations of educational programs currently under way (e.g., the evaluation of the Alternative Schools Initiative) are collecting only self-report data. Collection of official records for juveniles is difficult since juvenile records are not generally public records. However, it may be possible to collect aggregated official records for experimental and control groups. It would be quite valuable to collect such data and adult records that are available to supplement self-report information.

The second measurement issue relates to deterrent effects. It is important to incorporate variables that will reflect deterrent effects in crime models because failing to do so will impart omitted-variable bias to estimates of the effect of education.

Deterrence refers to the effect of possible punishment on individuals contemplating criminal acts. Deterrence may flow from both criminal justice system actions and the actions of friends and associates. The negative response of friends and associates to criminal behavior is believed to generate what is known as "social sanctions."

To date, attempts to measure deterrent effects have concentrated on the effects of the criminal justice system. The potential criminal's perceptions regarding social sanctions are difficult to measure, although work on peer group and community effects may be able to capture some aspects of perceived social sanctions. In terms of the effects of education, a consistent finding is that students who attend schools with strong ethical values (e.g., parochial schools) offend less than students attending modern urban high schools (see, e.g., Tauchen et al. 1994). This effect may stem from higher levels of social sanctions against crime in schools with strong ethical standards or from the better family and community settings of at least some students.

In the literature, deterrence is broken into two components. The first component, called specific deterrence, encompasses the effect of punishment on the individual punished. The second component, called general deterrence, encompasses the effect of punishment on the general public. Specific deterrence is generally reflected by including measures that reflect the individual's past experience with the criminal justice system (see, e.g., Witte 1980; or Trumbull 1989). The implicit assumption is that offenders form their perceptions regarding possible punishment based on their own experience with the criminal justice system.[3] For example, the offender's perceived probability of arrest might be proxied by the ratio of his past self-reported offenses to arrests and his perceived punishment as some sort of average of the punishments he has received in the past. There is an important potential difficulty in using this type of specific deterrence measure. If there is autocorrelation in criminal behavior, these measures of specific deterrence will be correlated with the error term in the crime equation. One might instrument these variables by using community-level or peer group measures.

It has proven much more difficult to obtain reasonable measures of general deterrent effects. As an example, consider the probability of arrest. In a standard model of criminal choice, an individual's probability of arrest depends upon his level of criminal activity, his ability to avoid arrest, and exogenous factors related to the criminal justice system. When contemplating a crime, the individual is faced with a schedule of probabilities that relates the nature and extent of his criminal activity to the probability of arrest. See Cook (1979) or Tauchen et al. (1994) for a discussion. An analogy would be to a taxpayer who, when making her labor supply and tax reporting decisions, is faced with a schedule that relates reported income to the schedule of tax rates.

Just as there is no single tax rate, there is no single probability of arrest. There is a different probability of arrest for each and every possible criminal choice. For example, we would expect that for a given individual the probability of arrest would be much higher for robbery than for petty theft.

Changes in criminal justice policy or in the level of criminal justice resources alter the probability schedule facing a potential criminal. For example, an increase in criminal justice resources such as that contained in the 1994 Crime Bill might raise the probability of being arrested for each criminal act, that is, it might cause the schedule relating the probability of arrest to criminal activity to shift up. The "war on drugs" caused certain sections of the probability schedule (the sections associated with drug offenses) to shift up and other sections to shift down (the sections associated with violent offenses). It is these types of exogenous changes in the criminal justice system that should be used to reflect

---

3. We know little about how individuals form their perceptions of likely sanctions if they offend, although Paternoster and his colleagues (see, e.g., Nagin and Paternoster, 1991) have done interesting empirical work, and Sah (1991) has developed a model for the perceived probability of punishment. In a study of institutionalized young adults (college students and prison inmates), Lattimore et al. (1992) find that individuals transform probabilities when making risky choices. Risk seeking is common over long-shot odds, and subjects are less sensitive to changes in midrange probabilities than is assumed by expected utility models.

deterrent effects and not a community-level probability of arrest. This approach to representing deterrence has been used by Block et al. (1981) and Tauchen et al. (1994).

7.4. Potential Economic Justification for Educational Programs to Combat Crime

As a society, we have made many involuntary exchanges criminal (e.g., robbery and rape) and have outlawed certain voluntary exchanges (e.g., drug sales and prostitution). These restrictions are part of the social contract. They are the rules of the game. Following the rules facilitates legal exchanges and restricts the consumption of goods that we deem "demerit" goods or those that we believe have sufficient negative externalities to merit social condemnation.

Rules concerning major involuntary exchanges change rarely and are found in most societies. Prohibitions regarding voluntary exchanges are more mutable. For example, gambling used to be illegal in most parts of the United States, but it is now not only legal but state supported in many areas. Laws against adultery and sodomy are gradually being repealed, and, where they are still on the books, they are generally not enforced. We allow changes in criminal laws through well-developed legal (common law) and political (legislative) processes. However, we expect and need most citizens to obey most laws while they are in effect.

Imparting the rules of the game to each new generation is an important function with pervasive technical externalities. When I impart the rules of the game to my children and supervise them so that they will obey them, I benefit other members of society as well as myself. Obedience to rules against involuntary exchanges gives us safe streets (a public good) and provides greater work and investment incentives. Obedience to the rules against buying and selling certain goods lowers self-destructive behaviors (i.e., decreases the destruction of human capital) and apparently makes the majority of us feel better.

Consider a world in which there were no public interventions aimed at socializing children. In such a world, each family would decide how much to educate its children in the rules of the game and how much to supervise its children's behavior. In making these decisions, the family would consider the socializing influence of education as it affects the family itself (e.g., better-behaved or more-future-oriented children). But it would be unlikely to give sufficient consideration to the benefit to the community as a whole of having young people who obey the rules of the game. As a result, children would probably be undersocialized.

One could imagine community members providing education and supervision directly or chipping in to subsidize socialization. Free riding would be pervasive because the benefits of educating children in the rules of the game are, by and large, nonrival and nonexcludable. For example, one person's enjoyment of safe streets does not preclude enjoyment by others. The exclusion of individuals not contributing to the socialization of children would be costly. Under a system with voluntary contributions to socializing the young, children would still be undersocialized. The level of trust and safety in our communities would be lower than optimal.

To overcome this problem, we have agreed as a group to raise taxes to subsidize the socialization of children. Many of the dollars raised go to education. Traditionally, we have spent most tax dollars supporting the public elementary and secondary schools. These schools were designed to teach basic skills and produce good citizens.

The family and other community organizations had the primary function of supervising children and teaching them "right from wrong." Changes in family and community structure that began in the 1960s have limited the degree to which parents and communities socialize and supervise the young today. For a vivid description of the problem in central city neighborhoods, see Anderson (1990), and for an excellent discussion of trends, see Maynard and McGrath (chap. 5, this volume).

We have tried erratically to fill the socialization gap left by absent parents (e.g., due to out-of-wedlock births, divorce, and increased labor force participation rates) and disorganized communities. We have by and large failed. The material surveyed earlier suggests some programs that may be successful in addressing the "socialization gap."

Pregnant women who use drugs (including tobacco), are involved in other dangerous activities (e.g., promiscuous sex or fights), or are exposed to environmental risks during pregnancy may damage their children in ways that increase the likelihood that the children will commit criminal acts. Prenatal care and education may play an important role in decreasing such behaviors.

Impoverished single parents have difficulty supervising or socializing their children. They are sometimes forced to raise children in areas where environmental pollution (such as exposure to lead) can cause the neurological damage, hyperactivity, attention deficits, and learning disabilities that are known to be associated with higher levels of crime. The intensive child and parent interventions described by Zigler et al. (1992) and Yoshikawa (1994) can lead to significantly lower levels of crime for children in these types of family circumstances.

Schools can be an important force for socializing and supervising children. Research suggests that successful schools are part of their communities, function with a set of shared values, have reasonable rules that are enforced and encourage interaction between adults and young people. Such schools can improve the behavior of children and may lower the crime rate (see Bryck et al. 1993; and Tauchen et al. 1994).

The public goods nature of supervised and socialized young people provides one potential justification for educational programs designed to lower crime. By providing training in parenting, early childhood education, school supervision of teenagers, and school-centered programs designed to promote community cohesion, schools may be able to lower crime rates.

Another potential justification for educational programs that reduce crime is equity. Crime is not distributed randomly but rather tends to be concentrated in poor, disorganized, minority neighborhoods. Educational programs that lower crime in such neighborhoods will increase the welfare of less-affluent members of society.

7.5. Comparative Institution Analysis

In the last section, I have argued that educational programs that reduce crime are likely to be underprovided by private markets. Further, I have argued that, because crime falls disproportionately on less prosperous members of our society, educational programs that reduce crime might be justified as a way of increasing the relative well-being of the poor.

Stating that private markets will provide suboptimal levels of educational programs designed to reduce crime does not imply that public programs are justified. As argued many years ago by Coase (1960), the discovery of market failure should call forth a careful analysis of the relative costs and benefits of alternative institutional approaches. This analysis should include the market and the current institutional structure among the institutional structures evaluated. The comparative institutional analysis may conclude that the market, although flawed, is better than any alternative institutional structure or it may conclude that some public program designed to address the market failure will lead to higher levels of social welfare.

This type of comparative institutional analysis could valuably inform public debate regarding the relative merits in terms of crime prevention of various institutions designed to provide education. Existing research suggests some insights that will be useful in designing institutional structures other than the market and current programs.

Research indicates that educational programs that seek to prevent the development of crime are likely to be more effective than programs that seek to deal with children after antisocial behavior has begun. For high-risk children, early childhood education programs and programs providing training in parenting are promising (e.g., the Perry Preschool Project). Educational programs for teens need to concentrate on keeping teens supervised and providing meaningful transitions to adulthood (e.g., the Job Corps). These programs have one important thing in common—they are intensive and relatively small. Less-intensive and larger programs such as Head Start and JTPA have not been shown to decrease crime.

Teenagers need to be supervised and given adult role models. Educational institutions can play an important role in doing this. Single parents and dual-career couples have limited time to supervise their teenagers and may not provide role models that teenagers find palatable.

Community organization can be a method of reducing crime. Poor neighborhoods and suburban neighborhoods with both parents at work all day need educational institutions that help to provide cohesion by becoming actively involved in their communities and proactively involving families and older adults in the education and supervision of children.

A large literature suggests that existing educational programs are not likely to significantly reduce the recidivism of convicted youthful offenders. Measures of educational attainment have not been shown to be related to recidivism. However, we have convicted offenders under our supervision and we need to provide productive uses for their time. Education and work are two needed activities.

7.6. Directions for Research

Developing educational programs that effectively reduce crime requires a number of things. First, it requires theoretical models that explicitly incorporate the role of education. These models need to be more firmly grounded in the stylized facts. These facts suggest that the major crime-reducing effects of education come not from providing either general or vocational education but are more likely to flow from the socializing, and supervisory activities of educational programs.

Second, programs that explicitly and innovatively incorporate the socialization, supervisory, and community development role of education will need to be developed. There are many innovative educational and vocational programs. However, the crime literature suggests that the credentials and job skills these programs provide will have little effect on crime. Not only are measures of educational attainment found to be unrelated to crime, but higher wage rates and higher incomes also appear to be unrelated to the level of criminality. If education is to have a major crime-reducing impact, it appears that the impact will arise from the educational programs' socializing and supervisory roles and not from their primary educational activities. As far as I am aware, little thought has been given to developing educational programs that specifically and creatively incorporate instruction in the rules of the game. Further, the importance of supervising teenagers and organizing the community has not been carefully embedded in the innovative educational programs that have been implemented nationwide. The CAR program does contain many of the requisite activities.

Once innovative programs incorporating socialization, supervision, and community organization have been developed, we need to carefully assess the effects of these programs on crime. Such programs are probably best evaluated using an experimental design when they are small. However, recent work by Heckman, Manski, and others suggests that other methods may produce equally valid estimates of program effects (for a discussion, see Manski and Garfinkel 1992). These methods require that the rules for assigning individuals to programs be explicit and quantifiable. These new methods appear particularly well designed to evaluate large programs.

Although not explicitly designed to evaluate the effect of education on crime, correlational studies have improved our understanding of crime and suggest important directions for the development of educational programs. These studies indicate that the crime-reducing role of education does not flow from greater educational attainment or the higher income this can provide. Rather, they indicate that greater time in school (possibly a supervisory effect) and attendance at parochial schools (possibly a socialization effect) decrease crime. As detailed previously, these results are open to serious question because of measurement and statistical problems, among other things.

New correlational studies based on carefully constructed theoretical models that explicitly incorporate the role of education and use carefully collected and extensive longitudinal data bases and appropriate statistical methods may provide new insights open to fewer questions. Such insights are important because they form a basis for both theory and program development. A number of new longitudinal data bases now available can be drawn upon to further explore the role of education in preventing crime.

REFERENCES

Anderson, E. 1990. *Streetwise: Race, Class, and Change in an Urban Community.* Chicago: University of Chicago Press.
Becker, G. 1968. Crime and Punishment: An Economic Approach. *Journal of Political Economy* 76:169–217.
Becker, G., and K. M. Murphy. 1988. A Theory of Rational Addiction. *Journal of Political Economy* 96:675–700.
Block, M., F. Nold, and J. Sidak. 1981. The Deterrent Effect of Antitrust Enforcement. *Journal of Political Economy* 89:429–45.
Blumstein, A., et al. 1978. *Deterrence and Incapacitation.* Washington, DC: National Academy Press.
Borjas, G., and G. Sueyoshi. 1993. A Two-Stage Estimator for Probit Models with Structural Group Effects. Working paper, Department of Economics, University of California-San Diego. Mimeo.

Bryck, A., V. Lee, and P. Holland. 1993. *Catholic Schools and the Common Good.* Cambridge: Harvard University Press.

Carr-Hill, G., and R. Carr-Hill. 1972. Reconviction as a Process. *British Journal of Criminology* 12:35–43.

Coase, R. 1960. The Problem of Social Cost. *Journal of Law and Economics* 3:1–44.

Collins, J. 1985. The Disposition of Adult Arrests. Working Paper, Wharton School, University of Pennsylvania. Mimeo.

Cook, P. 1979. The Clearance Rate as a Measure of Criminal Justice Effectiveness. *Journal of Public Economics* 11:135–42.

Couch, K. 1992. New Evidence on the Long-Term Effects of Employment Training Programs. *Journal of Labor Economics* 4:380–88.

Cushing, M., and M. McGarvey. 1985. Identification by Disaggregation. *American Economic Review* 75:1165–67.

Davis, M. L. 1988. Time and Punishment Again: An Intertemporal Model of Crime. *Journal of Political Economy* 96:383–90.

Dickens, W. T. 1986. Crime and Punishment Again: The Economic Approach with a Psychological Twist. *Journal of Public Economics* 30:97–107.

Donohue, J., and P. Siegelman. 1994. Is the United States at the Optimal Rate of Crime? Working paper, Northwestern School of Law, Chicago. Mimeo.

Earls, F. 1994. Violence and Today's Youth. *The Future of Children* 4:4–23.

Earls, F., and J. McGuire. 1993. *Third Annual Progress Report: Developmental Epidemiology Research Unit.* Boston: Judge Baker Children's Center, Harvard School of Public Health, Harvard Medical School.

Ehrlich, I. 1975. The Deterrent Effect of Capital Punishment: A Question of Life and Death. *Journal of Political Economy* 65:397–417.

Elliott, D., D. Huizenga, and S. Menard. 1988. *Multiple Problem Youth.* New York: Springer-Verlag.

Evans, W., W. Oates, and R. Schwab. 1992. Measuring Peer Group Effects: A Study of Teenage Behavior. *Journal of Political Economy* 100:966–91.

Farrington, D., et al. 1986. Unemployment, School Leaving and Crime. *British Journal of Criminology* 26:335–56.

Farrington, D., and P. Wikstroem. 1994. *Criminal Careers in London and Stockholm: A Cross-National Comparative Study,* ed. E. Weitkamp and H. Kerner.

Felson, M. 1993. Social Indicators of Criminology. *Journal of Research in Crime and Delinquency* 30:400–411.

Flinn, C. 1986. Dynamic Models of Criminal Careers. In *Criminal Careers and "Career Criminals,"* ed. A. Blumstein, et al. Washington, DC: National Academy Press.

Gendreau, P., and R. Ross. 1987. Revivification of Rehabilitation: Evidence from the 1980s. *Justice Quarterly* 4:349–407.

Good, D., M. Pirog-Good, and R. Sickles. 1986. An Analysis of Youth Crime and Employment Patterns. *Journal of Quantitative Criminology* 2:219–36.

Gottfredson, D. C. 1985. Youth Employment, Crime, and Schooling. *Developmental Psychology* 21:419–32.

Grogger, J. 1994. Criminal Opportunities, Youth Crime, and Young Men's Labor Supply. Working paper, Department of Economics, University of California-Santa Barbara. Mimeo.

Harrell, A. 1995. *Impact of the Children at Risk Program: Preliminary Findings on the First Year. Report to the National Institute of Justice and the Center on Addiction and Substance Abuse.* Washington, DC: Urban Institute.

Heckman, J. J. 1981. Statistical Models for Discrete Panel Data. In *Structural Analysis of Discrete Data with Econometric Applications,* ed. C. F. Manski and D. F. McFadden. Cambridge: MIT Press.

Karni, E., and D. Schmeidler. 1990. Fixed Preferences and Changing Tastes. *American Economic Review* 80:262–67.

Lattimore, P. K., and A. D. Witte. 1986. Models of Decision Making under Uncertainty. In *The Reasoning Criminal: Rational Choice Perspectives on Offending,* ed. D. B. Cornish and R. V. Clarke. New York: Springer-Verlag.

Lattimore, P., J. Baker, and A. Witte. 1992. The Influence of Probability on Risky Choice: A Parametric Examination. *Journal of Economic Behavior and Organization* 17:377–400.

Lattimore, P. K., A. D. Witte, and J. Baker. 1990. Experimental Assessment of the Effect of Vocational Training on Youthful Property Offenders. *Evaluation Review* 14:115–33.

Mallar, C., et al. 1982. *Evaluation of the Economic Impact Job Corps Program.* Princeton, NJ: Mathematica Policy Research.

Manpower Development Research Corp. 1980. *Summary and Findings of the National Supported Work Demonstration.* Cambridge, MA: Ballinger.

Manski, C., and I. Garfinkel. 1992. *Evaluating Welfare and Training Programs.* Cambridge, MA: Harvard University Press.

Moffitt, Terrie. 1993. Adolescence-Limited and Life-Course-Persistent Antisocial Behavior: A Developmental Taxonomy. *Psychological Review* 100:674–701.

Montmarquette, C., and M. Nerlove. 1985. Deterrence and Delinquency. *Journal of Quantitative Criminology* 1:37–58.

Moulton, B. 1990. An Illustration of a Pitfall in Estimating the Effects of Aggregate Variables on Micro Units. *Review of Economics and Statistics* 72:334–38.

Nagin, D., D. Farrington, and T. Moffitt. 1995. Life-Course Trajectories of Different Types of Offenders. *Criminology* 33:111–40.

Nagin, D., and R. Paternoster. 1991. The Preventive Effect of the Perceived Risk of Arrest. *Criminology* 29:561–73.

Orr, L., et al. 1994. *The National JTPA Study: Impacts, Benefits, and Costs of Title II-A.* Bethesda, MD: Abt Associates.

Phlips. L. 1983. *Applied Consumption Analysis.* Amsterdam: North-Holland Publishing Co.

Pollak, R. 1978. Endogenous Tastes in Demand and Welfare Analysis. *American Economic Review* 68:374–79.

Reiss, A., and J. Roth. 1993. *Understanding and Preventing Violence.* Washington, DC: National Academy Press.

Rivers, D., and Q. Vuong. 1988. Limited Information Estimators and Exogeneity Tests for Simultaneous Probit Models. *Journal of Econometrics* 39:347–66.

Rutter, M. 1983. School Effects on Pupil Progress: Research Findings and Policy Implications. *Child Development* 54:1–29.

Rutter, M. 1985. Resilience in the Face of Adversity: Protective Factors and Resistance to Psychiatric Disorder. *British Journal of Psychiatry* 147:598–611.

Sah, R. 1991. Social Osmosis and Patterns of Crime. *Journal of Political Economy* 99:1272–95.

Sampson, R., and W. Groves. 1989. Community Structure and Crime: Testing Social-Disorganization Theory. *American Journal of Sociology* 94:774–802.

Schmidt, P., and A. D. Witte. 1984. *An Economic Analysis of Crime and Justice.* New York: Academic Press.

Sellin, T., and M. Wolfgang. 1964. *The Measurement of Delinquency.* New York: John Wiley.

Shaw, C., and H. McKay. 1969. *Juvenile Delinquency and Urban Areas.* Chicago: University of Chicago Press.

Sickles, R., and P. Schmidt. 1978. Simultaneous Equations Models with Truncated Dependent Variables: A Simultaneous Tobit Model. *Journal of Economics and Business* 31:11–21.

Tarling, R. 1993. *Analyzing Offending.* London: HMSO.

Tauchen, H., and A. D. Witte. 1995. The Dynamics of Domestic Violence: Does Arrest Matter? *American Economic Review* 85:414–18.

Tauchen, H., A. D. Witte, and H. Griesinger. 1994. Criminal Deterrence: Revisiting the Issues with a Birth Cohort. *Review of Economics and Statistics* 76:399–412.

Theil, H. 1980. *The System-Wide Approach to Microeconomics.* Chicago: University of Chicago Press.

Thornberry, T., and R. Christenson. 1984. Unemployment and Criminal Involvement. *American Sociological Review* 49:398–411.

Thornberry, T., and M. Farnworth. 1982. Social Correlates of Criminal Involvement: Further Evidence of the Relationship between Social Status and Criminal Behavior. *American Sociological Review* 47:505–18.

Trumbull, W. 1989. Estimation of the Economic Model of Crime Using Aggregate and Individual Data. *Southern Economic Journal* 94:423–39.

Viscusi, W. K. 1986. Market Incentives for Criminal Behavior. In *The Black Youth Employment Crisis,* ed. R. B. Freeman and J. J. Holzer. Chicago: University of Chicago Press.

Weiss, J. 1986. Issues in the Measurement of Criminal Careers. In *Criminal Careers and "Career Criminals,"* ed. E. A. Blumstein, et al. Washington, DC: National Academy Press.

Weitkamp, E., and H. Kerner. 1994. *Cross-National Longitudinal Research on Human Development and Criminal Behavior.* Dordrecht: Kluwer.

Wilson, J. Q., and R. J. Herrnstein. 1985. *Crime and Human Nature.* New York: Simon and Schuster.

Witte, A. D. 1980. Estimating the Economic Model of Crime with Individual Data. *Quarterly Journal of Economics* 94:59–87.

Witte, A. D., and H. Tauchen. 1994. Work and Crime: An Exploration Using Panel Data. *Public Finance* 49:155–67.

Wolfgang, M., et al. 1987. *From Boy to Man, From Delinquency to Crime.* Chicago: University of Chicago Press.

Yoshikawa, H. 1994. Prevention as Cumulative Protection: Effects of Early Family Support and Education on Chronic Delinquency and Its Risks. *Psychological Bulletin* 115:28–54.

Zigler, E., et al. 1992. Early Childhood Intervention: A Promising Preventative for Juvenile Delinquency. *American Psychologist* 47:997–1006.

CHAPTER 8

Conclusion

Jere R. Behrman, David L. Crawford,
and Nevzer Stacey

This book considers the social benefits of education—defined to be the benefits of education other than the enhancement of labor market productivity and earnings. Though the primary argument in justifying education has been based on direct economic effects more narrowly defined, it is widely perceived that the effects of education spread beyond these direct economic effects to include such social benefits for individuals and society at large. The quantification of these social benefits is difficult, which Arrow suggests in chapter 2 is part of the reason that they may have been underemphasized relative to narrowly defined economic productivity and earnings benefits. But more systematically analyzing these benefits would improve our understanding of the full effects of education and would improve the informational basis for considering policies related to education.

This book includes a series of chapters on measuring these effects of education. As noted in the introduction, three common themes regarding the analysis of the social benefits of education emerge. First, there are measurement issues with regard to what is meant by education and outcomes affected by education. Second, there are basic analytical issues regarding how to use behavioral data to assess the causal impact of education on these social outcomes. Third, there is the question of whether the social benefits of education provide rationales for public policy interventions. Our contributors' reviews of the literature in chapters 4 through 7 indicate, however, that the sensitivity to these themes varies considerably across the literatures on different types of social benefits of education. Chapter 4 suggests that the literature on the impact of education on health is relatively well attuned to these issues compared with the literatures on parenting, the environment, and crime. There would be substantial gains in our understanding of the social benefits of education if the literatures on other social benefits were as sensitive to these issues as is at least some of the recent literature on the health effects of education.

Measurement of Education and of Outcomes Affected by Education

There are numerous data inadequacies that may affect the analysis of the social benefits of education. The data used to represent education in many studies are crude. Random measurement errors may bias the estimated effects toward zero. Systematic measurement errors, such as the use of schooling attainment with no information on school quality, may bias estimates of educational effects in either direction.

Some studies report that empirical estimates of the impact of schooling on earnings change substantially if schooling is measured by cognitive achievement or if measures of school inputs are added as control variables along with the simple years of schooling variable (chap. 3, sec. 3.2). The inclusion of school quality measures in the analysis of the social benefits of education would seem essential for improving our understanding of the true social benefits of education and for making sound policy decisions regarding the intensive margin of education. Yet, as reviewed in chapters 4 through 7, virtually none of the studies in the current literature on the social benefits of education use measures of learning or inputs into learning processes other than the years spent in school.

While cognitive achievement represents an important product of schooling and an important dimension of education, there may be other dimensions— such as self-discipline, problem-solving capabilities, specific skills, general knowledge, and learning how to learn—that also are important in assessing the social benefits of education. Unfortunately, the reviews of the current literature in chapters 4 through 7 have uncovered no efforts to assess such possibilities systematically.

The data on outcomes potentially affected by education, particularly for some of the outcomes of interest for this volume, are often very crude, may be available only for selected subsamples, and only partially represent the outcomes of interest. Such data problems can affect what we think we know about the social benefits of education and our choice of strategies for attempting to estimate them (chap. 2). For our interest in this book, the critical point is not whether some benefit or outcome indicators have more or less random measurement error than others (which is the focus of much of the data validation literature). Random errors in these indicators may diminish statistical significance, but they do not cause biases in the estimated impacts of education.

The critical point is whether there are systematic errors, particularly related to education. These measurement problems, unfortunately, have barely been touched in the literature on the social benefits of education (though the comparisons of self-reported versus officially reported crime summarized in chap. 7 is an exception). This lacunae leaves open the possibility of substantial contributions to our empirical understanding of the social benefits of education in future studies that explore such measurement problems for outcomes that are affected by education. For example, it would appear that the data on the social benefits of education related to crime lead to a focus on "blue collar" rather than "white collar" crime, though casual observations suggest that the latter is quite important and perhaps even more important than the former from the point of view of efficiency and distribution. Likewise it appears that the data on health lead to relative overemphasis on physical as opposed to mental health problems and that the data on the environment lead to underemphasis on environments in homes and workplaces. As Arrow emphasizes in chapter 2, which outcomes are measured has an important impact on what we perceive to be important and value as a society. Therefore, better measures of the multiple dimensions of the social effects of education may alter our perceptions of what are the more important benefits.

A pervasive data/estimation problem for all the alleged social benefits of education is the difficulty of capturing external effects. A few recent studies have shown that education can both create and facilitate the transmission of certain economic externalities. For example, a better-educated farmer may provide his neighbor with a better example of the application of new technology and thereby provide a positive externality. In addition, a better-educated farmer may find it easier to learn from a neighbor, so the transmission of the externality may be facilitated. Similar phenomena may be at work in the cases of health, parenting, the environment, or crime. Better longitudinal data on individuals and on their neighbors or coworkers from whom they may learn may permit identification of some of the external social benefits of education.

A further pervasive data problem is that available data primarily are nonexperimental or behavioral cross-sectional data, though some exceptions are discussed in chapters 5 through 7. This raises the analytical problems that constitute the second major theme of this book. But it also raises important possibilities for data improvements. Longitudinal behavioral data permit much better control for endogenous choices and unobserved factors such as preferences and abilities in the analysis of the social impact of education than do the cross-sectional data that primarily have been used in analysis to date. Longitudinal data are more costly to collect and may present estimation problems because of selective attrition, but they have the potential for substantial gains in our understanding of the social benefits of education. In some contexts the use of special data such as those on twins also can be used to control for unobserved family background and community school characteristics. And, of course, in some contexts experimental data with random assignment to treatment and control groups can be used to assess the social benefits of education. There would be gains in understanding if more efforts were made to obtain good experimental data, but for some questions experiments are precluded by costs or ethical concerns.

Analytical Problems in the Assessment of the Impact of Education

A second common theme of the chapters in this volume concerns the difficulties of ascertaining the causal effects of education from behavioral data given that education reflects choices in the presence of unobserved factors such as abilities and preferences. Education might generate effects in at least three ways: by changing individuals' preferences, by changing the constraints that those individuals face, or by augmenting the knowledge or information on which individuals base their behavior. Ascertaining the causal impact of education, as opposed to associations of education with various outcomes, is extremely difficult precisely because education reflects choices of individuals, families, communities, and policymakers. These choices are made in the presence of important factors that are not measured in most data sets used to analyze the effects of education.

For example, a recurring theme of the chapters in this volume is the enormous importance of family background as a determinant of children's eventual health, treatment of their own children, dealings with the environment, and illegal activity. Systematic empirical analysis, anecdotes, personal experience, and common sense about the importance of family background are so compelling as to be undeniable. Because education is also correlated with family background, it is difficult to measure the independent effects of education apart from those of family background.

To obtain good estimates of the social effects of education from behavioral data, it is essential that the analyst be mindful of the data generation process. That means that explicit models of the determination of education and the relation of education to the social benefits of interest are necessary in order to guide the estimation and interpret the results. Whether recognized explicitly or not, interpretation of estimates from behavioral data are conditional on models of underlying behavior. Explicit modeling makes possible the assessment of assumptions necessary to obtain the estimates and thus facilitates the evaluation of their credibility. Researchers who analyze behavioral data without using explicit models typically make strong implicit assumptions about the nature of the underlying behavior such as the assumption that education is independent of preferences and abilities that affect the outcome of interest.

In some of the areas considered in this book—probably most so in the case of the analysis of the impact of education on health (chap. 4)—the literature has moved increasingly toward recognizing and acting on this fundamental point about the analysis of behavioral data. But most of the empirical studies using behavioral data considered in this book ignore this critical point. Therefore, it often is hard to know how to interpret the available empirical estimates pertaining to the social benefits of education in many, probably the majority, of these studies.

To improve our understanding of the social benefits of education based on behavioral data, it is essential to develop integrated approaches with (1) better explicit modeling of the determinants of education as well as of the social benefits under investigation; (2) better data, including improved indicators of education and of outcomes and longitudinal information to control for behavioral choices and dynamic processes; and (3) appropriate estimation techniques to control for the underlying behavior and assess the robustness of the results. In some cases, as noted, substantial gains in understanding may be obtained from collecting good experimental data.

Basis for Policy Interventions

A third common concern of the literature reviewed in this book is that the social benefits of education may have important policy implications. The basic rationales for policy interventions are concerns about the efficiency of economic behavior and the equity of the distribution of income and other benefits. It is desirable to achieve distributional aims as efficiently as possible because there often are tradeoffs between distributional and efficiency goals. That is, it is preferable to use policies that create the smallest possible distortion costs to pursue distributional goals.

That education may have some strong positive social benefits is *not* in itself an efficiency reason for policy intervention and support. In addition, there must be a presumption of "market failures," in the sense that the total effects differ from the private effects, and some presumption that "policy failures" will not be of such magnitude as to swamp possible gains from policy interventions. In the analysis of the welfare effects of education, such "market failures" are thought to arise possibly because of imperfect capital and insurance markets (e.g., difficulties in obtaining financing for educational investments and in pooling risks), information problems, and the public goods or external aspects of education (e.g., effects on persons other than the individual being educated that are transferred other than through markets). As discussed in chapter 2, there is a difficult question of how to evaluate the welfare effects of policies if they affect preferences.

In addition to the problems in identifying market failure reasons for efficiency-based policy interventions, analyzing policies is further complicated by some difficult intergenerational distributional and efficiency issues relating to children. Generally adults—parents and other relatives—act as stewards for children, which raises questions about allocations to children on both efficiency and distributional grounds. For such reasons, many argue that the state has an important role in assuring adequate and appropriate allocations to children. But our opportunities to influence family environments are extremely limited. We can pump in resources but we can't be sure that those resources will get to the children. We can offer family support services, but we can't be sure that parents will use them. And it is virtually impossible to use public policy to induce parents to love and look out for their children. Public policy does have direct access to children for significant periods of time when those children are in school. The basic policy question is whether we can use that time to enhance the futures of our children.

Most of the applied literature, reviewed in chapters 4 through 7 of this volume, that purports to evaluate the policy implications of the social impact of education is not sensitive to the analytical reasons for policy interventions. The focus, instead, is almost exclusively on policy effectiveness in the sense of attempting to explore whether particular policies change behaviors related to social outcomes. Most of this literature, moreover, does not address the possibly important question of what determines policy choices, control for which in some cases alters considerably estimates of the effectiveness of policies (chap. 3, sec. 3.1.3). There are some exceptions in the form of experimental programs that are reviewed in chapters 5 through 7. But these experiments do not directly address the efficiency and distributional rationale for policy interventions related to the social benefits of education. Moreover, some of the most frequently cited of them (e.g., the Perry Preschool Project in Ypsilanti, Michigan) have questionable generalizability because of problems such as small samples, intensive interventions, and changes in control and experimental groups during the experiment.

Some of the health literature, once again, is an exception in which there is some concern about the analytical reasons for policies—namely, possible externalities of behaviors related to smoking, alcohol, and exercise, given public subsidies for health care. Even this literature, however, does not consider how better education fits into the policy hierarchy for improving efficiency—and it well may be the case that higher in the hierarchy is improving the pricing and insurance arrangements for health care. More generally, there is almost no persuasive systematic evaluation of the possible efficiency implications of measured social impacts of education. Nor is there systematic consideration of the difficult intergenerational issues or those raised by endogenous preferences.

The very limited systematic evidence on which to base policies related to the social benefits of education does not mean that there should be no policy interventions in this area. Policies always have to be made on the basis of imperfect information and a priori analysis—and taking no action is an implicit policy decision. But the very limited systematic evidence on which to base such policies does mean that there are considerable potential gains to further research that (1) assesses the efficiency basis for policy interventions related to the social benefits of education, (2) estimates the efficiency-distributional tradeoffs, and (3) deals with the difficult intergenerational and endogenous preference issues. Systematic modeling with integrated data and estimation methods of the types described in this volume would seem to have a high payoff in improving the information basis for policies related to the social benefits of education.

Index